Quiet Period
1934-2007

p. 11

Slapped by the Invisible Hand

FINANCIAL MANAGEMENT ASSOCIATION

SURVEY AND SYNTHESIS SERIES

Managing Pension Plans: A Comprehensive Guide to Improving Plan Performance
Dennis E. Logue and Jack S. Radar

*Efficient Asset Management: A Practical Guide to Stock Portfolio
Optimization and Asset Allocation*
Richard O. Michaud

Real Options: Managing Strategic Investment in an Uncertain World
Martha Amram and Nalin Kulatilaka

*Beyond Greed and Fear: Understanding Behavioral Finance and the
Psychology of Investing*
Hersh Shefrin

Dividend Policy: Its Impact on Firm Value
Ronald C. Lease, Kose John, Avner Kalay, Uri Loewenstein, and Oded H. Sarig

Value Based Management: The Corporate Response to Shareholder Revolution
John D. Martin and J. William Petty

Debt Management: A Practitioner's Guide
John D. Finnerty and Douglas R. Emery

*Real Estate Investment Trusts: Structure, Performance, and
Investment Opportunities*
Su Han Chan, John Erickson, and Ko Wang

Trading and Exchanges: Market Microstructure for Practitioners
Larry Harris

Valuing the Closely Held Firm
Michael S. Long and Thomas A. Bryant

Last Rights: Liquidating a Company
Ben S. Branch, Hugh M. Ray, Robin Russell

*Efficient Asset Management: A Practical Guide to Stock Portfolio Optimization
and Asset Allocation,* Second Edition
Richard O. Michaud and Robert O. Michaud

Real Options in Theory and Practice
Graeme Guthrie

Slapped by the Invisible Hand: The Panic of 2007
Gary B. Gorton

Slapped by the Invisible Hand

The Panic of 2007

GARY B. GORTON

OXFORD
UNIVERSITY PRESS
2010

OXFORD
UNIVERSITY PRESS

Oxford University Press, Inc., publishes works that further
Oxford University's objective of excellence
in research, scholarship, and education.

Oxford   New York
Auckland   Cape Town   Dar es Salaam   Hong Kong   Karachi
Kuala Lumpur   Madrid   Melbourne   Mexico City   Nairobi
New Delhi   Shanghai   Taipei   Toronto

With offices in
Argentina   Austria   Brazil   Chile   Czech Republic   France   Greece
Guatemala   Hungary   Italy   Japan   Poland   Portugal   Singapore
South Korea   Switzerland   Thailand   Turkey   Ukraine   Vietnam

Copyright © 2010 by Oxford University Press, Inc.

Published by Oxford University Press, Inc.
198 Madison Avenue, New York, New York 10016

www.oup.com

Oxford is a registered trademark of Oxford University Press

Library of Congress Cataloging-in-Publication Data
Gorton, Gary.
Slapped by the invisible hand : the panic of 2007 / Gary B. Gorton.
p.   cm. — (Financial Management Association survey and synthesis series)
Includes bibliographical references and index.
ISBN 978-0-19-973415-3
1. Banks and banking—United States—History—21st century.
2. Financial crises—United States—History—21st century.
I. Title.
HG2491.G674 2010
332.10973—dc22   2009026403

3 5 7 9 8 6 4

Printed in the United States of America
on acid-free paper

Contents

May 2009

{ #2 Aug 2009

 # 1

Slapped by the Invisible Hand

.

1

Introduction

I want to talk for a few minutes with the people of the United States about banking—to talk with the comparatively few who understand the mechanics of banking, but more particularly with the overwhelming majority of you who use banks for the making of deposits and the drawing of checks.
—Franklin Roosevelt, first fireside chat, March 12, 1933

I am by no means an alarmist. I believe that our system, though curious and peculiar, may be worked safely; but if we wish so to work it, we must study it. We must not think we have an easy task when we have a difficult task, or that we are living in a natural state when we are living in an artificial one. Money will not manage itself, and Lombard Street has a great deal of money to manage.
Walter Bagehot, *Lombard Street: A Description of the Money Market* (1877)

WHEN THE PANIC OF 2007 BROKE OUT IN AUGUST OF THAT YEAR, I WAS IN a unique position to observe the events. For 25 years, my academic career—in the Federal Reserve System, at the Wharton School of the University of Pennsylvania, and at Yale School of Management—focused on banking, financial crises, and banking panics. My 1983 PhD dissertation was on the subject of banking panics. One paper from my thesis was the first (and, as far as I know, the only) econometric study of panics to this day. But, starting in 1996, I also consulted for AIG Financial Products, where I worked on structured credit, credit derivatives, and commodity futures. During the panic, AIG became a focal point of anger because of its sheer size and the extent of the resources needed to maintain the company as a going concern.

When I wrote my PhD thesis in the early 1980s about banking panics, I never dreamed that I would live through one. Who could possibly have imagined what would transpire? The lived experience of the current banking panic would be surreal if it were not so tragic. Certainly the events are confusing, and the reality of what happened is hard to accept. But what exactly did happen? How could it happen? Answering these questions is important because the narrative of what happened provides a framework for new regulations, laws, and policies, ones that are relevant and effective.[1] Central bank lender-of-last-resort policies in the future need a record of what happened in the Panic of 2007. As A. Piatt Andrew argued a century ago about the Panic of 1907, "The unique dimensions of the recent panic among the experiences of the present generation render important the preservation for future study of all records concerning its phenomena" (1908A, p. 291).[2] In this book, I attempt to explain what happened. I do this from the viewpoint that the details matter; the details about certain financial markets and certain financial products need to be understood. Although I recognize that such details are probably rather boring for most people, I argue that understanding the details of how the actual securities, structures, and markets involved are designed and intertwined is essential for addressing the most important questions. Without the details, explanations are invariably simplistic and superficial, though they may be politically expedient.

Besides articulating the details of what happened, I also view American financial and banking history as important to provide context. Crises do not just happen. Financial crises have been the norm in U.S. financial history. As I will argue, in the United States, the period from 1934 to 2007 was special compared to the previous banking history. The earlier history has been forgotten, except for the Great Depression, and for many even that is a dim memory. Even professional economists tend to focus on the post–World War II era and on the stock market. But the earlier history offers important clues about how to think about what a "systemic event" is and what happened in the current crisis. Indeed, another way to understand what happened is to ask why was it a systemic event. Like many terms, this one has lost any precise meaning and has come to signify "bad financial events." It is important to recover some precision about this because its meaning is so closely linked to lender-of-last-resort policies, that is, what the central bank does in a financial crisis.

The modern financial system is complex, but still it is surprising that it has been so difficult to figure out what happened. One reason may well be that the events themselves were largely invisible to all but the participants in certain financial markets. I hope to convince you that the Panic of 2007 is not so different from, for example, the Panic of 1907 or that of 1893. But there is one big difference; the earlier panics were visible to all. In the Panic of 2007, most people had never heard of the markets that were involved, didn't know how they worked or what their purposes were. Terms like subprime mortgage, asset-backed commercial paper conduit, structured investment vehicle, credit derivative, securitization, or repo market were meaningless. These markets were obscure and esoteric for most, including economists. In the earlier panic episodes, not only could everyone see the runs on banks, most people likely participated, rushing to their bank to withdraw their money.

In the earlier panics, individuals, fearing for their savings and not knowing if their bank would survive the coming recession, rushed to their banks to withdraw their money. These runs would occur at all banks, usually starting in New York City and spreading from there. Everyone knew that the panic had happened, and then consequences would follow; firms would fail and there would be difficulties making transactions.

The visibility of earlier panics did not make the event itself explicable, but it did provide clarity about what had happened in a direct sense. In the Panic of 2007, the "bank run" was invisible to almost everyone because it was a run by banks and firms on other banks. These interbank markets were invisible to the public, journalists, and politicians. Without observing the bank run, what became visible were only the effects of the run and, in many cases, the effects were mistaken for the cause. Without the details of what happened, new policies may end up addressing effects rather than the cause.

If we think about a 19th-century bank run, like the one on the Seaman's Savings Bank in 1857 (see figure 1.1), we can get a sense of the problem. When everyone demands to withdraw cash from their banks, it is not possible for the banking system to meet these demands. The money has been lent out, and banks do not hold enough cash (because it does not earn a return). The

FIGURE 1.1 Run on Seaman's Savings Bank during the Panic of 1857. (Provided courtesy HarpWeek, LCC)

banking system becomes insolvent because it cannot meet the contractual demands of the depositors; that is, banks are simply unable to pay back all the cash that depositors want. Because the banks have lent the money out, there is no easy way to get it back. The banks cannot sell their loans—the assets of the banking system are simply too large for anyone to buy. This is what makes a banking panic a systemic event. One bank could possibly sell its loans and pay off its depositors. But when all banks have to sell loans, there are no other banks to buy them.

Banks understood that panics were systemic events. Trying to sell the loans of the bank system would be a disaster, so banks as a group, would suspend convertibility. In other words, they would refuse to give back the cash to their depositors. This saved the banking system from destruction, since with suspension of convertibility banks would then not have to sell their loans. But when suspension happened, bank checks were no longer accepted at stores and to meet payrolls. There was a "currency famine," the term that contemporary observers coined to describe a situation where there is no transaction medium to use to buy goods or pay employees. Bank checks were no longer acceptable, and cash was hoarded. The inability to transact was a big problem, as you might imagine.

So what caused people to run to their banks and demand their cash? People were rational, but lacked some important information. As I documented in my thesis (see Gorton, 1988), people learned that a recession was coming, and if they learned that the recession was going to be particularly bad, then they would panic ("panic" meaning that they would want to protect their savings so that they would have the money during the recession). If you become unemployed, for example, you spend your savings. Withdrawing money from the bank was rational because the bank might fail during the recession. You could lose all your savings in that event. The problem was that no one outside the banking system knew which banks were the weak banks, which banks were risky. Even other banks might not have known. Without knowing which specific banks were the riskiest, depositors were cautious and withdrew their cash from all banks. But the banks did not fail because convertibility was suspended. Over time, the panic would subside and convertibility would resume. In the Panic of 2007, I use the term "counterparty risk" to denote this concern about bank risk.

Now comes a crucial issue, which will reappear later in the Panic of 2007 aftermath. One way of addressing the depositors' information problem, that they lacked precise bank-specific information, would be to try to provide that information. In the viewpoint of modern finance theory, there is a lack of market discipline, and information is needed. For example, the government could dictate that bank information be disclosed. But that was already happening during the 19th century, and there were still panics. And there is another problem.

Bank deposits are not like stocks (equities) because checks are used for trans-actions. Imagine going to the store and paying with ABC Company shares. The first question would be what the stock was worth on that day at that time. Second, the question could arise as to whether one party to the transaction had secret information about ABC Company, information unknown to the other party. It would be difficult to transact with stock. Perhaps the stock is actu-ally worth more than the value of the goods you are buying. Transactions are best conducted with a security that has a known value that's easy to determine and immune to gaming by one side of the transaction. In particular, a security where no one can profitably find secret information, so they don't bother try-ing. Securities like demand deposits are information insensitive, while securi-ties like equities are information sensitive.

The idea of deposit insurance, passed in the United States in 1934, is that bank runs and the currency famine would not arise if people never had to worry about their money in banks. Government deposit insurance made checks com-pletely information insensitive. If there is no uncertainty about the value because of the government guarantee, then no one would ever run on banks and bank-ing crises would be a thing of the past. And that is what happened, until 2007.

The alternative policy that could have been adopted in 1934 would have been one that was aimed at more transparency about bank balance sheets, so that depositors would know which banks were weakest. The government could have decided that efficient markets would work if checks were more informa-tion sensitive. Then, when depositors learned that a recession was coming, they would—in theory—only run on the weakest banks. This is the idea of "market discipline," that is, that depositors with precise information would run only on the weakest banks and leave the other banks alone. The experience of the 19th century suggests that the necessary precision for such transparency was not possible. Not only are today's banks much more complicated and opaque; the problem of transacting with stock-like securities further complicates the situation. Information-sensitive securities are not good for transacting. They provide speculators with an incentive to produce secret information and trade on this information. This is what made the Free Banking Era in the United States problematic. During the period 1837–1862, banks issued private (paper) money; there was no government money. So imagine a person carrying money issued by a bank in New Haven, Connecticut, goes to visit Boston. This per-son's New Haven Savings Bank ten-dollar bill would not be worth ten dollars in Boston, but would be discounted.[3] The discount changed, so store owners had to determine the market value of the money, which they did by referring to newspapers that printed the local prices. Transacting with such private money was similar to what it would be like to transact with stock.

Today it seems clear that deposit insurance was overall a better idea than the alternative of using information-sensitive securities to transact. Deposit insurance is not as controversial today as it was when it was proposed in the 1930s.[4] Nevertheless, it is astounding that deposit insurance passed. At the time, for example, Senator Robert Bulkley (D, Ohio) said of deposit insurance: "Such a guarantee as that would indeed have put a premium on bad banking. Such a guarantee as that would have made the government pay substantially all losses which had been accumulated, whether by misfortune, by unwise judgment, or by sheer recklessness, and it might well have brought an intolerable burden upon the federal treasury."[5] The arguments of opponents and proponents were moralistic. Opposition came largely from bankers who were blamed for the Great Depression and vilified. Opponents included the Roosevelt administration, segments of the banking industry and from some members of Congress. The issues were framed in terms of the small naive depositors against the sophisticated bankers. See Flood (1992) and FDIC (1998).

The events of 2007 are essentially a repeat of the problem of the 19th-century bank runs, only in 2007 some firms ran on other firms. What has become known as the "shadow banking system" is, in fact, genuine banking and, it turns out, was vulnerable to the same kind of bank runs as in previous U.S. history. While the details are provided later, here is a short summary. Where do firms and institutional investors save their money when they do not want to make long-term investments? In other words, what is the equivalent of a checking account for firms? There are no insured deposit accounts large enough for these depositors. But they have large amounts of money that they would like to deposit safely and with easy access, like a checking account. Over the last 25 years, a number of forces led to a banking solution. The solution is banking, but it does not happen in the familiar form of a depository institution.

Firms "deposit" in the sale and repurchase ("repo") market, a short-term market for firms, banks, and institutional investors. Here's how it works. Imagine a large institutional investor wants to save $500 million short-term. The investor wants to earn some interest, wants the money to be safe (no risk), and wants to have easy access to the money. One thing this investor could do is buy U.S. Treasury bonds. But there are many demands for U.S. Treasury bonds. Not only do foreign governments and foreign investors want to invest in U.S. Treasury bonds, but there are many domestic demands for them, as well. As discussed later, the demands for this type of (information-insensitive) bond are enormous. U.S. Treasury bonds are used as collateral for derivatives positions and in clearing systems.[6] There is a shortage of such collateral. So our institutional investor may well engage in the following transaction: the $500 million is "deposited" overnight with a bank (investment bank or commercial bank, foreign or domestic). The institutional investor will receive bonds (not necessarily government bonds) with a market value of $500 million; in other words, he receives collateral. In the panic, the collateral most likely will be securitization-related bonds, which represent claims on the portfolios of loans held by special legal entities that only hold that portfolio—all of which will be discussed later. The institutional investor will earn interest on the deposit. The bonds have to be given back when the institutional investor withdraws his money by not renewing (not "rolling") the transaction. Note that the firm receiving the deposit of $500 million has just financed the bonds that were given as collateral.

This transaction has some notable features. It resembles checking in that it is short-term, often lasts overnight; it is backed by the collateral; and the bond received as collateral can be "spent," that is, it can be used as collateral in some other transaction that the institutional investor may undertake. And that party can pass it on, as well. This process of reusing the collateral repeatedly is called "rehypothecation."[7] In short, repo is banking. You can see why the Federal Reserve System counted these transactions as "money" when it computed a measure of money called M3, now discontinued.[8]

The problem that will arise stems in part from the demands for collateral and how the private sector responds to this, by producing and supplying collateral. Simply put, there is a shortage of information-insensitive collateral that can be used in repo. For various reasons that will be discussed later, the financing of bank loans began to move out of the regulated bank sector and into capital markets. Many important forces have led to the evolution of the banking system, but in this case, the private sector began to produce bonds that could be used as collateral in repo.

You can see the possibility of a panic; it could occur if the depositors in the repo market decide not to renew their deposits and withdraw instead. Once a panic occurs, things get complicated fast. Transactions (or "liquidity") are best accomplished with information-insensitive securities, like demand deposits or repo with collateral. These markets are defined by the fact that individuals do not perform due diligence on the credit risk precisely because they have confidence in the value of the securities and because they are sure the other side does not know more than they do about the security's value. Common knowledge that this is the case is called "confidence in the system." No one needs to know the details of the securities precisely because they don't matter.

It's a bit like electricity. When you wake up in the morning, you put your lights on. And when you leave for work, you turn them off. Return from work, turn them on; go to sleep, turn them off. You don't need to know anything about electricity for this system to work. In fact, the idea is that you shouldn't have to know; you don't need to be an electrician. But if it happens that there is a blackout in which the whole electrical grid breaks down (this came close to happening in August 2003), then there is a problem. No one saw what happened to the grid, and many people do not actually know what electricity is. For the consumers of electricity, thinking about electricity for the first time seems incredibly complicated. And it is. Of course, the solution is not for everyone to become an electrician, rather, it is to restore the credibility of the system so that no one has to think about electricity.

Once the Panic of 2007 happened, the complexity was slowly revealed. When we start to probe into the underlying chains of securities and structures, the complexity can be dizzying. But that is not the point. It is not that financial wizards have created some complex house of cards, any more than the electrical grid is one. That complexity is what confronted market participants when securities that they took as information insensitive became information sensitive, due to the panic. Again, think of a 19th-century panic. Suppose there had not been suspension of convertibility and all the banks tried to sell their loans. Potential buyers do not know anything about the loans or the borrowers. No one may want to buy the loans, even at very low prices. The complexity of loan terms and information about borrowers would overwhelm the potential buyers of the loans. But no one other than banks needed to know all this in the 19th century, even when there was a panic. That was why banks suspended convertibility. Similarly, the repo markets involve counterparties and complex structured bonds. Much of that was designed to be information insensitive, but the design is very complicated.

How the repo market is related to the subprime housing market, and how that led to a panic in the modern wholesale banking (repo) market, is what this book is about. The book is based on three papers; two were written during the crisis for two Federal Reserve System conferences, and the third paper, written in the early 1990s, expresses concerns about the shadow banking system, although it had not yet developed fully. Still, the problems were already apparent. For the most part, little about the papers has been changed or rewritten. Each is a document of its moment.

The papers are presented in reverse chronological order. The oldest paper, chapter 5, was written over 15 years ago when it was clear to me that what is now called the "shadow banking system" had developed and was presenting serious issues with regard to bank regulation. It seemed clear to me then that the evolution of the banking system was challenging the regulatory paradigm of bank regulation. My academic work described these changes—loan sales, securitization, and the rise of derivatives.

The second paper was written for the Federal Reserve Bank of Kansas City's Jackson Hole Conference in August 2008. I was commissioned to write this paper some months prior to the conference. The crisis was full blown at the time of the writing, having started in August 2007. By late 2007, it was clear that the crisis was going to lead to a recession or depression. When I started writing in 2008, I wanted to write down everything I knew that I thought was relevant to understanding the complexity of the financial nexus that was the panic. I also wanted to convey a sense of financial history, that panics are not events that are completely unfamiliar—we have been through this before. I viewed writing this paper as producing a record for posterity. When I was writing my PhD thesis, I read many old academic articles about the earlier panics in U.S. history. Many of these were written by the eminent economists of the age, and a lot of what they wrote was narrative. O.M.W. Sprague, one of the most famous of these, wrote the classic *History of Crises under the National Banking System*. Sprague was the first chaired professor at Harvard Business School. Another famous chronicler of panics was Alexander Dana Noyes, a reporter and editor.[9] There are many more who could be mentioned.[10] Fifty to one hundred years after they were written, their articles struck me as very enlightening, and I set out to write a paper that someone could read in one hundred years and get a sense of the events of August 2007 to August 2008. Here, this paper has been split into two parts, chapters 3 and 4.

The Jackson Hole Conference, where this paper was delivered, is attended by invitation only, and the attendees consist of central bankers, bank regulators, economists from banks and academia, some members of the financial press, and bankers from the private sector. It is usually about monetary policy and topics that might impact central banks' policies.[11] I had never been to this conference before, presumably because my academic research is not on monetary policy. For the last 30 years, academic research related to central banks has concentrated almost exclusively on monetary policy, that is, on interest rates and inflation. The lender-of-last-resort role of central banks has not really been a focus.

The conference itself was somewhat strange in a number of respects. It seemed to me that it had an undercurrent of anxiety, but this appeared to me to be unspoken. On the one hand, participants did not act like we were in the middle of a terrible crisis that seemed out of control and not understood. On the other hand, the speed with which existing paradigms in economics were dropped as if they had never existed was breathtaking. In an instant, Keynesianism was revived, and the lender of last resort was the focus of central bank policy. By the time of the conference, central bankers had a narrative for the crisis, the so-called originate-to-distribute story, which argued that securitization per se was bad because incentives were not aligned.[12] It is interesting that central bankers as a group all used this catchphrase, and I wondered how they had coordinated this. No serious evidence was offered for this viewpoint, and my paper critiqued it (see chapter 4). As the crisis progressed, central bankers dropped this narrative and, unfortunately, they did not offer another, more accurate narrative to explain what had happened. In that sense, Jackson Hole did not produce any clarity. (In that regard, my paper did not help, either.) Soon, the dominant narrative became that of the press and the politicians, in which the crisis was due to a "reckless few" who "gamed the system" and got big bonuses. The lack of visibility of the core aspect of the crisis—the run in the repo market that I will shortly describe—allowed this to happen, and so we were plunged into dangerous demagoguery. Academics later were also unable to articulate a credible narrative for what happened and tended to speak in vague generalities.

After the Jackson Hole Conference of August 2008, things did not get better. Lehman failed on September 15, 2008. Sometime thereafter, I agreed to write another paper, this time for a conference sponsored by the Federal Reserve Bank of Atlanta to take place in May 2009 on Jekyll Island, Georgia, the place where the idea for the Federal Reserve System was originally hatched in 1910 by, among a few others, Senator Nelson Aldrich, the above-mentioned A. Piatt Andrew, and J.P. Morgan and Company partner Henry Davidson. By the time of the writing of this new paper, I had reflected more on what had happened, and this paper tries to convey the overall picture in a clearer way, along the lines I summarized above. The clarity is no doubt due partly to work I had started with academic coauthors Tri Vi Dang, Bengt Holmström, and Andrew Metrick; the ideas from this joint work influenced my thinking.

The Jekyll Island paper also has a slightly different tone than the Jackson Hole paper. By the time of the Jekyll Island conference, the crisis had been going on for almost two years, and momentous events had occurred. The atmosphere of the Jekyll Island Conference was almost one of fatigue. There was no end in sight. Fed Chairman Ben Bernanke, who had spoken at Jackson Hole about the Fed's response to the crisis, spoke again.[13] At Jekyll Island, Bernanke spoke about the bank stress tests that the Fed and other regulators had recently conducted, very impressively and in a short amount of time.[14]

I have tried to preserve the feeling of the historical moment in which each of my papers was written by not rewriting them to unify the style and feel. Quite the opposite: while I have tried not to be repetitious, there is overlap, some of which I have not eliminated. For example, I did not change the opening to the Jackson Hole paper, where I tried to convey some of the raw fear that was felt on trading floors in August 2007 and the subsequent realization of what was happening.

I have included the third paper specifically to indicate that the dangers associated with the rise of the shadow banking system did not appear suddenly. They were visible a long time ago, but they were simply not noticed. I thought there was a problem, as I indicate in chapter 5 (the third paper). The chapter title is the original title of the paper, "Bank Regulation When 'Banks' and 'Banking' are Not the Same." It seemed clear then (the paper was published in 1994 and written earlier) that changes in banking were presenting dangerous challenges to the bank regulatory system. The focus of the paper is on how banks can be effectively regulated.

One issue discussed in "Bank Regulation When 'Banks' and 'Banking' Are Not the Same" bears highlighting. In a capitalist system, firms ultimately face competition, and the owners of capital make decisions about how to allocate their capital. Regulations that are inconsistent with that competition result in exit from the industry. For example, capital requirements that are too high, in the absence of any countervailing benefit, will result in firms choosing to invest elsewhere. As I discuss (in two different chapters), the countervailing benefit historically was a valuable bank charter, which limited entry into banking and gave banks monopoly profits in exchange for abiding by regulations. If the charter becomes less valuable, there is an incentive to exit, via securitization, for example. This is the tension between a capitalist system and the need for regulation. It is a fine balance, which, if not finely tuned, can result in problems. While this paper was written over 15 years ago, prior to credit derivatives, for example, this tension was very palpable as the shadow banking system was emerging. It is even more pressing now. The period from 1934 to 2007, which I subsequently call the "Quiet Period" in U.S. banking history, was a period where this balance was achieved. Retuning the system depends on the narrative of the crisis, which sets the framework for new regulations. There is a lot at stake.

Many people have been very generous and helpful in the writing of the papers that appear here. Some of them gave comments and suggestions. Some of them helped obtain data or helped on specific details or examples. Some answered questions or gave advice. I thank the following people: James Aitken, David Andolfatto, Geetesh Bhardwaj, Omer Brav, Markus Brunnermeier, Adam Budnick, Charles Calomiris, Jared Champion, Tri Vi Dang, Craig Furfine, Kristan Blake Gochee, Itay Goldstein, Richard Grossman, Ping He, Bengt Holmström, Lixin Huang, Matt Jacobs, Ananth Krishnamurthy, Arvind Krishnamurthy, Tom Kushner, Bob McDonald, Maury Obstfeld, Maureen

O'Hara, Hui Ou-Yang, Ashraf Rizvi, Rich Rosen, Gabe Rosenberg, Geert Rouwenhorst, Amit Seru, Hyun Shin, Manmohan Singh, Marty Wayne, Axel Weber, and also those who wished to remain anonymous. Thanks to Meggi Persinger for help with the illustrations. Thanks to my students, whose never-ending questions forced clarity and disciplined thinking. Also, I thank Yale University for the support shown when the going looked like it was going to be very tough. Finally, my family was very kind with their love and support.

2

Slapped in the Face
by the Invisible Hand

Banking and the Panic of 2007

The American panic of 1907...gave the lie directly to those who in recent years have contended that we should never again witness experiences like those of the memorable years 1837, 1857, 1873, and 1893.
—Andrew (1908a, p. 290)

ECONOMISTS VIEW THE WORLD AS BEING THE OUTCOME OF THE "invisible hand," that is, a world where private decisions are unknowingly guided by prices to allocate resources efficiently.[1] The credit crisis raises the question of how it is that we could get slapped in the face by the invisible hand. What happened? Many private decisions were made over a long time, which created the shadow banking system. That system was vulnerable to a banking panic. The U.S. had a banking panic starting in August 2007, one that continues today. But, you say, banking panics, like the one in the movie *It's a Wonderful Life*, don't happen anymore.[2] Indeed, until these recent events, most people did not think of banking panics as something to be concerned about. After all, the panics of the Great Depression are a dim memory. Since 1934, when deposit insurance was adopted, until the current panic—a span of almost 75 years—there had been no banking panics.

The period from 1934, when deposit insurance was enacted, until the current crisis is somewhat special in that there were no systemic banking crises in the United States.[3] It is the "Quiet Period" in U.S. banking (see figure 2.1).[4] The figure shows the Great Depression very dramatically, but this event was very special, as discussed below. Looking at the figure, the Quiet Period in banking following the Great Depression is also clear. This Quiet Period led to the view that banking panics were a thing of the past. The year 2008 does not show much because the figure is in terms of number of failures, not total assets of failed institutions; and it does not include failed investment banks or distressed mergers.

The period of quiescence is related to what macroeconomists call "The Great Moderation," a view associated with the observation that the volatility of aggregate economic activity has fallen dramatically in most of the industrialized world.[5] One explanation for this is that there were no longer banking panics.[6] From a longer historical perspective, however, banking panics are the norm in American history. And obviously the world is different now; recent events are likely to lead to a revision of this view.

What gave us almost 75 years of relative quiet in banking? What has changed? How could problems in one part of the housing sector cause a banking panic in the 21st century? The banking system metamorphosed in the last 25 to 30 years, and this transformation re-created the conditions for a panic. But what does that mean exactly? What is the "shadow banking system"?

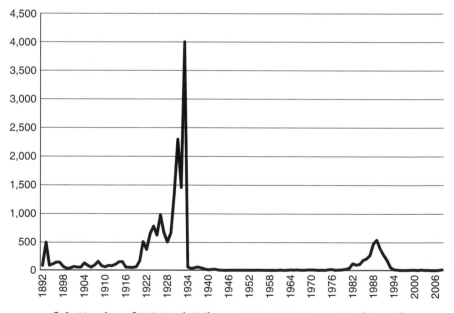

FIGURE 2.1 Number of U.S. Bank Failures, 1892–2008. Source: *Banking and Monetary Statistics* and FDIC.

Understanding that the shadow banking system is, in fact, real banking and that current events constitute a banking panic is vital to thinking about the future of the financial system. The failure to understand the transformation of banking has led to a great deal of confusion about the state we are in now. The functions of "banks" and "banking" remain, and these must be understood to see how a banking panic can occur. Understanding this is the only reasonable basis for new policies.

The lived experience of the current banking panic is confusing, and the reality of what has happened is hard to accept. The concept of a "systemic event" seems somewhat vague, seemingly referring casually to "bad things" happening. It is important to be clear on this. A banking panic means that the banking system is insolvent. The banking system cannot honor contractual demands; there are no private agents who can buy the amount of assets necessary to recapitalize the banking system, even if they knew the value of the assets, because of the sheer size of the banking system. When the banking system is insolvent, many markets stop functioning, and this leads to very significant effects on the real economy. This paper makes the case that the ongoing "credit crisis" is actually a banking panic.

The essential function of banking is to create a special kind of debt, debt that is immune to adverse selection by privately informed traders.[7] The leading example of this is demand deposits. More generally, this kind of debt is very liquid because its value rarely changes, and so it can be traded without fear that some people have secret information about the value of the debt.[8] If speculators can learn information that is private (only they know it), then they can take advantage of those less informed in trade. This is not a problem if the value of the security is not sensitive to such information. This information-insensitive debt originally was limited to demand deposits.

But demand deposits are of no use to large firms, banks, hedge funds, and corporate treasuries, which may need to deposit large amounts of money for a short period of time. These depositors are not willing to deposit, say, $500 million in a bank because it cannot be insured. But in the repo market, it can be "deposited" with a firm and collateralized with bonds, which the depositor receives and which can be used elsewhere (rehypothecation).[9] Rehypothecation is somewhat akin to being able to write checks. Like demand deposits, repo is short-term and can be withdrawn at any time. The "bank" backs the deposits with bonds as collateral, and often that collateral takes the form of securitized products (that is, bonds issued by special-purpose vehicles to finance portfolios of loans). The demand for collateral grew to include securitized products because of the growing need for collateral in the repo banking system for collateralizing derivatives positions and for settlement purposes.[10]

Historically, only banks (and, of course, the government) created information-insensitive debt, but the demand for such debt has grown. And now there is a range of securities with different information sensitivities. The notion of information-insensitive debt corresponds to the institutions that surround debt, as distinct from equity. Equity is very information sensitive. It is traded on centralized exchanges, and individual stocks are followed by analysts. Because debt is senior, and because securitized debt is backed by portfolios (see Gorton and Pennacchi, 1993a and Gorton and Souleles, 2006), senior "tranches" (bonds based on seniority) of securitizations are information insensitive, but not riskless, like demand deposits.[11] Information-insensitive debt does not need extensive institutional infrastructure, like equity. So, for example, the job of rating agencies need not be as in-depth as that of equity analysts.

The current crisis has its roots in the transformation of the banking system, which involved two important changes. First, derivative securities have grown exponentially in the last 25 years, and this has created an enormous demand for collateral, i.e., information-insensitive debt. Second, there has been the movement of massive amounts of loans originated by banks into the capital markets in the form of securitization and loan sales. Securitization involves the issuance of tranches that came to be used extensively as collateral in repo transactions, freeing other categories of assets, mostly treasuries, for use as collateral for derivatives transactions and for use in settlement systems. As discussed above, repo is a form of banking in that it involves the short-term (mostly overnight) "deposit" of money on call, backed by collateral. The current panic centered on the repo market, which suffered a run when "depositors" required increasing haircuts due to concerns about the value and liquidity of the collateral if the counterparty "bank" were to fail.[12] (A "haircut" refers to overcollateralization. For example, if the depositor provides $90 in cash and receives $100 worth of bonds as collateral, there is said to be a 10% haircut.) This interpretation is developed below, and evidence is provided for this viewpoint. Also, see and Gorton and Metrick (2009a,b).

Uninsured bank debt is vulnerable to panic. In the 19th century, before deposit insurance, periodic real shocks caused depositors to be anxious about their banks, described below. In such cases, they would run to their banks en masse demanding cash.[13] In the current period, there was shock as house prices began to fall. Gorton (2008, 2009) argues that this shock to fundamentals was revealed by the ABX, an index that started trading in January 2006 and which is linked to subprime securitization transactions. This is reviewed below. The panic starting in August 2007 involved firms "withdrawing" from other firms by increasing repo haircuts. So a "banking panic" occurs when information-insensitive debt becomes information sensitive due to a shock, in this case, the shock to subprime mortgage values due to house prices falling.

Understanding that the current crisis is a banking panic is important for thinking about the future of the financial landscape. The reality is that the so-called shadow banking system is, in fact, banking. It serves an important function, which should be recognized and protected. In order for that to happen, it is useful to ask why the U.S. banking system was panic-free between 1934 and 2007. The key features of that period provide some insight about how to re-create a period of quiescence in banking. There are two important features to be discussed. First, starting in 1934, bank debt was insured. Second, in addition to bank regulation, bank charters were valuable because of subsidies in the form of limited entry into banking, local deposit monopolies, interest-rate ceilings, and underpriced deposit insurance. In other words, bank regulation not only involved the "stick" of restrictions (reserve requirements, capital requirements, limitations on activities), but also the "carrot," that is, the subsidies. Both the restrictions and the subsidies have varied over time. But the value of a bank charter eroded in the 1990s with increased competition from nonbanks and, faced only with the stick, the shadow banking system developed out of the regulated banking system. Creating a new Quiet Period requires that "bank" debt be insured to assure that it is information insensitive and that will require that a valuable charter be re-created for firms that are deemed "banks." A brief proposal along these lines is sketched out as an example.

The paper proceeds as follows. It begins with a brief review of the function of "banks," a necessary prelude to understanding what happened. Next is a review of the history of banking panics, identifying the crucial characteristics that will again be seen in the current panic. Also, the endogenous response of the banks themselves to panics is briefly discussed. The historical response of banks provides some clues about the problem of panics and the best responses. I then describe the evolution of the shadow banking system. The increase in the demand for collateral, the rise of the repo market, and securitization are discussed. The nexus of these activities constitutes the shadow banking system. The key point is to understand that these activities constitute banking. This is important for thinking about what future regulations should look like. I then briefly describe the panic that started in 2007. In chapter 3, I provide much more detail on the panic itself than is explained here. This section draws on and reviews the evidence in Gorton (2009) and Gorton and Metrick (2009a,b). I very briefly review the history of bank regulation and the features that allowed for the Quiet Period from 1934 to 2007. Some possible new regulation is very briefly discussed, followed by a conclusion.

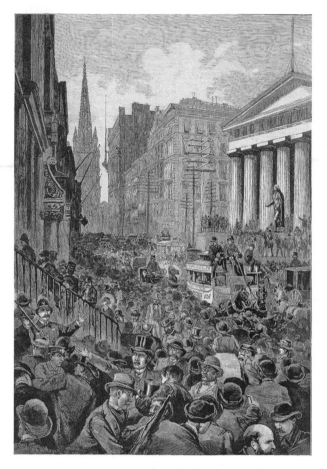

FIGURE 2.2 The Panic—Scenes in Wall Street Wednesday Morning, May 14, 1884, Harper's Weekly. (Provided courtesy HarpWeek, LCC)

Banks and Banking

During the panic of 1907, a bank run was an almost daily occurrence.

It was a horrible sight and one to make your heart ache with the pathos of it. Hard-working men and women whose deposits in the trust company represented years and years of savings and self-denial being suddenly stripped of all their earnings through no fault of their own. None of them understood what it was about, either.

And hardly ever does the layman understand what it is all about. All he knows is that he put his money in the bank for safe keeping, and it ought to be there when he wants to draw it out. (Seward, 1924)

In order to understand what a banking panic is about, it is necessary to know what banks do and, in particular, whether their functioning makes the banking system vulnerable to panic. Here is a brief review.

Bank Creation of Information-Insensitive Debt

There is a large academic literature on the functions of banking (see Gorton and Winton (2003) for a review). Most of this academic literature focuses on the bank's asset side of the balance sheet, namely, loans. The basic argument is that bank loans are special because they involve monitoring of the borrower by the bank and the production of private information about the borrower when the loan is made initially. Bank loans have more detailed covenants than bonds so the bank can monitor by enforcing these constraints. Bank loans are usually the first source of external finance for firms, and bond issuance usually comes next, and so issuing bonds seems to depend on the firm first having a loan (a kind of certification). The implication of these arguments about banking is that bank loans cannot be sold by the bank because then the bank would have no incentive to produce the information when it first made the loan, or to monitor the borrower during the life of the loan. Reality contradicts these descriptions of banking because loans are, in fact, sold in significant quantities, as discussed below. This is part of the development of the shadow banking system. So these academic arguments cannot be the primary reason for the existence of banks, as least today.

On the liability side of the balance sheet, however, banks produce special securities, that is, information-insensitive debt that can be used for transactions. Demand deposits are the leading example of this. Their special features are designed to make checks easy to use to conduct transactions. But the main point about demand deposits is that counterparties accepting checks written to them need not worry about the value of the check, unlike in the Free Banking Era. Many features of checks contribute to this. Demand deposits are short-term; they essentially have no maturity. Depositors have the right to withdraw their currency at any time. Today, this is because of deposit insurance, the purpose of which is precisely to ensure that no party to the transaction need be concerned about the value of the check. This is the feature of demand deposits that make them a currency. This point was not obvious in the 19th century. For example, Dunbar (1887) wrote: "The ease with which we ignore deposits as a part of the currency seems the more remarkable, when we consider that few men in business fail to recognize the true meaning of this form of bank liability; that it is a circulating medium in as true a sense and in the same sense as the bank-note, and that, like the bank-note, it is created by the bank and for the same purposes" (p. 402). Dunbar argues that a demand deposit is like currency, which means that it has the basic feature of currency: it is information insensitive (though, of course, Dunbar does not say that).

Banks create liquidity by producing securities that have this property. Bank debt is designed to be small bonds that are not subject to adverse selection when traded because it is not profitable to produce private information to speculate in these bonds. In the extreme, the securities are riskless, like insured demand deposits. "Banking" corresponds to the process of creating this type of debt. Clearly, if the debt is a senior claim on a diversified portfolio, like a portfolio of bank loans, it is likely less risky. But, as we will see, this portfolio need not reside at a regulated commercial bank.

In the 19th century, before demand deposits were insured, banks went to great lengths to create nearly riskless demand deposits through the use of clearinghouse arrangements, discussed below. But these arrangements ultimately did not prevent banking panics. The need for information-insensitive debt is the logic behind deposit insurance.[14]

But what about other kinds of debt? More broadly, studies of corporate bond returns and bond yield changes have mainly concluded that investment-grade bonds behave like Treasury bonds, reacting to interest rate movements rather than measures of the issuer's default risk, while below-investment-grade bonds (junk bonds) are more sensitive to the firm's stock returns, reacting to information about the firm.[15] The difference in behavior is notable and is a sort of dividing line between degrees of credit risk information sensitivity. Nevertheless, even investment-grade debt can suffer losses if the issuer defaults. Corporate debt is senior, but it is not (typically) a claim on a diversified portfolio. Senior corporate debt has some features of the kind of debt that is needed for transactions; it is an intermediate case.

A firm, however, may be financed by issuing securities that are claims on the general credit of the corporation; that is, they are backed by the assets of the company (bonds), or the firm can finance itself by segregating specified cash flows and selling claims specifically linked to these specified cash flows. The latter strategy is accomplished by setting up another company, called a Special Purpose Vehicle (SPV) or Special Purpose Entity (SPE), and then selling the specified cash flows to this company. The SPV, in turn, issues securities into the capital market to finance the purchase of the cash flows from the company (called the "sponsor"). The sponsor services the cash flows, that is, makes sure that the cash flows are arriving, etc. The SPV is not an operating company in the usual sense. It is more of a robot company in that it is a set of rules. It has no employees or physical location. As we will see, an SPV has some special properties that make it different in other ways, as well. The latter process is called securitization.

Securitization involves seniority and large portfolios. Figure 2.3 shows the general process of securitization. The figure shows how the cash flows from assets (loans) created by an originating firm are sold to a special purpose vehicle, which finances this by issuing securities in the capital markets. These seniority-based securities are called "tranches." Gorton and Souleles (2006) provide more details. As shown in the figure, securitization involves two conceptual steps. First, underlying cash flows from assets are put into a pool. In other words, the specific assets that are generating the cash flows, usually loans of some sort, are identified and sold (in a specific legal sense) to the SPV. As mentioned above, an important distinguishing feature of asset-backed securities (ABS) is that they rely upon the cash flows from a specified pool of assets for payment, rather than on the general credit of an issuing corporation. The cash flows emanate from assets originally created by a sponsoring corporation. When they are securitized, the cash flows from these assets are sold into a separate legal entity, the SPV (often its legal structure is a master trust) that finances the purchase of the assets through issuance of securities to investors.

The second conceptual step in securitization is that the pool of cash flows sold to the SPV is tranched; that is, securities with different seniorities are designed and issued against the pool. Another way to say this is that the SPV has to have a capital structure, so its liability side must be designed. This is called tranching.

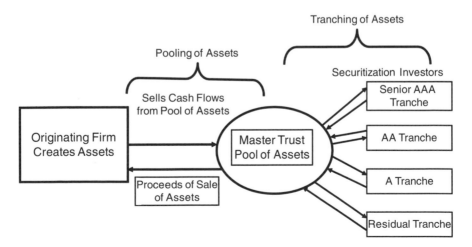

FIGURE 2.3 The Securitization Process: Pooling and Tranching

In addition to home mortgages, many other asset classes have also been securitized (see table 2.1). Securitized asset classes, e.g., mortgages, credit card receivables, and auto loans, may be examples of relatively information-insensitive debt, created by the private sector without government insurance.[16] Several features make securitization debt potentially immune from adverse selection. First, most of the debt is senior and investment-grade. Second, with securitization, the debt is backed by portfolios (see Gorton and Pennacchi, 1993a, and Gorton and Souleles, 2006). Third, a by-product of many structured products is that they are complex (as explained in chapter 3). Complexity raises the cost of producing private information. Finally, securitization does not involve traded equity; this is important because there is no information leakage or externalities from the equity market, as with corporate bonds. In summary, senior tranches of securitizations are information insensitive, though not riskless, like demand deposits. The most senior tranches of securitization transactions have never experienced defaults.

The outstanding amounts of major asset classes that are securitized are provided below. They are very significant. The nonmortgage securitization issuance has exceeded U.S. corporate bond issuance in recent years. Securitization is far from a trivial amount or an exotic asset class.

Because of the security design, information-insensitive debt is surrounded by a different set of trading and related infrastructure and institutions compared to information-sensitive asset classes, in particular, equity. Broadly speaking, this debt does not really correspond to the textbook descriptions of "efficient markets," a notion that is basically about stock markets. The primary

TABLE 2.1 Examples of Securitized Asset Classes

Aircraft leases	Health club receivables
Auto loans (prime)	Home equity loans
Auto loans (subprime)	Intellectual property cash flows
Auto leases	Insurance receivables
B & C MBS	Motorcycle loans
Commercial real estate	Music royalties
Computer leases	Mutual fund receivables
Conforming first-lien mortgages	Manufactured housing loans
Non-conforming mortgages	Small business Loans
Consumer loans	Stranded utility costs
Credit card receivables	Student loans
Equipment leases	Trade receivables
Equipment loans	Time share loans
Franchise loans	Tax liens
"Future" receivables	Taxi medallion loans
Healthcare receivables	Viatical settlements

market is over-the-counter, where debt is sold based almost exclusively on its rating.[17] There is no organized secondary market; instead, the secondary market is organized around dealer banks and depends on intermediation via the repurchase market.

Intuitively, information-insensitive debt is debt that no one need devote a lot of resources to investigating. It is designed to avoid exactly that. Consumers do not spend a lot of time doing due diligence on the bank holding the money of someone buying something from them. Analogously, firms and institutional investors will not need to do due diligence because of the presence of collateral, i.e., information-insensitive debt. Again, think of it as like electricity. Millions of people turn their lights on and off every day without knowing how electricity really works or where it comes from. The idea is for it to work without every consumer having to be an electrician.

The current crisis was caused by a shock which led to the collapse of debt, because the banking system broadly has evolved to be susceptible to such a shock. This is discussed below. Continuing the analogy from above, when the shock hits, suddenly the electricity stops working. When that happens, an event no one really contemplated, it is too late for everyone to become an electrician. Because the event of losing electricity is so rare, no one understands how it could happen, but the solution of everyone becoming an electrician in the future makes no sense.

The Demand for Collateral

Collateral is the currency for firms; that is, firms need to both post collateral to mitigate default risk as well as obtain collateral that can be reused or "spent." "Posting collateral" is a way to make good on a promise to pay, as long as the collateral does not lose value while it is posted to the counterparty. We will see that collateral is almost synonymous with information-insensitive debt, although obviously there are degrees of sensitivity.

The use of collateral has expanded rapidly in the last decade or so. This is due, in large part, to the use of bilateral collateral agreements to address counterparty risk. There is a huge demand for collateral. Financial firms, such as dealer banks and commercial banks, have large needs for collateral, and this has grown to an enormous extent. First, collateral is needed in repo markets, where the transaction involves the "deposit" of cash in exchange for a bond as collateral. Second, collateral is also needed in derivatives markets, where it is used to offset counterparty credit risk. Finally, collateral is needed in payment and settlement systems. See, for example, Bank for International Settlements (BIS) (2001). Probably, the largest demands for collateral come from the repo market, discussed in a subsequent section below. Here the second and third sources of demands for collateral are very briefly discussed.

In the last 25 years, the use of derivative securities has grown dramatically.[18] (See figure 2.4.) Derivatives trade under International Swap and Derivative Association (ISDA) master agreements, which often involve a Credit Support Annex (CSA), specifying the conditions under which parties must post collateral. While counterparty risk is mitigated in a variety of ways, the most important credit enhancement is the posting of collateral in the amount of the current mark-to-market value of the derivative contract.[19] An ISDA master agreement and the CSA contain a number of provisions which allow each party to protect its position. These provisions are negotiated between the parties when entering into an ISDA agreement. The provisions specify credit support, events of default and termination events, among others things.

The Credit Support Annex outlines collateral posting requirements, which are among the most significant issues in the original negotiations. The parties

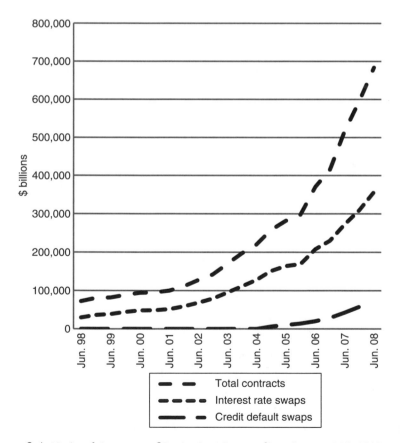

FIGURE 2.4 Notional Amounts of Derivatives Outstanding. Source: BIS (2008a).

may agree to collateralize their exposure to one another only to the extent that such exposure exceeds a certain dollar amount, namely, the threshold. Hedge funds generally must agree to post collateral based on a zero threshold amount, so that the dealer is fully collateralized, while dealers generally have to agree to post only above a specified amount. Collateral posting is also usually related to various triggers about the credit risk of a party (e.g., ratings triggers) and market-to-market thresholds on the position. For example, Ambac Financial Group, Inc., the bond insurer, lost its AAA credit ratings in 2008 and announced that the downgrade triggered $776 million of collateral posting and termination payments at its investment division.

In 2009, the International Swaps and Derivatives Association (ISDA) reported that "the amount of collateral used in connection with over-the-counter derivatives transactions grew from $2.1 to $4.0 trillion during 2008, a growth rate of 86 percent, following 60 percent growth in 2007" (p. 2). According to ISDA (2009):

> Collateral coverage continues to grow, both in terms of trade volume subject to collateral agreements and of credit exposure covered by collateral. This reflects a long-term trend toward increased collateral coverage. For all OTC derivatives, 65 percent of trades are subject to collateral agreements, compared with 63 percent last year and 30 percent in 2003. Further, 66 percent of OTC derivative credit exposure is now covered by collateral compared with 65 percent last year and 29 percent in 2003. (p. 2)

Cash is the most important form of collateral for derivatives (see ISDA 2008). But, that means that that collateral is not available for other purposes. Figure 2.5 shows the growth in collateral, based on ISDA surveys of its members. The figure shows the effect of the crisis; collateral usage in 2008 shot up.

Collateral is also needed for purposes of settlement in securities transactions. Delivery versus payment settlement eliminates the settlement risk between parties to a transaction (because the trade and settlement occur simultaneously). Without this, the risk is a possible loss of cash or securities during the time it takes to settle; that is, there is the risk that the promised payment/deliveries do not actually occur. Collateralized intraday credit is one way to mitigate this type of risk. See Zhou (2000) for background. On central bank collateral policies, see Chailloux, Gray, and McCaughrin (2008).

In the last 15 years or so, there has been a shift toward real-time gross settlement (RTGS) systems, usually involving accounts at a central bank. See BIS (2005a, b). "Real-time" means that there is no waiting period; the transaction is settled as soon as it is processed. There is no netting of transactions; rather,

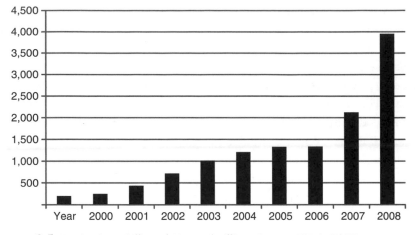

FIGURE 2.5 Derivatives Collateral Usage, $Billion. Source: ISDA (2009).

under "gross settlement," the transaction is settled without regard to any other transaction. Under RTGS systems, transactions are only completed if the paying bank has sufficient funds. Central banks usually provide intraday credit, but only on a fully collateralized basis.[20] According to the Federal Reserve (2006): "In 2005, 64 percent of the approximately 270 depository institutions that paid daylight overdraft fees had assets pledged to the Reserve Banks for discount window purposes" (p. 35683).[21] Figure 2.6 shows the average daylight overdraft amounts, most of which would be collateralized.

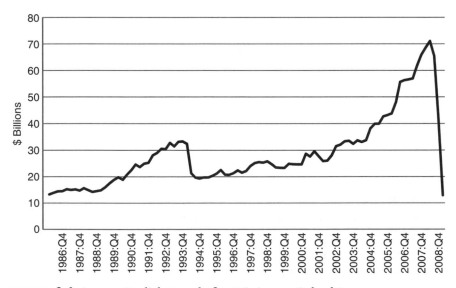

FIGURE 2.6 Average Daylight Overdrafts, U.S. Source: Federal Reserve.

The figure, of course, is only for the U.S., and does not cover the Clearing House Interbank Payments System (CHIPS) or collateral pledged on other futures, options, or stock exchanges.[22] Also, it shows the average, rather than the peak daylight overdrafts. But the main point is to get a sense of the size and growth of the demand for collateral for settlement purposes. Similar data for other countries is provided by the Bank for International Settlements (2009).

Shadow Banking

Creation of information-insensitive debt is the function of the banking system. In the regulated bank sector, this corresponds to insured demand deposits. The characteristics of demand deposits are: (1) demand deposits have no fixed maturity; they can be exchanged for cash at par on demand; (2) they are senior claims; (3) they are claims on a portfolio; (4) they can be used in transactions. This form of debt is created by depository institutions and by money market mutual funds that offer checking.

Shadow banking combines repo with securitization (or other forms of information-insensitive debt) to accomplish the same function for firms. Senior tranches of securitized debt and commercial paper (not discussed here) are also quite information insensitive. The shadow banking system, the combination of repo and securitized debt, is a kind of bank, as follows: (1) repo has a short maturity; it is typically settled overnight and can be withdrawn (not rolled over) on demand; (2) it is senior in that the collateral is senior, but also senior in the sense that there may be a haircut on the collateral (this is discussed below); (3) repo collateral is backed by a portfolio if the collateral is securitization-based debt; (4) the collateral can be used in other transactions, i.e., it can be rehypothecated. Repo is discussed further below.

The shadow banking system is different from depository institutions in that the activity involves the repo market, where depositors and lenders are individually matched; all depositors get their own collateral. So the shadow banking system involves a market, the repo market. Securitization enters via the need for collateral. If securitization debt is information insensitive, it can be input into the repo system, creating a kind of transaction medium, i.e., collateral that can be rehypothecated.

The demand for collateral for purposes of mitigating counterparty risk in derivatives and settlement systems appears large, though the evidence is scanty. Aggregate evidence about the demand for treasuries is provided by Krishnamurthy and Vissing-Jorgensen (2008), who discuss the demand for treasury collateral and provide evidence of a "convenience yield" associated with treasuries, i.e., evidence of their value in use as "cash" rather than just as a store of value. Also, Caballero (2006) discusses the macroeconomic implications of a shortage of collateral.

Prior to the current panic, there was also evidence on the potential scarcity of collateral. For example, the BIS (2001) warned of the problems of a scarcity of collateral, concluding that "Current issuance trends suggest that shortfalls of the stock of preferred collateral may eventually lead to appreciable substitution into collateral having relatively higher issuer and liquidity risk" (p. 2). Also, see Domanski and Neumann (2001). In a "Letter to the European Central Bank," November 28, 2003, from The Bond Market Association:

> ...the increasing market focus on collateralisation—a focus encouraged by central banks, by supervisors in encouraging the use of collateral in risk management, by payment and settlement systems in their own endeavours to ensure the integrity of their systems and by market participants' own risk management efforts—means that the demands for collateral within the financial markets are rapidly increasing and can be expected to increase very significantly in the future.

The topic of demands for collateral reappears below when the repo market is discussed.

Debt and Systemic Events: The Lessons of History

> The causes of crises are so subtle in nature that any attempt to foretell fluctuations in the financial world might well be considered hazardous. No one in the opening months of the year 1860 thought of doubting the continuance of the rising tide of prosperity which had begun to gather strength the year before. And yet the closing months of the year saw such a destruction of trade and credit, and the downfall of so many powerful houses, that the financial situation in New York and, indeed, throughout the United States generally, occasioned deep anxiety to the financiers of the world. (Swanson, 1908a, p. 65)

> Everywhere the banks suddenly found themselves paying out money in response to the demands of frightened depositors, and were in turn forced to draw upon their reserves with other banks. The evidence of lack of confidence in the banks is clear, and points to a serious problem in American banking....Seven times during the last century the banks suspended payment in some measure, and there has been a currency premium...(Sprague, 1908, p. 363)

Understanding that the current crisis is a banking panic can be made easier by first looking at past panics. While there were banking panics as early as

1792 in the U.S. (see Cowen, Sylla and Wright, 2006), the U.S. National Banking Era, 1863–1913, is a very useful laboratory for studying banking panics because there was no central bank during this period, that is, no government lender of last resort. Also, there was little regulation or deregulation of banks by the federal government (though national banks were chartered by the federal government), but data about national banks was systematically collected.[23] The period is useful too because there are no peso-type problems with respect to the government (that is, reactions by firms and consumers to the possibility of a government action, which then does not occur). Finally, there is a "large" sample, in the sense that panics were a fairly regular event during this period. Gorton (1988) and Calomiris and Gorton (1991) study this period.[24]

What can we learn from the National Banking Era experience of panics? We can observe the central features of panics and try to understand the nature of the event. Also, we can get clues about the causes of panics by looking at the endogenous response of banks themselves, before there was a government lender of last resort. Lastly, the historical experience of panics provides some clarity as to what a systemic event is.

FIGURE 2.7 Scene in the New York Stock Exchange during the Panic of 1873 (1875). (Picture Collection, The New York Public Library, Astor, Lenox and Tilden foundations)

U.S. National Banking Era Panics, 1864–1913

The National Banking Act was passed in 1863, creating a system of national banks and a uniform national currency. The act also established the Office of the Comptroller of the Currency. Table 2.2 lists the banking panics that occurred in the United States during the National Banking Era. The first two columns show the National Bureau of Economic Research (NBER) business cycle dates and the date of the panic. The NBER dates were determined by Burns and Mitchell (1946). There has been subsequent work based on new data that has made some of the dates slightly suspect.[25] The panic dates are based on when clearinghouses issued loan certificates, discussed below, and on contemporary sources stating when depositors were observed running on banks. This usually started in large cities and spread across the country.[26] Looking at the panic dates, it is notable that they occur very near the peak of the business cycle, in most cases. In fact, based on the discussion below, the panic date may be a better indicator of the business cycle peak date.

The panics are associated with recessions, some with very serious recessions. See Grossman (1993). The panics of 1873 and 1907 are notable in this regard.[27] The declines in real economic activity, as proxied for by the change in pig iron production and the length of the recession, are very significant.

The table also shows the percentage change in the currency-deposits ratio, the percentage change in pig iron production, the loss per dollar of deposits, and the percentage and number of national bank failures. These variables are measured from panic date to trough date. Pig iron production is a common measure of monthly economic activity during the National Banking Era. Looking at

TABLE 2.2 U.S. National Banking Era Panics

NBER Business Cycle Dates Peak–Trough	Panic Date	%Δ(C/D)	%Δ(Pig Iron)	Loss per Deposit $	% and # of U.S. National Bank Failures
Oct. 1873–Mar. 1879	Sep. 1873	14.53	−51.0	0.021	2.8 (56)
Mar. 1882–May 1885	Jun. 1884	8.8	−14.0	0.008	0.9 (10)
Mar. 1887–Apr. 1888	No Panic	3.0	−9.0	0.005	0.4 (12)
Jul. 1890–May 1891	Nov. 1890	9.0	−34.0	0.001	0.4 (14)
Jan. 1893–Jun. 1894	May 1893	16.0	−29.0	0.017	1.9 (74)
Dec. 1895–Jun. 1897	Oct. 1896	14.3	−4.0	0.012	1.6 (60)
Jun. 1899–Dec. 1900	No Panic	2.78	−6.7	0.001	0.3 (12)
Sep. 1902–Aug. 1904	No Panic	−4.13	−8.7	0.001	0.6 (28)
May 1907–Jun. 1908	Oct. 1907	11.45	−46.5	0.001	0.3 (20)
Jan. 1910–Jan. 1912	No Panic	−2.64	−21.7	0.0002	0.1 (10)
Jan. 1913–Dec. 1914	Aug. 1914	10.39	−47.1	0.001	0.4 (28)

Source: Gorton (1988).

the change in pig iron production, it is clear that panics are associated with very serious subsequent recessions. By this measure, the three worst panics, 1873, 1907, and 1914, were followed by declines of 51%, 46%, and 47%, respectively. The currency-deposit ratio also rises, reflecting withdrawals at banks, but this is tempered by the suspension of convertibility, which was the first act of banks faced with a generalized panic. On suspension, see Gorton (1985a).

The final two columns are remarkable in showing that the losses per deposit dollar and the percentage of national banks failing were quite low. In contrast, for example, losses as a percent of deposits over the period 1921–1933 averaged 45 cents (0.45) per year—an order of magnitude higher (see FDIC, 1998, table 5, p. 21). The reasons for this have to do with the response of private bank clearinghouses to panics, discussed below.

These historical banking panics had four important characteristics. First, the banking system is insolvent. Depositors run to their banks en masse seeking to withdraw money from checking and savings accounts.[28] The banking system cannot honor these demands because the money has been lent out. The loans are illiquid; that is, there is no one capable of buying a sufficient amount of assets to recapitalize the banking system, and so banks cannot honor depositor demands. The evidence for the insolvency of the banking system during a panic is discussed below, when clearinghouse loan certificates are discussed.

Second, because of the hoarding of cash and despite the efforts of bank clearinghouses, discussed below, there was a shortage of transaction mediums, repeatedly described by contemporary observers as a "currency famine." Transactions were disrupted because of a lack of means of payment. For example, firms could not meet payrolls because employees would not accept bank checks. Checks could not be used at stores because they were not accepted. Certified checks were exchanged at deep discounts. And this currency famine occurred despite the issuance of clearinghouse loan certificates (discussed below), as well as many other kinds of money substitutes. See, for example, Andrew (1908b).

Third, the hoarding of cash led to a currency premium. That is, currency sold at a premium to certified checks, and sometimes a premium was paid for a large amount of cash (by a country bank to a city bank, for example). Dwyer and Gilbert (1989) contain figures showing the evolution of the currency premiums during the panics of 1893 and 1907. Also, see Andrew (1908a), Sprague (1910), Noyes (1894).[29]

The final point concerns the timing of the panics and was noted above. Panics occurred at business cycle peaks. The observation about timing is related to explaining the cause of panics. Gorton (1988) analyzes the causes of panics empirically, estimating a model of a representative agent facing a cash-in-advance constraint. The agent saves by depositing in a risky bank. This agent cares about the intertemporal marginal rate of substitution, so the pricing kernel weights the expected returns on the demand deposits in determining the currency-deposit ratio. In other words, the agent cares about possible losses on his savings should the bank fail and, to the extent that these losses are to come in bad times, the agent will hold more currency relative to deposits. Bank losses that come in bad times are particularly bad because consumption is lower in bad times. Just when the agent is worse off in terms of consumption, the bank might fail. So, in a recession, income and consumption decline and banks tend to fail because their borrowers also tend to fail. If the agent anticipates this, then he will withdraw from the bank to avoid losses on his bank savings occurring during the recession.

Gorton (1988) estimates this model and, in particular, asks what information arrives that causes the agent to forecast the coincidence of consumption being low and banks failing. The answer is that a leading indicator of recession—the cyclical component of the liabilities of failed businesses spikes—indicates that a recession is coming and, acting on this information, agents in the economy rush to their banks to withdraw money, in a panic. During the National Banking Era, every time this leading indicator was greater than 0.83, there was a panic. There are no cases of a panic when the indicator is not higher than this threshold.

The information that depositors received was aggregate information, not specific information about individual banks. People knew that a recession was coming and that in a recession some banks were likely to fail, but no one knew which banks. So it was rational to take the precautionary action of withdrawing cash from all banks. The shock threshold was literally large enough to cause a panic.

This is related to the function of banks, discussed above. Banks try to produce securities that are useful for transacting, namely bank debt—demand deposits. But, in a panic, people lose confidence in the value of bank debt. Bank debt that was previously viewed as "safe" becomes viewed with suspicion. In this context, "safe" means two related, things. First, the value of the bank debt does not change much, a ten-dollar check is pretty much always worth ten dollars. And, second, because of this it is not susceptible to adverse selection when it is used in transactions (traded in markets). That is, it does not pay anyone to produce private information about the value of the bank debt and speculate on that information.

A panic is a situation where a shock occurs that is large enough for bank debt to become information sensitive. It loses its most important feature, and so agents do not want it anymore; they want an asset which is surely information insensitive—cash. When that happens, the banking system cannot honor the demands and is insolvent.

How did banks respond to panics during the National Banking Era? Their response will give us clues as to the causes and remedies for panics.

The Private Bank Clearinghouse Response to Panics

During the National Banking Era, there was no central bank to act as a lender of last resort. So what happened during a panic? During the 19th century, the banks themselves developed increasingly sophisticated ways to respond to panics. The response was centered on private bank clearinghouses. Originally organized to be an efficient way to clear checks, these coalitions or clubs of banks evolved into much more. Toward the end of the National Banking Era, the clearinghouse response was essentially as follows.[30]

In response to a panic, banks would jointly suspend convertibility of deposits into currency. Coincident with this, clearinghouse member banks joined together to form a new entity overseen by the Clearinghouse Committee. As Swanson (1908b, p. 221) put it, describing the crisis of 1860, there was "the virtual fusion of the fifty banks of New York into one central bank" (p. 221). The clearinghouse would also cease the publication of individual bank accounting information (which banks were normally required by the clearinghouse to publish in the newspapers) and would instead only publish the aggregate information of all the members. Finally, banks issued loan certificates, which were first used to replace currency in the clearing process, starting with the Panic of 1857. But in the panics of 1893 and 1907, the clearinghouse issued new money, called clearinghouse loan certificates, directly to the public, in small denominations. See Gorton (1985b). These were liabilities of the clearinghouse members jointly and served the purpose of providing a kind of deposit insurance. The clearinghouse loan certificate was a remarkable innovation, resulting from individual private banks finding a way to essentially become a single institution, responsible for each other's obligations during a panic and issuing a hand-to-hand currency.

Table 2.3 shows the amounts of clearinghouse loan certificates issued by the New York City Clearinghouse Association. The details of how the clearinghouse required collateral and set rates on the collateral are provided in Gorton (1985b) and Canon (1910). Other cities typically followed New York and also issued certificates. Sprague (1903): "The position of the more important New York banks is entirely analogous to that of the great central reserve banks of Europe, such as the Bank of England and the Bank of France. Any unusual demand for actual cash...is certain sooner or later to bring about a withdrawal of money from the New York national banks" (p. 34).

FIGURE 2.8 Making the Exchange in Six Minutes, at the Clearing House.
(From J. S. Gibbons, *The Banks of New York, Their Dealers, The Clearing House and the Panic of 1857* [1859], illustration by Herrick)

TABLE 2.3 Clearinghouse Loan Certificates Issued by the New York Clearinghouse ($millions)

Year	Date First Issued	Months until Redeemed	Maximum Amount Created	Bank Deposits
1860	November 23	3.5	$6.9	$99.6
1861	September 19	7.25	22	99.3
1863	November 6	2.75	9.6	159.5
1864	March 7	3.25	16.4	168.0
1873	September 22	3.75	22.4	174.8
1884	May 15	4.25	21.9	317.2
1890	November 12	2.75	15.2	386.5
1893	June 21	4.66	38.3	398.0
1907	October 26	5	88.4	1023.7
1914	August 3	4	109.2	—

Sources: Report of the Comptroller of the Currency, 1907, p. 63; Dwyer and Gilbert (1989); Swanson (1908b).

In 1893 and 1907, depositors unsure of the risk of their own single bank failing were not able to obtain cash, but received instead a claim on the clearinghouse member bank jointly. Thus, depositors were insured against their own bank failing, but were not insured against the entire clearinghouse failing. The issuance of clearinghouse loan certificates was not insignificant. In the

Panic of 1893, about $100 million of hand-to-hand currency was issued (2.5% of the money stock). During the Panic of 1907, about $500 million was issued, which was about 4.5% of the money stock. See Gorton (1985b) and Dwyer and Gilbert (1989).

In 1893 and 1907, when clearinghouse loan certificates were issued to the public in small denominations, they traded initially at a discount to par, reflecting the belief that there was some chance that the clearinghouse was insolvent. This is evidence of the "insolvency" of the banks in the clearinghouse, essentially the banking system since this occurred nationwide. Over time, the discount was reduced, and suspension was lifted afterward. Following the return to normalcy, the clearinghouse might announce the insolvency of a member bank.

The clearinghouse response did not prevent panics. But clearinghouse actions prevented wholesale liquidation of the banking system in the face of system insolvency. Still, there were real effects from the crisis. The most important real effect, based on the writings of contemporaries, concerned the disruption of transactions due to a shortage of cash. How much this contributed to the recession is not known.

Clearinghouse actions in response to panics offer clues to the causes of a panic. First, it is notable and somewhat counterintuitive that the clearinghouse, after suspending convertibility, would suspend the release of bank-specific information. This is completely contrary to an "efficient markets" view of the world. The logic of the clearinghouse response to a panic was to form a single institution, the coalition, and only information about this entity was relevant. See Gorton and Huang (2006). Second, the issuance of clearinghouse loan certificates was started; these were financial claims on the coalition of banks, not the liability of any single bank. Essentially, what happened was that the clearinghouse tried to make bank liabilities more information insensitive by replacing bank-specific deposits with certificates that were claims on the whole coalition.[31] This meant that bank-specific information was not relevant. Clearinghouses attempted to provide a kind of deposit insurance, by issuing loan certificates in times of panic.

The clearinghouse response to panics was exactly the opposite of the view that it is important to "mark-to-market" the assets of the banking system. The clearinghouse decisively recognized that the assets could not be sold and that such "marking" was meaningless. (Adrian and Shin (2009a, b) have studied the effects of marking-to-market.) The clearinghouse was an incentive-compatible mechanism for agreeing on when suspension should occur, including the change in the information regime. This is an important clue for understanding panics.

The clearinghouse system continued to evolve until the Federal Reserve System came into being. For example, by the early part of the 20th century, the clearinghouse had its own bank examiners, starting in Chicago in 1906 and "introduced in St. Paul and Minneapolis in 1907, Kansas City, Los Angeles, and San Francisco in 1908; St. Joseph and Philadelphia in 1909, Milwaukee, Oklahoma City, and Nashville in 1910; Portland (Ore.), Cleveland, Louisville, Cincinnati, and New York in 1911, and Columbus, New Orleans, and Muskogee in 1912."[32] Given the mutual obligations adopted by clearinghouse members, banks thought "they were entitled to know the conditions of each member bank."[33] "The examiner is not burdened with rules or instructions. He is interested principally in determining the solvency and healthfulness of an institution and the character of its management."[34]

How successful was the clearinghouse in dealing with panics? Obviously, clearinghouses did not prevent panics. But they did prevent wholesale liquidation of banks due to insolvency caused by the runs. Banks were not forced to sell assets. Table 2.4 shows the causes of bank failures based on the Comptroller of the Currency's classification of failures, which were categorized into three groups by Thomas (1935). The numbers in the table are the ratio of occurrences of each cause to the total occurrences of all causes, i.e., each number is a percentage. The data are expressed as a percentage because the number of banks changes over this long period. The data show that the cause of bank failures during normal times is poor management and illegal activity. During panics or recessions, more banks fail, but as a percentage of the total failures the causes of failure are still largely poor management and illegal activity. During the Panic of 1873 and the aftermath, the two categories are almost equally

TABLE 2.4 Causes of Failure of National Banks (percentage of total failures)

Years	Poor Management (1)	Fraud and Violation of the Law (2)	All Internal Bank Causes (1) Plus (2)	Depression and Depreciation of Assets
1865–1872	47%	32%	79%	20%
1873–1879 Panic	26	23	49	50
1880–1889	21	41	62	37
1890–1900 Panic	31	29	60	38
1901–1905	21	48	69	30
1906–1908 Panic	25	48	73	26
1909–1913	20	55	75	25
1914–1920 Panic	25	63	88	12
1921–1922 Recession	23	18	41	58
1923–1929 West of Miss.	31	9	40	60
1923–1929 East of Miss.	32	26	58	41
1930–1931 Recession	51	1	52	47

Source: Thomas (1935), based on Annual Reports of the Comptroller of the Currency. The data concern national banks placed in the hands of receivers.

likely. During the Panic of 1907, mostly trusts failed, not national banks. During the Panic of 1914, 88% of the failures were due to poor management and illegal activity. Thomas (1935) wrote: "One may conclude…that a prevention of operation of these 'internal causes' consisting of incompetent management, fraud, and violation of established banking law would be far in abolishing bank failure even in bad times" (p. 299).

Summary

What can we conclude about the National Banking Era panics?

- Banking panics during the National Banking Era were caused by shocks, information about the real economy that came at business cycle peaks. The information indicated that a recession was imminent, a time when consumers would want to dissave to smooth consumption (i.e., draw down their savings at banks to try to maintain their consumption level). But recession is a time when their bank is more likely to fail. So, as a precaution, they sought to withdraw cash.[35]
- Depositors were confused about which banks were really at risk and consequently ran on all banks. How do we know depositors were confused about which banks were at risk? One indication was that the clearinghouse prohibited individual bank information from being published. The idea was that weak banks were not to be exposed. In fact, ex post, few banks failed.
- The response of clearinghouses—issuing loan certificates to replace cash in the clearing process—was a method of conserving cash collateral. When the certificates were handed out directly to the public to honor withdrawals, they were designed as claims on the entire clearinghouse, which is consistent with the motivation of creating information-insensitive claims.
- A banking panic is a systemic event because the banking system as a whole is insolvent. How do we know that the banking system was insolvent? For the panics of 1893 and 1907, when clearinghouse loan certificates were issued directly to depositors, these financial claims traded at a discount to par, reflecting the expected losses on the coalition of banks.
- Did asset prices fall during these panics? Bank asset prices did not fall because there was no need to sell assets. Banks suspended convertibility, i.e., failed to honor their deposit contracts. Consequently, they did not have to sell loans and mortgages, and there was no market anyway.
- In a panic, cash is hoarded, and there is a shortage of transactions mediums.

The response of private bank clearinghouses was to suspend convertibility, cut off the flow of bank-specific information, and issue private money in the form of clearinghouse loan certificates that were the joint liability of clearinghouse member banks. This did not prevent panics from occurring. But it was very successful in preventing massive liquidations of banks.

The Evolution of Banking in the Last 25 Years—
The Rise of "Shadow" Banking

Actually, throughout these decades (1882–1910) National Banks continuously tried to expand the scope of their activities beyond the traditional commercial banking...some banks organized bond departments...the financing of stock speculation on call...the profits of some of the biggest banks were tremendous, especially those which entered investment banking. (Redlich, 1947, pp. 180, 183)

Banking has always been in a constant process of change.[36] The evolution of banking in the last 25 years is due to a number of forces, but the main point here is that the shadow banking system that emerged is a real banking system. Above, the shadow banking system was defined as a combination of the repo market and the necessary collateral, including securitization debt. This section describes the development of the shadow banking system and explains a bit more about how it operates to provide banking services.

The Development of the Shadow Banking System

The banking system evolved over the last 25 years in a number of fundamental ways. This evolution was a product of increased competition from nonbanks, decreased regulation, and innovation in financial products. Increased competition came from money market mutual funds, on the liability side of the bank balance sheet and from junk bonds on the asset side of the bank balance sheet.[37] In the early 1970s, interest rate ceilings on deposits were phased out; banks were allowed to engage in a variety of other financial activities; restrictions on geographic scope were eliminated.[38] Innovation came in many forms. Derivative securities became an important product line (e.g., see Gorton and Rosen, 1995). Loans became more liquid; they could be sold in secondary markets (see Gorton and Pennacchi, 1990b, 1993c). And securitization allowed portfolios of loans to be sold into the capital markets. For our purposes, securitization is the most important development. Later, loan sales are briefly discussed.

As discussed above, securitization is a form of off-balance-sheet banking. Loans originated by banks are sold to a legal entity known as a special-purpose vehicle (SPV), which finances the purchase of the portfolio of loans by issuing investment-grade securities in the capital markets. The SPV is robotic in the sense that no one works there, and there is no physical location for the SPV. Servicing the loans is outsourced, and the cash flow from the loans is allocated according to prespecified rules. It's important to note that SPVs are bankruptcy remote, meaning that the failure of the originator of loans is not relevant to the investors in the securitization bonds, called "tranches." The loans that were sold to the SPV cannot be clawed back by an originator that is in bankruptcy. Also, the SPV itself cannot go bankrupt. If the cash flow from the loan portfolio that constitutes the assets of the SPV is insufficient to make the payments on the tranches, then early amortization is triggered. This is not an event of default. See Gorton and Souleles (2006) for more details.

Table 2.5 shows issuance of various asset classes over the period 1996–2008. The two relevant columns with regard to securitization are the columns labeled "mortgage-related" and "asset-backed." The column labeled "mortgage-related"

TABLE 2.5 Issuance of Various Types of Securities in the U.S., 1996–2008 ($bil.)

	Municipal	Treasury[a]	Mortgage-Related[b]	Corporate Debt[c]	Federal Agency Securities	Asset-Backed	Total
1996	185.2	612.4	492.6	343.7	277.9	168.4	2,080.2
1997	220.7	540.0	604.4	466.0	323.1	223.1	2,377.3
1998	286.8	438.4	1,143.9	610.7	596.4	286.6	3,362.7
1999	227.5	364.6	1,025.4	629.2	548.0	287.1	3,081.8
2000	200.8	312.4	684.4	587.5	446.6	337.0	2,568.7
2001	287.7	380.7	1,671.3	776.1	941.0	383.3	4,440.1
2002	357.5	571.6	2,249.2	636.7	1,041.5	469.2	5,325.7
2003	382.7	745.2	3,071.1	775.8	1,267.5	600.2	6,842.5
2004	359.8	853.3	1,779.0	780.7	881.8[d]	869.8	4,642.6
2005	408.2	746.2	1,966.7	752.8	669.0	1,172.1	5,715.0
2006	386.5	788.5	1,987.8	1,058.9	747.3	1,253.1	6,222.1
2007	429.3	752.3	2,050.3	1,127.5	941.8	901.7	6,202.9
2008	389.1	1,037.3	1,344.1	706.2	1,114.9	163.1	4,754.7
YTD '07	429.3	752.3	2,050.3	1,127.5	941.8	901.6	6,202.8
YTD '08	389.1	1,037.3	1,344.1	706.2	1,114.9	163.1	4,754.7
% Change	−9.4%	37.9%	−34.4%	−37.4%	18.4%	−81.9%	−23.3%

[a] Interest-bearing marketable coupon public debt.
[b] Includes GNMA, FNMA, and FHLMC mortgage-backed securities and CMOs and private-label MBS/CMOs.
[c] Includes all non-convertible debt, MTNs and Yankee bonds, but excludes CDs and federal agency debt.
[d] Beginning with 2004, Sallie Mae has been excluded due to privatization.
Sources: U.S. Department of Treasury, Federal Agencies, Thomson Financial, Inside MBS & ABS, Bloomberg.

includes all securitized mortgages: privately securitized product but also securitizations by the government-sponsored housing entities. By issuance, mortgage-related bonds are the largest category of traded debt in the United States. Also of particular note is the fact that nonmortgage asset-backed securities ("asset-backed") exceeded the issuance of U.S. corporate debt in 2004–2006. These securities are the obligations of SPVs holding a variety of loan types, such as credit card receivables, auto loans, student loans, and so on. Securitization is a very significant form of financing.

Securitization is banking in the sense that the SPVs hold loans and finance these loans with high-grade debt, which is largely information insensitive. This debt is investment-grade and has an information advantage over equivalently rated corporate debt. Speculation can occur in corporate bonds based on information from the company's stock. Capital structure arbitrage involves taking long and short positions in different instruments of a company's capital structure; see Yu (2005). Implementation of this strategy involves comparing credit derivative swap spreads to the firm's equity price with a structural model.

In contrast, securitization does not involve any traded equity. The SPV only issues bonds rated investment-grade. As mentioned above, studies of corporate bond returns have mainly concluded that investment-grade bonds behave like Treasury bonds, while below-investment-grade bonds are more sensitive to stock returns. These results were prior to credit derivatives, which now allow for speculation in corporate bonds without having to find the cash instrument.

The securitization bonds will play an important role in what follows. Securitization is, or was, quantitatively significant, as shown in table 2.6. The table shows issuance levels, not outstanding amounts. To provide a sense of the significance of these numbers, they can be compared to the amounts that remain on the banks' balance sheets, for example. Figure 2.9 shows the ratio of the securitized amounts of credit card receivables to the amount of receivables not securitized and remaining on bank balance sheets. In 2002 and 2003, the ratio is about 1.7 in favor of off-balance-sheet financing, though more recently it has fallen to just less than one. A ratio of 1.7 means that for every dollar of on-balance-sheet credit card receivables, there are 1.7 dollars of off-balance-sheet credit card receivables.

Why did securitization arise? We do not know for sure. One possibility, discussed further below, is that it was a response to bank capital requirements, which created a cost without a countervailing benefit. Banks, being private institutions, can exit the industry if it is not profitable. Another possibility is that the demand for collateral made securitization profitable, and this could

TABLE 2.6 Outstanding Amounts of Various Non-Mortgage Asset-Backed Securities ($bil.)

	Automobile Loans	Credit Card Receivables	Home Equity Loans	Manufactured Housing	Student Loans	Other	Total
1996	71.4	180.7	51.6	14.6	10.1	76.0	404.4
1997	77.0	214.5	90.2	19.1	18.3	116.7	535.8
1998	86.9	236.7	124.2	25.0	25.0	233.7	731.5
1999	114.1	257.9	141.9	33.8	36.4	316.7	900.8
2000	133.1	306.3	151.5	36.9	41.1	402.9	1,071.8
2001	187.9	361.9	185.1	42.7	60.2	443.4	1,281.2
2002	221.7	397.9	286.5	44.5	74.4	518.2	1,543.2
2003	234.5	401.9	346.0	44.3	99.2	567.8	1,693.7
2004	232.1	390.7	454.0	42.2	115.2	593.6	1,827.8
2005	219.7	356.7	551.1	34.5	153.2	640.0	1,955.2
2006	202.4	339.9	581.2	28.8	183.6	794.5	2,130.4
2007	198.5	347.8	585.6	26.9	243.9	1,069.7	2,472.4
2008	137.7	314.1	395.5	20.0	239.5	1,565.0	2,671.8

Source: Bond Market Association, Bloomberg.

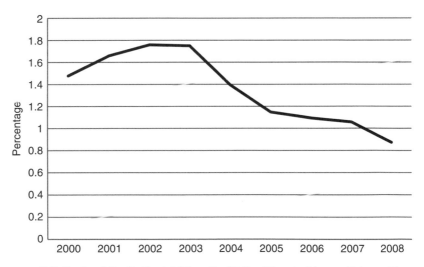

FIGURE 2.9 Ratio of Credit Card ABS to Credit Card Receivables on Balance Sheet. Sources: Federal Reserve System, Bond Market Association.

not be accomplished on-balance-sheet because deposit insurance was limited. That is, as discussed above, the demand for information-insensitive securities to use as collateral for various purposes may also have played a role. Third, bankruptcy costs are minimized with off-balance-sheet financing. But the off-balance-sheet debt is not tax-advantaged for the originator. See Gorton and

Souleles (2006). Thus, one would expect that companies with lower credit ratings would find it optimal to securitize. Finally, the innovation in structuring the special-purpose vehicle as an off-balance-sheet vehicle may have been the driving force for growth. Whatever the cause, securitization has become a very significant form of financing.

Another aspect of the development of off-balance-sheet banking is loan sales, which refers to the sale of secondary participations in commercial and industrial loans to firms. This is not the way that banks operated for hundreds of years. Instead, bank loans resided on bank balance sheets until maturity. And, as mentioned above, academic theory says that only if the bank holds the loan will it have an incentive to produce information and monitor, an argument which also suggests that securitization should not occur.

Table 2.7 shows the extent of commercial and industrial loan sales. Figure 2.10 shows the ratio of loans sold to loans retained on-balance-sheet. The ratio peaks at about one-quarter in 2006. That is, for every dollar lent, one quarter is sold. In fact, loans are now rated, and trade like bonds.

Table 2.7 and figure 2.10 contradict the prevailing academic paradigm for the existence of banks, in which banks cannot sell loans because then they

TABLE 2.7 Commercial and Industrial Loans
On-Balance-Sheet and Loan Sales ($bil)

Year	C&I Loans ($bil)	Secondary Market Volume ($bil)
1991	632.8	8.0
1992	607.3	11.1
1993	593.9	15.0
1994	619.6	20.8
1995	695.2	33.8
1996	750.4	39.5
1997	816.3	60.6
1998	896.2	77.6
1999	956.3	79.1
2000	1046.5	102.0
2001	1062.8	117.5
2002	982.5	112.5
2003	917.7	144.6
2004	893.8	155.0
2005	900.7	176.3
2006	1126.4	238.6
2007	1295.3	342.0
2008	1521.1	318.4

Sources: Commercial and Industrial Loans from Federal Reserve H.8 release; loan sales from Reuters Loan Pricing Corporation.

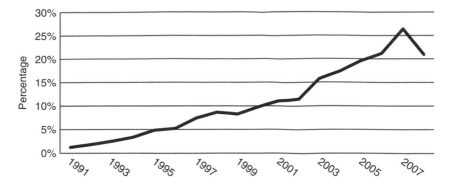

FIGURE 2.10 Ratio of Secondary Market Loan Sales to Commercial and Industrial Loans Outstanding. Sources: Reuters Loan Pricing Corporation, Federal Reserve Board, H.8.

have no incentive to behave, produce initial information, and monitor borrowers. There is little evidence that these incentives have broken down or that this plays an important role in the panic.[39] As Gorton and Metrick (2009a) argue, nonsubprime-related asset classes, such as credit card securitization and loan sales, show no problems until the interbank repo market panics. We turn to repo next.

The Rise of Repo

The rise of securitization coincided with (was caused by?) the increased demands for collateral, discussed above. Further, securitization required changes in the financial infrastructure. Investment and commercial banks that sponsored securitizations often bought loan portfolios to sell to SPVs and then held the SPV-issued bonds until they could be sold. This meant that the balance sheets of dealer banks, in particular, had to increase in size, and this had to be financed somehow. Gorton and Metrick (2009a) show this to be the case. Firms also, apparently, had a need for a place to deposit short-term cash. These factors led to an enormous growth in the sale and repurchase, or repo, market, a short-term collateralized lending market. The repo market traditionally was confined to U.S. Treasury securities, but in the last 25 years it has grown to accept a broad range of securitized bonds as collateral. Asset classes that came to be eligible for repo included all manner of securitized products, as well as tranches of structured products like collateral debt obligations.

The importance of the repo market is suggested by its immense size: primary dealers reported financing $4.5 trillion in fixed income securities with repos as of March 4, 2008. These numbers, while large, do not include all the

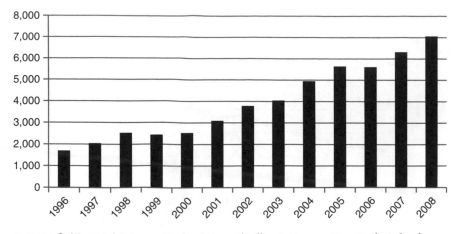

FIGURE 2.11 Total Primary Dealers' Repo ($Billion). Source: New York Federal Reserve Bank.

repo that nonprimary dealers undertake. There are no official statistics about the size of the overall repo market, but unofficial guesses put the market at somewhere around $10 trillion, though that may include double counting of repo and reverse repo (i.e., both sides of the transaction).[40] For comparison, the total assets of the regulated U.S. banking sector are also about $10 trillion.

Repo is essentially depository banking built around information-insensitive debt. In a repo transaction, one side of the transaction wants to borrow money and the other side wants to save money by "depositing" it somewhere safe. Think of the borrowers as a bank and the lender as a depositor, although the lender is another firm, such as a bank, insurance company, pension fund, institutional investor, or hedge fund. The depositor receives a bond as collateral for his deposit.

When the depositor deposits money, the collateral may involve a "haircut," or margin. The haircut is the percentage difference between the market value of the pledged collateral and the amount of funds lent. For example, a haircut of 5% means that a "bank" can borrow $95 for each $100 in pledged collateral. A haircut further protects the depositor against the risk of borrower default by the "bank." The size of the haircut reflects the credit risk of the borrower and the riskiness of the pledged collateral.

Another important feature of repo is that the collateral can be rehypothecated. In other words, the collateral received by the depositor can be used— "spent"—in another transaction, i.e., it can be used to collateralize a transaction with another party. Intuitively, rehypothecation is tantamount to conducting transactions with the collateral received against the deposit. There is no data on the extent of rehypothecation.

Summary

The shadow banking system is, in fact, a real banking system. The "depositors" are firms seeking a place to save cash in the short term, often money market funds and corporations. The "lenders" are financial firms seeking cash to finance themselves. The deposits are designed to be information insensitive by backing them with information-insensitive collateral. Often that collateral is securitization bond. The collateral can be "spent," i.e., rehypothecated. Depositors can "withdraw" their funds by not rolling over their repo agreements and returning the bond, or they can withdraw by increasing the haircut on the collateral.[41] This is depository banking in a different form, but banking nevertheless. Like demand deposits at regulated commercial banks, this system is vulnerable to panic.

It is easy to summon up the old adage that one should not borrow short to finance long assets, but the reality is that banking inevitably involves that because part of making the "deposit" nearly riskless is for it to be short maturity. Note that with insured deposits, the debt is effectively long maturity because depositors have no need to run their banks to try to withdraw cash. The shadow banking system resembles the pre-FDIC U.S. banking system in some ways.

The Panic

> That astonishing disturbance and collapse of credit (during the Panic of 1907) was one of the most unbecoming, if not disgraceful, episodes in our financial history. Popular clamor followed. When the air had cleared it was seen that the trouble was due to the banking system, which, ill-adapted to supply the needs of a progressive industrial nation under normal conditions, was utterly inadequate for the preservation of business equilibrium and the allaying of distrust in times of business accident and unexpected strain. (Weston, 1922, p. 17)

What caused the panic? The short answer is that there was a shock and, like panics in the National Banking Era, there was asymmetric information about where the exposures to this shock were located. The Panic of 2007 chronology has been outlined by Gorton (2008), and the details will not be repeated here. The key question to be addressed to understand the panic is why asset classes completely unrelated to subprime asset classes saw their spreads rise to distress levels. The fundamentals of subprime deteriorated, so asset classes linked to subprime should have declined in value. But that is not a systemic event. The systemic event concerns the collapse of the prices of other asset classes. Gorton and Metrick (2009a,b) and Gorton (2009) address the question of why asset classes other than those related to subprime suffered declines in value. This section draws on those studies.

As explained in the next chapter, the particular design of subprime mortgages made them especially sensitive to house prices. The shock to fundamentals was the failure of home prices to rise. Indeed, they later fall. This shock was revealed in the only market that was widely observable within the nexus of derivatives and structured products involved in the panic. Dealer banks launched the ABX.HE (ABX) index in January 2006. The ABX index is a credit derivative that references 20 equally weighted subprime RMBS tranches. There are also sub-indices linked to a basket of subprime bonds with specific ratings: AAA, AA, A BBB, and BBB-. Each subindex references the 20 subprime RMBS bonds with the rating level of the subindex.[42]

The introduction of the ABX indices opened a (relatively) liquid, publicly observable market, which priced subprime risk. See Gorton (2009). The other subprime-related instruments, RMBS and CDOs, did not trade in publicly observable markets. In fact, securitized products generally have no secondary trading that is publicly visible. Thus, for our purposes, the ABX indices are important because of the information revelation about the value of subprime mortgages, which in turn depends on house prices.[43]

Gorton and Metrick (2009a) track the timing of movements in the ABX. The ABX.HE indices showed a steady deterioration of subprime fundamentals, starting in early 2007. Gorton and Metrick also show that subprime-related asset classes and firms also deteriorated along with the ABX. Examples of these deteriorating asset classes include tranches of collateralized debt obligations, BBB subprime tranches, and BBB commercial mortgage-backed securities. Countrywide, Washington Mutual, and the monoline insurance companies are example of firms whose fates moved with the ABX.[44]

However, significantly, other asset classes did not show deterioration (spreads rising) with deterioration in the ABX. That is, the shock to subprime per se was not the cause of the panic. Other asset classes only experienced difficulties when there were problems in the interbank market, starting in August 2007. Gorton and Metrick (2009a) studied the spread between three-month LIBOR and the three-month overnight index swap (OIS).[45] As they explain, this spread should be zero by no-arbitrage, except for transaction costs. Indeed, this spread historically has been about eight basis points.

The LIBOR-OIS spread jumped in August 2007, and again when Lehman failed. Other securitized asset classes with nothing to do with subprime, like credit card receivables, auto loans, and student loans, all moved with the proxy for the state of the interbank market, not with the ABX. See Gorton and

Metrick (2009). The key question for understanding the panic is: why were non-subprime-related asset classes affected? Subprime mortgage originations in 2005 and 2006 totaled about $1.2 trillion (see Gorton (2008)), a large number to be sure, but not large enough to cause a systemic crisis. How was the shock turned into a panic?

The shock was combined with asymmetric information about the locations and sizes of exposures to subprime. Like the panics during the National Banking Era, it was not clear which firms had the largest exposures. During the National Banking Era, depositors did not know which banks were more likely to fail during the recession. They just knew that they were exposed to the risk that their bank would be insolvent during the recession, just when they might be unemployed. So they "ran" to their bank to withdraw cash. The banks' equity cushion and their assets—the collateral—were not to be trusted.

The same mechanism operated this time. The "depositors" were firms that deposited money in the form of (reverse) repo and received a bond as collateral. Prior to the panic, repo haircuts were zero. The run occurred in the repo market.

The Run on Repo

Uncertain about the solvency of counterparties, repo depositors became concerned that the collateral bonds might not be liquid; if all firms wanted to hold cash—a flight to quality—then collateral would have to decline in price to find buyers. This is the crucial link between the subprime shock and other asset categories. Gorton and Metrick showed that the other asset classes started to deteriorate in August 2007, when the LIBOR-OIS spread jumped, even though the subprime fundamentals as measured by the ABX had been deteriorating for months prior to that.

Repo rates spread to OIS increased as banks tried to retain funding. So one effect is that depositors were compensated with higher rates. But higher rates do not address the uncertainty about the value of the collateral, should the counterparty fail. In that case, the depositor can unilaterally terminate the agreement and keep the collateral. But to obtain cash, the collateral must be sold. Gorton and Metrick (2009a) show that this uncertainty about collateral value led to an increase in repo haircuts, which had been zero for all asset classes.

The run on repo is, again, akin to previous panics. "Withdrawal" corresponds to an increase in haircuts. So, previously, when $100 was "deposited," collateral in the form of a bond worth $100 in the market was acceptable. In August 2007, the haircuts went up in some important asset classes. Say the

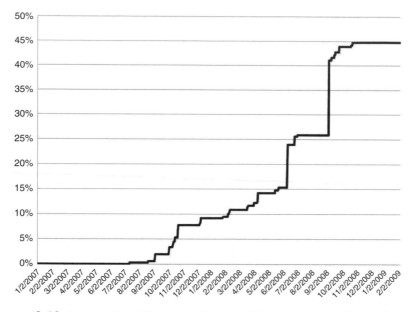

FIGURE 2.12 Average Repo Haircut on Structured Debt. Source: Dealer Bank.

haircut increases to 5%. Then the depositor deposits only $95 in exchange for collateral worth $100.

Figure 2.12 shows the average repo haircut on seven categories of structured debt. The figure is based on data from Gorton and Metrick (2009a), which also has the details underlying this figure. Also see Gorton (2009). The figure is a picture of the panic. Haircuts were zero until August 2007. After that, haircuts rise and continue to rise. The increasing haircuts are tantamount to withdrawals from the "bank." What does this mean? Figure 2.13 provides a stylized balance sheet for the "banking" system. Inititally, the banking system has assets of $100 financed by equity capital of $10, long-term debt of $40, and short-term financing in the form of repo of $50.[46] In the panic, repo haircuts rise to 20%, amounting to a withdrawl of $10, so the system has to either shrink, borrow, or get an equity injection to make up for this. As we saw, after some early equity injections during the fall of 2007 (often from sovereign wealth funds), this source dried up, as did the possibility of borrowing. That leaves asset sales. So the system as a whole needs to sell $10 of assets. But this causes prices to go down (and collateral values to fall). In panel C of the figure, some assets were sold and the prices fell on others. Assets are now worth $80; equity is wiped out. The system is insolvent. There is nothing corresponding to suspension of convertibility for the repo market.[47] The reality is that there is no private agent large enough to buy enough of the assets of the system to solve

A. The initial state of the "banking" system, with 10% equity.

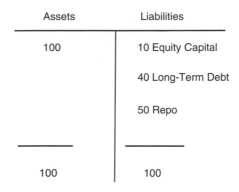

Assets	Liabilities
100	10 Equity Capital
	40 Long-Term Debt
	50 Repo
100	100

B. Repo haircuts increase from 0 to 20% — not an equilibrium.

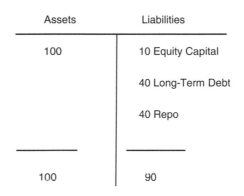

Assets	Liabilities
100	10 Equity Capital
	40 Long-Term Debt
	40 Repo
100	90

C. The System sells assets, causing asset prices to fall.

Assets	Liabilities
80	0 Equity Capital
	40 Long-Term Debt
	40 Repo
80	80

FIGURE 2.13 The Systemic Effects of the Repo Market Panic

the problem. Left with the only alternative, namely, selling assets, the outcome is simply that prices fall.

There are no official figures for the size of the repo market, beyond primary dealers. Also, there are no official data on repo haircuts. Consequently, it is hard to put hard numbers on the above stylized example. Estimates of the size of the repo market are that it is roughly $8 trillion to $10 trillion. If repo haircuts increase to an average 20% (a guess), then between $1.6 and $2 trillion must be raised by the banking system. Without investors willing to finance this by investing in these firms, the only alternative is to sell assets. As in panics during the National Banking System, the system is insolvent. It is worth recalling the clearinghouse loan certificate process. The *New York Times* (November 17, 1890, p. 4) explained as follows:

> [Clearinghouse loan certificates] use may be compactly defined as the protection of values against panic. They accomplish that by enabling the several banks to obtain and give credit to real value of securities, instead of being forced to throw those securities upon a panic-stricken market, which would be certain slaughter and inevitable ruin for creditors and debtors alike. In other words, the banks as a body, the "Associated Banks," the "Clearing House," offer their joint guarantee of the real value of property and they can judge of soundly and wisely and enable that property to be used at its real value when no individual could know its worth, or could act on if he thought he knew it. The simplicity of the process…conceals its immense importance. But, it is, in reality, one of the most marvelous developments of modern commercial life.

The Shortage of Collateral—The "Currency Famine"

> Quite understandably, [central bank counterparties] have economized on the use of central government bonds which has been often almost the only collateral counterparties could still use in interbank repo markets. Instead they have brought forward less liquid collateral…including ABSs, for which primary and secondary markets have basically dried up." (José Manuel González-Páramo, ECB Executive Board Member, June, 2008. Quoted by Chailloux, Gray, and McCaughrin, 2008)

The increase in haircuts means that there is a shortage of collateral. There is an excess demand for U.S. Treasuries because of the flight to quality generally. The evidence of this is provided by Gorton (2009), who points to the very large increase in Treasury repo "fails." A repo fail occurs when the party with the bond has rehypothecated the bond and then cannot find an acceptable bond to return when the repo matures. A repo fail is not an event of default. See Fleming and Garbade (2005). Total fails in Treasury repos reached a record $5.1 trillion in October 2008. For comparison, total fails averaged $165 billion per week between 1990 (when the Fed started collecting data) to July 2007.

Gorton and Metrick (2009a) document that an even larger spike upward in the LIBOR-OIS spread occurs just after Lehman failed. As shown in the figure on repo haircuts, haircuts continued to increase, with some asset classes becoming simply unacceptable in repo. The aftermath of Lehman wreaked further havoc in the interbank market. One effect was that the extent of rehypothecation significantly declined; see Singh and Aitken (2009). Singh and Aitken examine 10Q filings of major firms and find "that since end-2007, the decline in rehypothecation (i.e., total collateral received that can be pledged) by the largest four broker-dealers was $1.774 trillion" (p. 5).

The other effect of the Lehman failure was the fear about daylight risk exposure. This is a kind of settlement risk that occurs when a party faces possible loss between the time a settlement payment is made and a corresponding payment is received (usually in another currency) on the same business day. In over-the-counter markets, settlement sometimes takes between a day to three days, but after Lehman, firms hoarded cash, only trading on a delivery-versus-payment basis, i.e., no delay between exchange of cash and the security. It is difficult to document this, but the BIS (2008b, p. 26) reported a contraction of $423 billion in the U.S. dollar interbank borrowing market. The analysis of Gorton and Metrick (2009a) shows that the spike in the LIBOR, overnight index swap spread upon the collapse of Lehman is consistent with the idea that "global interbank markets seized up, curbing banks' access to short-term funding" BIS (2008, p. 9).

Complexity Revealed When Debt Becomes Information Sensitive

A panic is an event where information-insensitive debt becomes information sensitive. It is a switch because it becomes profitable to produce private information about the debt. That is, some agents are willing to spend resources to learn private information to speculate on the value of these securities, a practice that was not profitable before the panic. This leads to a "lemons market," in which everyone needs to suddenly produce information to trade.[48]

This is a devastating regime switch because market participants are not prepared to cope with the sudden information requirements for understanding, valuing, and trading securities that are suddenly information sensitive. Part of the crisis is the aftermath, in which securities that previously were information insensitive become information sensitive. This makes them illiquid. Not only does information now have to be produced, but the expertise is lacking. In the current environment, given the panic, the complexity of the underlying structure (described in chapter 4 as a chain of structures) matters a great deal. Chapter 4 discusses this complexity in detail.

Summary

Perhaps a useful way to summarize the Panic of 2007 is to contrast it with the panics of the National Banking Era.

- Like the banking panics during the National Banking Era, the Panic of 2007 was caused by a shock, in this case, to housing prices. The panic started in August 2007. The National Bureau of Economic Research dates the peak of the business cycle to December 2007.
- "Depositors" were firms that lent money in the repo market (engaged in reverse repos). The location of subprime risks among their counterparties was not known. Depositors were confused about which counterparties were really at risk and consequently ran all banks. In other words, repo haircuts increased, tantamount to withdrawal. How do we know depositors were confused about which banks were at risk? The evidence is that non-subprime-related asset classes saw their spreads rise significantly only when the interbank market started to break down.
- A banking panic is a systemic event because the banking system as a whole is insolvent. How do we know that the banking system was insolvent? There is no direct evidence, although back-of-the envelope calculations suggest that the banking system needed to replace about $2 trillion of financing when the repo market haircuts rose.
- Did asset prices fall during the Panic of 2007? Asset prices did fall. To the extent that they can be measured, the prices of non-subprime-related assets fell significantly. See Gorton and Metrick (2009). Financial firms could only de-lever in response to the increase in haircuts by selling assets. There was no suspension of convertibility (or of mark-to-market accounting). Consequently, financial firms had to try to sell loans and mortgages.
- In a panic, cash is hoarded, and there is a shortage of transaction mediums. In the Panic of 2007, U.S. Treasuries were hoarded. We know this from repo fails. And there was a shortage of collateral.

The similarities and differences between the National Banking Era panics and the Panic of 2007 are revealing. On the one hand, the similarities strongly suggest that the interpretation of repo as banking is correct. On the other hand, the main difference was that there was no clearinghouse response, no suspension of convertibility. And obviously there was no "deposit" insurance in either case.

FIGURE 2.14 Book cover of *Wasn't the Depression Terrible?* by Otto Soglow and David George Plotkin (1934). (Picture Collection, The New York Public Library, Astor, Lenox and Tilden foundations)

The Future Financial Landscape

> A study of the crises of 1873, 1893, and 1907 and of the numerous minor critical periods in the financial history of the last generation is not calculated to impress one with the smooth working of our banking machinery. No other advanced country in the civilized world has experienced such a disastrous series of financial collapses, suspensions, disrupted exchanges, and currency makeshifts during the past 40 years as the United States....I am not one of those who have a panacea for currency and banking ills, and the few rather commonplace suggestions I have to make at this time are tentative, and, like railroad time tables, "subject to change without notice." (Kemmerer, 1911)

It is very difficult to see what the financial landscape will look like in five or ten years. Surely that will depend, in large part, on new regulations. What should be the new regulations? The answer to that question depends on what the problem is that resulted in a panic. In this section, two related issues are very briefly addressed. First, answers to these questions are discussed: what explains the Quiet Period in U.S. banking that was experienced from 1934–2007; why did it end and can it be reproduced?[49] And, second, what should be done about the shadow banking system?

Explaining the Rise and Fall of the Quiet Period in U.S. Banking

Following the introduction of deposit insurance in 1934, the long period of quiescence in U.S. banking started, broken by the savings and loan (S&L) crisis and bank failures during the business cycle, starting in July 1990. But there was no systemic event in banking until 2007. Some explanation for how society achieved the long period of quiet in banking may provide some clues to how to once again obtain that goal. Since financial innovation is inevitable, whether such a period can be made permanent or not is hard to determine.

In the Quiet Period in U.S. banking, demand deposits were insured, and entry into banking was limited.[50] Firms called "banks" were well defined; they took in deposits and made loans. To do this, banks had to obtain a charter from either the federal or state government, and this was very restrictive (see Peltzman, 1965). Until the Monetary Control Act of 1980, there were interest-rate ceilings of deposits (Regulation Q). Due to limited entry, banks had local monopolies on deposits, see, for example, Neumark and Sharpe (1992), who show that "banks in concentrated markets are slower to raise interest rates on deposits in response to rising market interest rates, but are faster to reduce them in response to declining market interest rates" (p. 657). Also, see Hannan and Berger (1991). Bank charters were valuable, providing an incentive for banks to self-regulate. This explains why banks do not appear to have engaged in the moral hazards that are alleged to follow from government deposit insurance. See Keeley (1990) and Marcus (1984). The Quiet Period followed from a combination of "sticks" and "carrots." Banks faced the "stick" of bank regulations and examinations, but also had the "carrot," in the form of monopoly rents that made the charter valuable.

In the early 1990s, competition from nonbanks (e.g., money market mutual funds, junk bonds), and deregulation (e.g., of interest-rate ceilings) caused bank charter values to decline, which in turn caused banks to increase risk and reduce capital. This has been documented by Keeley (1990). Also, see Berger, Kashyap, and Scalise (1995). Keeley noted an increase in risk-taking and a decline in capital levels. The carrot essentially disappeared and regulators increasingly relied on the stick, and that was increasingly capital requirements. Whether this caused "banking" to move out of banks or not is less clear. Gorton and Winton (2000) argue that if regulators impose capital requirements that are binding when there is no carrot in the form of a valuable charter, then bank capital will exit the (chartered bank) industry. Again, we do not know for certain if that, in fact, caused capital to exit regulated banking for the shadow banking system. But, in any case, the shadow banking system developed coincidentally with the disappearance of charter value. This development was fairly long in the making, but was not hidden. It was there for all to see.[51] Gorton (1994), in a paper entitled "Bank Regulation When 'Banks' and 'Banking' Are Not the Same," noted that banking had significantly metamorphosed into something different.

Without the carrot of a valuable charter providing an incentive to self-regulate and monitor risk, it seems unlikely that the stick alone can create a new period of quiet.

What Should Be Done About the Shadow Banking System?

What should be done about bank regulation? A good starting point is the recognition that (1) there is a demand for collateral by firms for many purposes and, (2), there is the need for a safe way for firms to save cash in the short term. The shadow banking system arose to meet these demands. Securitization created collateral, and the repo market provides a banking mechanism for firms and institutional investors. Collateral means information-insensitive debt. Firms could be provided a safe savings location with large insured accounts at banks. But forcing previously securitized asset classes back onto banks' balance sheets does not solve the collateral problem. Collateral is needed for derivatives and settlement, as well as for savings in the form of repo. Forcing everything back on balance sheet seems like an attempt to return to the Eden of the Quiet Period without recognizing that the world has changed.

Further, as discussed above, a key part of the Quiet Period was a valuable bank charter, which provided an incentive to self-regulate. If the shadow banking system is recognized as a genuine banking system, then perhaps the Quiet Period for this banking system can be achieved by creating charter value and information-insensitive debt. Very broadly, this would mean three things:

1. Senior tranches of securitizations of approved asset classes should be insured by the government.
2. The government must supervise and examine "banks," i.e., securitizations, rather than rely on ratings agencies. That is, the choices of asset class, portfolio, and tranching must be overseen be examiners.
3. Entry into securitization should be limited, and any firm that enters is deemed a "bank" and subject to supervision.

Information-insensitive debt is created by points 1 and 2, which then provides a way for repo to serve as a short-term savings mechanism for firms. Point 3 creates charter value for firms that engage in the production of the new information-insensitive debt. Being able to securitize is valuable.

These three points simply highlight the kind of thinking needed if it is agreed that shadow banking is real banking which needs to be protected. The alternative viewpoint seems somewhat problematic because the rise of securitization and repo as very significant parts of the capital markets cannot be explained as a bubble or as the product of greed, and so on. The "originate-to-distribute" viewpoint, discussed by Gorton (2008), is the view that argues that securitization per se is the problem, again an attempt to rationalize going back to the view of pushing everything back onto banks' balance sheets.

The demands for more information-insensitive debt to serve as collateral have been hard to satisfy, and the economy needs more of it. That is the modern equivalent of saying that consumers need insurance for their demand deposits. Imagine that we had had the broad system outlined above. Under point 2, would the government have rejected subprime securitization as eligible for insured collateral? Probably not. The government probably cannot do better than private entities. But the effects of the mistake would have been different. The government would have borne the losses on the AAA- and AA-rated tranches (assuming those were insured), and a systemic event would have been avoided.

It is important to emphasize the implications of "information-insensitive" debt. Whenever debt is created, by definition, a residual security is also created. So, to the extent that there is a demand for information-insensitive debt, there must also be a residing place for the very information-sensitive residuals (equity) that are a byproduct of this debt creation. Creation of a valuable charter is intended to address that risk. As Keeley (1990) highlights, the usual "moral hazard" argument about banks and deposit insurance did not have any force during the Quiet Period because of the valuable charter.

The History of Bank Regulatory Policy

If there is anything to be learned from U.S. history, it is that the Quiet Period was rare and that it is hard to create. Every time a major banking reform was enacted, it was hailed and then failed. When the National Banking Act replaced the Free Banking Era (see Gorton, 1996, 1999), it was hailed. For example, the *New York Times* wrote:

It is now more than twelve years since the national banking system went into operation in this country....It requires but a moderate knowledge of the banking system now in force to see that, whatever may be its defects, and whatever the errors of the managers doing business under it, it can never inflict the same kind of loss on the country as that which came from the old system.[52]

What followed were the periodic panics of the National Banking Era.

Banking history is replete with many such examples. But in each case there were problems, perhaps inevitably so. When the Federal Reserve System came into being in 1914, the clearinghouse mechanisms for dealing with panics were eliminated, and the money issuance features under the Aldrich-Vreeland Act were also eliminated.[53] When the Great Depression occurred, none of the previous methods were available to deal with the panic. Clearinghouse loan certificates were not issued and, as Silber (2007a, footnote 4 on page 288) points out, the discount window was not the same as credit creation under the Aldrich-Vreeland Act. These were mistakes that could have been avoided. Gorton (1988) looks at the counterfactual experiment of what would have happened during the Great Depression had the clearinghouse mechanisms been in place. The conclusion is that "if there had been a panic in December 1929, [bank] failure and loss percentages would have been an order of magnitude lower" (p. 247). Policy errors can be devastating. It was not until 1934 that the controversial idea of deposit insurance was enacted.

Of course, it is easy to observe things ex post. But surely the lessons of history have something to offer. That history is the long search for institutions that can ensure a "sound currency," and that is still the search. Now it requires the recognition that shadow banking is, in fact, banking, creating a "currency" for firms. The sketch of banking reform outlined above, while no more than a sketch, suggests that policy should be firmly based on an understanding of the problem, not just a reaction to the crisis.

Conclusion

Each panic teaches us something new and this accumulating experience should in time enable us to prolong the interval of recurrence if not eventually to prevent the recurrence entirely, just as epidemics of disease, formerly thought inevitable, are now prevented. (Marburg, 1908, p. 55)

Concisely stated, the problem before us at the present time is to develop a sound banking system in the United States...why has the United States not found a satisfactory solution to its banking problems during the long period

of agitation and reform that stretches back to 1836? Perhaps the chief reason
is our habit of application—of being content with immediate remedies for
pressing problems...To find a permanent solution we must first analyze the
fundamental bases of the problem—not merely its superficial inconveniences.
(James, 1934, p. 1)

Periodic banking panics have been the norm in U.S. history. But the panics
appeared to end in the U.S. when deposit insurance was legislated in 1934.
Combined with valuable bank charters and oversight by bank examiners, the
Quiet Period was created. What changed? Bank charter values eroded under
competition. Securitization is a more efficient way to finance loans. The growth
of derivative securities caused an enormous demand for collateral. Over 25
years, the shadow banking system evolved to meet the needs of this modern
economy. Unfortunately, the vulnerability to panic was also produced.

The shadow banking system is, in fact, banking. Banking is about the
creation of information-insensitive debt. Securitized products serve the function of collateral for many purposes, but serve an especially important role in
the repo market. Although the shadow banking system has been present for
roughly 25 years, it was never understood to be "banking" because that was
associated with chartered depository institutions. So while the development
of this system was noted, the vulnerability to panic was not noted. Keep in
mind that there are no official measures of the size of the repo market, or
repo haircuts or rates. There are no data on the identity of repo market participants like bank call reports, which banks are required to file. There are no
official measures of collateral usage in derivatives or settlement. There are
no official measures of securitization. The shadow banking system was, as
they say, "off the radar screen." But its presence has been obvious in a general
sense. No matter what new regulatory policy is proposed, discussed, debated,
contemplated, or considered, surely we would be better off with information to
make an informed decision.

A banking panic is a systemic event because the banking system cannot
honor commitments and is insolvent. The current panic appears to have this
feature, although the panic happened in the shadow banking system, not the
regulated system. Subprime-related products were shocked by the decline in
housing prices, but the location of these risks was not known. This shock is
reminiscent of the 19th-century shocks and had the same outcome. Worried
that their banks were not solvent, and concerned about the liquidity of their
collateral, repo depositors increased repo haircuts, essentially demanding more
equity financing of the collateral. Banks could not get enough new investment
though the sale of equity or new debt and decided to sell assets, since they could

not suspend convertibility. But the fundamental fact is that the private sector is too small to buy that amount of assets. Asset prices plummeted. The banking system became insolvent.

Understanding the role of the shadow banking system and the banking panic is fundamental to thinking about future regulation. Re-creation of a Quiet Period in banking depends on the existence of debt that is information insensitive for banking purposes. The economy has evolved to the point where more of this type of debt is needed by firms, rather than consumers. The "banking" in question is that provided by the shadow banking system via securitization and repo. This is banking. Policies need to be adopted to create a sufficient amount of the needed debt so that companies can engage in banking safely. The response of our predecessors to banking panics was not to outlaw demand deposits; rather, it was to take the proactive step of facilitating the creation of riskless debt through insured demand deposits, combined with valuable charters and oversight.

Paradoxically perhaps, this is somewhat contrary to modern finance theory, which focuses on equity markets and extols the virtues of "market efficiency," that is, the idea that equity prices contain lots of information. That may be fine for equity markets, but for much of the debt market there should be no reason for prices to reflect a lot of information. In fact, the needs of the economy are for precisely the opposite. Demand-deposit prices do not reflect the risk of the bank failing, nor do insured certificates of deposit.[54]

Reforms to the current system must address the reality of the shadow banking system as a banking system. It is important to get this right. We have been through this before.

> There are two conceivable methods by which banking reform in the United States may be achieved. The first might be defined as the cataclysm of panic method, being the possibility of securing legislation in the frightened desperation of an industrial panic or in the period of dull prostration which succeeds. As a mode of procedure, it is open to all of the indirection and waste of Elia's method of preparing roast pig—and to something of its uncertainty. On more than one occasion, experience has shown that panic leads to the swift adoption of a remedial device, but unfortunately of a wrong one. The other method is the slower, more prosaic one of popular education and effective propaganda. (Hollander, 1913)

3

The Panic of 2007, Part 1

With a full year elapsed since the panic of 1907 reached its crisis among this country's financial markets, its banking institutions, and its productive industries, it ought to be possible to obtain an insight into the nature of that economic event such as could not easily have been obtained when the phenomena of the crisis itself surrounded us.
—Alexander Noyes, "A Year after the Panic of 1907,"
Quarterly Journal of Economics, February 1909

WE ARE NOW ABOUT ONE YEAR SINCE THE ONSET OF THE PANIC OF 2007. The forces that hit financial markets in the United States in the summer of 2007 seemed like a force of nature, something akin to a hurricane or an earthquake, something beyond human control. In August of that year, credit markets ceased to function, like the sudden arrival of a kind of "no trade theorem" in which no one would trade with you simply because you wanted to trade with them.[1] True, thousands of people did not die, as in the recent natural disasters in Asia, so I do not mean to exaggerate. Still, thousands of borrowers are losing their homes, and thousands are losing their jobs, mostly bankers and others in the financial sector. Many blame the latter group for the plight of the former group; ironic, as not long ago the latter group was blamed for not lending to the former group ("redlining" it was called). The deadweight losses from bankruptcies, foreclosures, and job search are no doubt significant.

Indeed, the feeling of the Panic of 2007 seems similar to that described by A. Piatt Andrew (1908a) a century ago, who wrote: "The closing months of 1907...were marked by an outburst of fright as wide-spread and unreasoning as that of fifty or seventy years before" (p. 290). Andrew (1908b) wrote that: "The autumn of 1907 witnessed what was probably the most extensive and prolonged breakdown of the country's credit mechanism which has occurred since the establishment of the national banking system" (p. 497). The actions taken during that panic were extraordinary. They included legal holidays declared by governors and the extensive issuance of emergency currency through clearinghouses.[2]

It is true that today's panic is not a banking panic in the sense that the traditional banking system was not initially at the forefront of the "bank" run as in 1907, but we have known for a long time that the banking system was metamorphosing into an off-balance-sheet and derivatives world—the shadow banking system.[3] Still, I would say that the current credit crisis is essentially a banking panic. Like the classic panics of the 19th and early 20th centuries in the United States, holders of short-term liabilities (mostly commercial paper, but also repo) refused to fund "banks" due to rational fears of loss—in the current case, due to expected losses on subprime and subprime-related securities and subprime-linked derivatives. In the current case, the run started on off-balance-sheet vehicles and led to a general sudden drying up of liquidity in the repo market and a scramble for cash, as counterparties called collateral and refused to lend. As with the earlier panics, the problem at root is a lack of information.[4]

What is the information problem? The answer is in the details. Indeed, the details of the institutional setting and the security design are important for understanding banking panics generally. This should come as no surprise. Panics do not occur under all institutional settings or under all security designs. Contrary to most of the theoretical literature, historically it does not appear that panics are an inherent feature of banking generally. This point has been made by Bordo (1985, 1986), Calomiris and Gorton (1991), and Calomiris (1993), among others. Bordo (1985), for example, concludes that: "the United States experienced panics in a period when they were a historical curiosity in other countries" (p. 73). Indeed, the same observation was made a century ago, by Andrew (1908a): "In England no such general suspension of bank payments and no such premium upon money have occurred since the period of the Napoleonic wars; in France not since the war with Prussia..." (p. 290–91). Why is this point important? If one shares the viewpoint that panics are inherent to banking, then the details of panics perhaps do not matter. My viewpoint is that understanding panics requires a detailed knowledge of the setting.[5] That is what I will try to provide here in the case of the Panic of 2007.

How could a bursting of the house price bubble result in a systemic crisis?[6] I try to answer this last question in this and the next chapter. There are, of course, a myriad of other questions (many of them important, and some distractions from the real issues), but I focus on this one as the central issue for policy. I do not test any hypotheses in this paper, nor do I expound any new economic theory. I include some anecdotal evidence, as well as observations from my own and my colleagues' experiences. I focus on describing the details of the financial instruments and structures involved and supply some very simple, stylized examples to illustrate their workings. The details normally don't matter, as with electricity, but once the house price shock hits, the details suddenly matter. I develop the thesis that the interlinked or nested unique security designs that were necessary to make the subprime market function resulted in a loss of information to investors as the chain of structures—securities and special-purpose vehicles—stretched longer and longer. The chain of securities and the information problems that arose are unique to subprime mortgages—and that is an important message of this paper. This uniqueness is the source of vulnerability.

Subprime mortgages are a financial innovation intended to allow poorer (and disproportionately minority) people and riskier borrowers access to mortgage finance in order to own homes. Indeed, these mortgages were popular. Subprime mortgage origination in 2005 and 2006 was about $1.2 trillion, of which 80% was securitized.[7] The key security design feature of subprime mortgages was the ability of borrowers to finance and refinance their homes based on the capital gains due to house price appreciation over short horizons and then turning this into collateral for a new mortgage (or extracting the equity for consumption). The unique design of subprime mortgages resulted in unique structures for their securitization, reflecting the underlying mortgage design. Further, the subprime residential mortgage-backed securities (RMBS) bonds resulting from the securitization often populated the underlying portfolios of collateralized debt obligations (CDOs), which in turn were often designed for managed, amortizing portfolios of asset-backed securities (ABS), RMBS, and commercial mortgage-backed securities (CMBS).[8] CDO tranches were then often sold to (market-value) off-balance sheet vehicles or their risk was swapped in negative basis trades (defined and discussed below). Moreover, additional subprime securitization risk was created (though not on net) synthetically via credit default swaps as inputs into (hybrid or synthetic) CDOs. This nesting or interlinking of securities, structures, and derivatives resulted in a loss of information and ultimately in a loss of confidence since, as a practical matter, looking through to the underlying mortgages and modeling the different levels of structure was not possible. And while this interlinking enabled the risk to be spread among many capital market participants, it resulted in a loss of transparency as to where these risks ultimately ended up.

When house prices began to slow their growth and ultimately fall, the bubble bursting, the value of the chain of securities began to decrease. But exactly which securities were affected? And where were these securities? Who holds them? What was the expected loss? Even today, we do not know the answers to these questions. In 2007, there was a run on off-balance-sheet vehicles, such as structured investment vehicles (SIVs) and asset-backed commercial paper conduits (ABCP conduits), which were, to some extent, buyers of these bonds. Creditors holding the short-term debt, i.e., commercial paper, of these vehicles did not roll their positions, which was tantamount to a withdrawal of funds. A number of hedge funds collapsed. As of this writing, the crisis is not over.

An important part of the information story is the introduction, in 2006, of new synthetic indices of subprime risk, the ABX.HE ("ABX") indices. These indices trade over the counter. For the first time, information about subprime values and risks was aggregated and revealed. While the location of the risks was unknown, market participants could, for the first time, express views about the value of subprime bonds by buying or selling protection. In 2007, the ABX prices plummeted. The common knowledge created, in a volatile way, ended up with the demand for protection pushing ABX prices down.

The ABX information together with the lack of information about location of the risks led to a loss of confidence on the part of banks in the ability of their counterparties to honor contractual obligations. Securities wrapped by mono-line insurers, such as auction rate notes, failed to re-auction and lost value as monoline exposure to subprime was questioned. The entire financial system was engulfed when the ability to engage in repurchase agreements essentially disappeared. Collateral calls and the unwillingness to engage in repo transactions caused a scramble for cash. The bank-like system of off-balance-sheet vehicles is beyond the reach of regulators, but migrates back to regulated institutions when things go bad.[9] The assets of SIVs and conduits were absorbed back onto bank balance sheets. Liquidity for asset-backed securities and mortgage-backed securities, both cash and synthetic, dried up. Absent reliable market prices, accountants forced firms to "mark-to-market," causing massive writedowns and resulting in reduced GAAP-based capital.[10] Financial firms had to issue securities (at unfavorable terms) and sell assets, with the latter causing further declines in prices—and subsequent further writedowns. Meanwhile, underneath all of this, millions of Americans face foreclosure on their homes due to being unable to refinance their mortgages or to make payments on their current mortgages.[11]

The story is paradoxical. On the one hand, it is about securities that are information insensitive—highly rated securities with inner workings that no one really needs to bother about in normal times. But inside the securities and structures, things are complicated. I focus on the inner workings. The information setting is complicated, but I try to develop the following story. The sell side of the market (dealer banks, CDO and SIV managers) understands the complexity of the subprime chain, while the buy side (institutional investors) does not. Neither group knows where the risks are located, nor does either group know the value of every link in the chain. The chain made valuation opaque; information was lost as risk moved through the chain. The introduction of the ABX index revealed and aggregated values of the subprime bonds with centralized prices, until there was a breakdown of the index.[12]

At the root of the information story are the details of the chain. I detail the design of the various interlinked securities to develop the proposition that the uniqueness of these designs is at the root of the panic. No other securitization asset class works like subprime mortgages; that is, no other asset class (e.g., credit card receivables, auto loans) is linked so sensitively to underlying prices. This distinction is important relative to the view of the panic that seems to be coalescing into the common view. This view is known as the "originate-to-distribute" hypothesis, which very broadly claims that the last 25 years of change in banking has led to the current panic because originators, it is alleged, have no incentive to maintain underwriting standards. I briefly discuss this hypothesis in a later section.

In the first section of this chapter, I briefly look at some background on mortgage markets and the development of the subprime mortgage market. The following section is devoted to explaining how subprime mortgages work. The focus is on implicit contract features, which link the functioning of these mortgages to home price appreciation. Subprime mortgage originators financed their businesses via securitization, but the securitization of subprime mortgages is very different from the securitization of other types of assets (e.g. prime mortgages, credit cards, auto loans). Subprime securitization has dynamic tranching as a function of excess spread and prepayment and is sensitive to house prices as a result. This is explained in a later section. That is not the end of the story, because tranches of subprime residential mortgage-backed securities (RMBS) were often sold to collateralized debt obligations (CDOs). Later, I briefly explain the link to CDOs and the inner workings of these vehicles, the issuance of CDOs, links to subprime, and the synthetic creation of subprime RMBS risk. I provide a very simplified example of the interlinked payoff structure of the securities to show the complexity and loss of information. The crisis also involves a widespread problem of liquidity, which is a topic deserving of much more attention that I have space for here.

Some Background

65~73

In this section, I begin with a very brief description of the evolution of subprime mortgages. Then I briefly look at the definition of "subprime" and the closely related category of "Alt-A" and review the issuance volumes and outstanding amounts of these mortgages.

The Development of Subprime Mortgages

Home ownership for low income and minority households has been a long-standing national goal. Subprime mortgages were an innovation aimed at meeting this goal—and at making money for the innovators. The Harvard "1998 State of the Nation's Housing Report," put it this way:

> In addition to a buoyant economy, the overall housing industry owes its endur-ing vigor to innovations in mortgage finance that have helped not only expand homeownership opportunities, but also reduce market volatility. Under market and regulatory pressure to make home buying more accessible to low-income and minority households, financial institutions have revised their underwrit-ing practices to make lending standards more flexible. In the process, they have developed several new products to enable more income-constrained and cash-strapped borrowers at the margin to qualify for mortgage loans. (Joint Center for Housing Studies, 1998, p. 8).

In the same vein, Listokin et al. (2000) noted:

> America's housing and mortgage markets are in the midst of a dramatic transformation. After generations of discrimination and disinvestment, low-income and minority borrowers and neighborhoods now represent growth potential for homeownership and mortgage lending. In a movement that seems to reconcile socioeconomic equity with the imperatives of profitabil-ity in a competitive and turbulent industry, mortgage lending has emerged as the key to revitalizing the inner city, opening access to suburban housing markets, and promoting household wealth accumulation. Prodded by policy makers, the housing finance industry is now racing to tap new markets for homeownership by reaching traditionally underserved populations of racial and ethnic minorities, recent immigrants, Native Americans, and low- to moderate-income (LMI) households. (p. 19)

Subprime lending expanded during the 1990s, partly in response to changes in legislation affecting mortgage lending. See Temkin et al. (2002) and Mans-field (2000) for the earlier history of subprime lending.[13] Much of the change in mortgage products was due to technological change, which achieved effi-ciencies in standardizing loan products and allowed for the routinization of application procedures. For example, underwriting became automated, based on credit scoring models.[14]

The main issue to be confronted in providing mortgage finance for the unserved population was clearly that these borrowers are riskier. Subprime borrowers are, by definition, riskier than "prime" borrowers, so even if this risk is priced, there must be a decline in underwriting standards in order to provide mortgages to this segment of the population. But, more specifically, potential subprime borrowers have a number of issues which make them difficult bank customers. A Bank of America Mortgage study (cited by Listokin et al., 2000, p. 98) noted the following problems:

1. *Insufficient Funds for a Down Payment.* Low-income or minority customers often are not able to save enough money for a down payment, particularly in rapidly appreciating markets. Intermittent employment and employment at lower-paying jobs often make it hard for many such households to save (Smith 1998).

2. *Credit Issues.* BAMG [Bank of America Mortgage] finds that roughly two-thirds of the LMI [low- and middle-income] population that it deals with has either no credit or lesser-rated credit, as measured by bureau or FICO scores (Smith 1998). While it is the industry standard, the calibration of credit performance in bureau reports and FICO scores is deemed by BAMG to be far from a perfect measure when dealing with traditionally underserved populations.

3. *Undocumented Income.* The cash economy in many traditionally underserved communities means that "they [prospective home buyers] are earning income but cannot prove it in the way most lenders want them to, with a W-2" (Smith 1998).

4. *Lack of or Erroneous Information.* As previously described regarding the Hispanic focus group study, many LMI, ethnic, and immigrant households are totally unfamiliar with the home-buying process or, worse, are misinformed on such matters as how much house they can afford and the minimum down payments required. BAMG underscores that there is not a monolithic underserved community, but rather that different segments of that community have varying problems. Some have strong credit but low savings, while others have some credit issues but have been better savers. To meet these different needs, BAMG introduced two new Neighborhood Advantage mortgages, Zero Down (launched April 1998) and Credit Flex (launched July 1998).[15]

Obviously, such households are risky propositions for lenders. If mortgages were to be extended to these borrowers, the underwriting standards would have to be different, and the structure of the mortgages would have to be different. For example, in 1998, Bank of America initiated two products to address this issue. One product, called the Neighborhood Advantage Zero Down, allowed low-to-moderate income borrowers with good credit a 100% LTV, as well as gifts or grants, to cover closing costs. The other product, called the Neighborhood Advantage Credit Flex, provided some flexibility to low-to-moderate income borrowers subject to a documented alternative credit history. Other banks had similar products. See Listokin et al. (2000).

While the interest rate on a mortgage can be set to price the risk, such a rate is not likely affordable for these borrowers. So the challenge was (and remains) to find a way to lend to such borrowers. The basic idea of a subprime loan recognizes that the dominant form of wealth of low-income households is potentially their home equity. If borrowers can lend to these households for a short time period, two or three years, at a high but affordable interest rate, and equity is built up in their homes, then the mortgage can be refinanced with a lower loan-to-value ratio, reflecting the embedded price appreciation.[16] So, as detailed later, the mortgages were structured so that subprime lenders effectively have an (implicit) option on house prices. After the initial period of two or three years, there is a step-up interest rate, such that borrowers basically must refinance, and the lender has the option to provide a new mortgage or not, depending on whether the house has increased in value. Lenders are long real estate and are only safe if they believe that house prices will go up. This is detailed later.

Subprime and Alt-A Mortgages

The terms "subprime" and "Alt-A" are not official designations of any regulatory authority or rating agency. Basically, the terms refer to borrowers who are perceived to be riskier than the average borrower because of a poor credit history. However, the *Interagency Expanded Guidance for Subprime Lending Programs* defines a subprime borrower as one who displays one or more of the following features:

- Two or more 30-day delinquencies in the last 12 months, or one or more 60-day delinquencies in the last 24 months
- Judgment, foreclosure, repossession, or charge-off in the last 24 months
- Bankruptcy in the last five years
- Relatively high probability of default as evidenced by, for example, a FICO score of 660 or below
- Debt service-to-income ratio of 50% or greater, or otherwise limited ability to cover family living expenses after deducting total debt-service requirements from monthly income.

The market has adopted a somewhat larger, more ambiguous definition, one that is not standard across banks.[17] As shown in table 3.1, subprime borrowers typically have a FICO score below 640 and at some point were delinquent on some debt repayments in the previous 12 to 24 months, or they have filed for bankruptcy in the last few years.[18] Whatever the definition, the innovation was a successful, at least for a significant period of time. Tables 3.2 and 3.3, one for outstanding amounts and the other for issuance, show the size of the Alt-A and subprime mortgage markets relative to the total mortgage market and to the agency mortgage component of the market. The tables show:

- The outstanding amounts of subprime and Alt-A combined amount to about one-quarter of the $6 trillion mortgage market.
- Issuance in 2005 and 2006 of subprime and Alt-A mortgages was almost 30% of the mortgage market.

TABLE 3.1 Market Description of RMBS Categories

Attribute	Prime	Jumbo	Alt-A	Subprime
Lien Position	1st Lien	1st Lien	1st Lien	Over 90% 1st Lien
Weighted Average LTV	Low 70s	Low 70s	Low 70s	Low 80s
Borrower FICO	700+ FICO	700+ FICO	640–730 FICO	500–660 FICO
Borrower Credit History	No credit derogatories	No credit derogatories	No credit derogatories	Credit derogatories
Conforming to Agency Criteria?	Conforming	Conforming by all standards but size	Non-conforming due to documentation or LTV	Non-conforming due to FICO, credit history, or documentation
Loan-to-Value (LTV)	65–80%	65–80%	70–100%	60–100%

TABLE 3.2 Non-Agency MBS Outstanding

	Outstandings in $ Billions					Percent of Total MBS				
		Non-Agency Outstanding					Non-Agency Outstanding			
Year	Total MBS	Agency	Total	Jumbo	Alt-A	Subprime	Agency	Total	Jumbo	Alt-A	Subprime
2000	3,003	2,625	377	252	44	81	87%	13%	8%	1%	3%
2001	3,409	2,975	434	275	50	109	87%	13%	8%	1%	3%
2002	3,802	3,313	489	256	67	167	87%	13%	7%	2%	4%
2003	4,005	3,394	611	254	102	254	85%	15%	6%	3%	6%
2004	4,481	3,467	1,014	353	230	431	77%	23%	8%	5%	10%
2005	5,201	3,608	1,593	441	510	641	69%	31%	8%	10%	12%
2006	5,829	3,905	1,924	462	730	732	67%	33%	8%	13%	13%
2007Q1	5,984	4,021	1,963	468	765	730	67%	33%	8%	13%	12%

Source: Federal Reserve Board, Inside MBS&ABS, Loan Performance, UBS.

TABLE 3.3 Gross Mortgage-Backed Security Issuance

| Year | Agency | Non-Agency $ Tril. | | | | Total MBS $ Tril. | Percent of Total | | | | | | |
		Jumbo	Alt-A	Subprime	Other		Agency	Jumbo	Alt-A	Subprime	Other	Non-Agency
2000	0.479	0.054	0.016	0.052	0.013	0.615	78%	8.7%	2.7%	8.5%	2.2%	22.1%
2001	1.09	0.142	0.011	0.087	0.027	1.35	80%	10.5%	0.8%	6.4%	2.0%	19.7%
2002	1.44	0.172	0.053	0.123	0.066	1.86	78%	9.2%	2.9%	6.6%	3.6%	22.3%
2003	2.13	0.237	0.074	0.195	0.080	2.72	78%	8.7%	2.7%	7.2%	2.9%	21.6%
2004	1.02	0.233	0.159	0.363	0.110	1.88	54%	12.4%	8.4%	19.3%	5.8%	45.9%
2005	0.965	0.281	0.332	0.465	0.113	2.16	45%	13.0%	15.4%	21.6%	5.3%	55.3%
2006	0.925	0.219	0.366	0.449	0.112	2.07	45%	10.6%	17.7%	21.7%	5.4%	55.3%
7m 2007	0.654	0.136	0.219	0.176	0.047	1.23	53%	11.0%	17.8%	14.3%	3.8%	46.9%

Source: Inside MBS&ABS.

- Over the period 2000–2007, the outstanding amount of agency mortgages doubled, but subprime grew 800%!
- Since 2000 the subprime and Alt-A segments of the market grew at the expense of the agency share, which fell from almost 80% (by outstanding or issuance) to about half by issuance and 67% by outstanding amount.

Many seem to hold the view that subprime mortgages are homogeneous. Aside from the attributes in the table of characteristics above, this is not the case. Certainly, as is well known, vintage of the mortgage is important. But also, even cross-sectionally, subprime mortgages are not homogeneous. That is, while they are all "subprime," this does not mean that they are all the same across all dimensions, even holding vintage constant. Table 3.4 shows some of the heterogeneity of origination characteristics of the borrowers and the heterogeneity of experience of those borrowers across states from the 2006 vintage, as of November 13, 2007. Table 3.4 is from UBS (*Mortgage Strategist*, November 13, 2007, p. 31). The last row is the total for the balances and is the weighted average for the characteristics.[19]

Note:

- The combined loan-to-value ratio (Combo LTV) varies from about 80% to 91.5%.
- All the state FICO scores are around 620. They vary from a low of 604 in West Virginia to a high of 644 in Hawaii. Note, however, that West Virginia's percentage of loans that are 60 days or more delinquent is 6.67%, compared to a weighted national average of 16%.
- The percentage of mortgages that are full doc varies from a minimum of 43.6% in New York to a maximum of 80.9% in Indiana.
- Compared to "all," note that Minnesota, California, Florida, Nevada, Rhode Island, Georgia, and Ohio are worse that the weighted average, in terms of percentage, a cumulative 60 days delinquent. In terms of cumulative loss, the experience varies from three basis points of loss in West Virginia to a maximum of 1.2% cumulative losses in Missouri.
- House Price Appreciation (HPA) over the life of the loan, by state, shows a wide range of experience.
- These are state averages, so the dispersion is undoubtedly greater.

These observations are intended to convey the richness and complexity of the cross-sectional experience of different states. Even though subprime bond portfolios are fixed and RMBS investors cannot easily choose state concentrations, there is some variation, which is relevant assuming house prices rise and defaults are idiosyncratic. But portfolios tend to reflect the national concentrations of population, for example, in California.

TABLE 3.4

State	Original Balance	Current Balance	Factor	Combo LTV	FICO	% Full Doc	%60D+	%Cum Def	%Cum Loss	HPA Life	%Cum 60D+
AK	$526,218,473	$399,461,897	76.4	88.4	620	70.4	10.01	0.96	0.28	4.99	8.60
AL	$1,849,884,555	$1,550,451,687	85.1	89.5	606	76.1	13.53	1.24	0.44	6.05	12.76
AR	$815,652,588	$697,886,978	87.5	89.9	615	73.1	11.46	1.50	0.44	4.37	11.53
AZ	$14,428,873,327	$11,553,251,475	83.2	85.8	622	58.7	15.07	1.53	0.45	1.52	14.07
CA	$102,766,337,717	$82,358,162,338	82.3	86.3	638	46.6	22.92	2.33	0.84	-1.15	21.19
CO	$5,292,370,638	$4,441,089,856	86.9	91.4	627	70.4	15.99	2.50	0.84	1.44	16.39
CT	$4,669,164,260	$3,861,877,916	85.2	84.7	614	60.8	14.05	1.20	0.30	0.95	13.17
DC	$1,194,568,797	$777,630,979	65.8	79.3	618	52.5	19.50	1.81	0.70	0.63	14.65
DE	$991,186,352	$794,565,683	83.8	85.8	607	71.1	11.74	0.77	0.08	4.39	10.61
FL	$43,832,887,130	$36,621,751,851	86.4	85.5	621	50.8	21.37	1.26	0.45	1.33	19.73
GA	$8,695,861,284	$6,981,317,691	81.5	91.3	618	67.1	18.22	2.51	0.98	4.11	17.37
HI	$3,018,554,281	$2,321,907,957	78.7	83.0	644	46.2	11.73	1.14	0.32	4.21	10.38
IA	$858,318,756	$683,838,875	81.0	90.6	608	80.9	13.85	0.94	0.25	3.13	12.16
ID	$1,415,015,589	$1,130,897,876	82.4	86.7	617	70.2	11.14	1.58	0.27	7.32	10.76
IL	$17,296,689,870	$11,903,745,425	69.7	88.7	625	56.9	18.21	1.16	0.41	3.71	13.85
IN	$2,885,253,658	$2,512,373,695	88.7	90.7	614	76.0	15.74	1.45	0.64	2.42	15.41
KS	$903,577,781	$699,004,465	79.7	90.8	613	78.8	12.80	1.05	0.31	3.56	11.26
KY	$1,317,753,384	$1,141,425,298	89.8	90.4	610	78.7	14.47	1.24	0.31	3.36	14.23
LA	$1,781,601,486	$1,539,635,309	89.0	89.1	609	68.8	10.61	0.65	0.15	5.93	10.09
MA	$9,065,659,267	$6,577,633,279	73.8	84.9	623	55.8	18.60	1.70	0.53	-1.82	15.42
MD	$16,017,510,459	$10,727,182,750	68.5	84.9	615	62.7	14.93	1.00	0.30	2.35	11.22
ME	$1,097,914,180	$793,716,799	74.4	84.2	615	62.7	15.16	0.61	0.15	2.55	11.90
MI	$6,820,690,521	$5,744,089,563	85.4	89.8	613	66.5	22.31	1.79	0.86	-2.56	20.83
MN	$4,667,272,065	$3,835,369,086	83.6	89.6	626	64.5	23.92	1.72	0.70	0.61	21.73
MO	$3,654,696,377	$2,912,862,041	81.4	89.5	607	74.0	15.40	2.91	1.20	3.43	15.45
MS	$980,156,949	$855,069,697	89.1	89.8	605	74.7	15.19	1.69	0.56	5.56	15.23

MT	$410,267,389	$323,274,332	81.5	85.5	617	65.7	8.64	1.45	0.10	8.06	8.49
NC	$4,597,544,803	$3,520,500,657	78.1	89.7	613	73.5	11.16	1.31	0.31	6.89	10.03
ND	$93,805,229	$81,770,280	88.2	91.3	616	77.4	8.59	1.09	0.15	5.96	8.67
NE	$511,569,008	$448,252,110	89.6	91.4	614	77.7	10.98	1.28	0.51	2.19	11.11
NH	$1,361,125,986	$1,131,525,707	86.3	85.0	614	63.8	13.34	1.27	0.35	0.38	12.78
NJ	$14,963,091,591	$10,011,731,473	68.0	83.8	620	48.8	18.12	1.10	0.26	1.77	13.41
NM	$1,377,416,203	$900,206,794	66.9	87.1	615	68.7	9.01	0.69	0.12	7.46	6.72
NV	$7,448,696,508	$6,276,562,378	87.6	88.2	631	54.5	19.61	1.89	0.60	-1.60	19.06
NY	$22,383,244,240	$17,544,608,248	79.7	84.3	633	43.6	18.58	1.60	0.38	1.49	16.42
OH	$5,483,111,567	$4,690,730,151	87.1	90.6	613	76.3	17.89	1.08	0.36	0.32	16.66
OK	$1,221,051,933	$1,071,559,556	90.5	90.3	610	76.8	12.39	1.12	0.33	3.61	12.34
OR	$4,427,876,513	$3,595,736,620	83.7	87.2	629	70.3	9.59	1.17	0.23	7.93	9.20
PA	$6,978,493,823	$5,809,560,356	86.0	85.5	608	70.0	10.88	0.53	0.12	4.57	9.89
RI	$1,935,464,210	$1,506,722,871	79.6	84.9	621	55.5	19.87	2.53	0.95	-1.45	18.34
SC	$2,359,469,767	$1,805,802,326	78.0	88.1	612	70.7	13.18	1.14	0.29	6.41	11.42
SD	$143,990,678	$125,448,463	88.5	91.0	616	75.7	11.53	0.28	0.07	4.37	10.49
TN	$3,863,653,816	$3,350,306,516	88.5	91.5	615	75.7	12.38	2.21	0.74	6.09	13.16
TX	$14,544,490,634	$12,691,323,091	90.4	89.6	616	66.7	11.51	2.05	0.74	6.43	12.46
UT	$3,185,604,205	$2,423,726,305	77.7	90.6	631	68.3	8.24	1.60	0.26	14.70	8.00
VA	$10,125,147,122	$7,702,473,341	78.7	85.8	616	59.7	17.95	2.21	0.82	3.11	16.33
VT	$309,867,790	$213,999,934	71.7	81.7	615	64.4	13.75	0.52	0.10	3.06	10.38
WA	$9,550,742,478	$7,505,680,840	81.1	88.0	625	69.5	9.40	1.58	0.26	9.13	9.20
WI	$3,511,477,290	$2,533,979,690	72.9	88.7	613	72.4	15.44	0.82	0.23	2.79	12.08
WV	$454,297,185	$347,335,187	78.9	86.1	604	76.7	13.38	1.13	0.31	2.47	11.69
WY	$296,835,000	$236,406,395	82.9	90.1	615	79.9	7.43	0.51	0.03	9.97	6.67
ALL	$378,382,004,715	$299,265,424,087	81.1	86.8	625	56.5	18.35	1.71	0.57	1.72	16.60

Subprime Mortgage Design   74-82

The security design problem faced by mortgage lenders was this: how can a mortgage loan be designed to make lending to riskier borrowers possible? The defining feature of the subprime mortgage is the idea that the borrower and lender can benefit from house price appreciation over short horizons. The horizon is kept short to protect the lender's exposure. Conditional on sufficient house price appreciation, the mortgage is rolled into another mortgage, possibly with a short horizon, as well. The appreciation of the house can become the basis for refinancing every two or three years. In this section, I begin with an overview of subprime mortgages. The next subsection explains the details of how these mortgages work with a simple, stylized example.

Overview

The defining characteristic of a subprime mortgage is that it is designed to essentially force a refinancing after two or three years. Specifically, most subprime mortgages are adjustable-rate mortgages (ARMs) with a variation of a hybrid structure known as a "2/28" or "3/27." Both 2/28 ARM and 3/27 ARM mortgages typically have 30-year amortizations. The main difference between these two types of ARMs is the length of time for which their interest rates are fixed and variable.

In a 2/28 ARM, the 2 represents the number of initial years over which the mortgage rate remains fixed, while the 28 represents the number of years the interest rate paid on the mortgage will be floating. Similarly, the interest rate on a 3/27 ARM is fixed for three years, after which time it floats for the remaining 27-year amortization. The margin that is charged over the reference rate depends on the borrower's credit risk, as well as prevailing market margins for other borrowers with similar credit risks.[20]

These mortgages are known as "hybrids" because they incorporate both fixed- and adjustable-rate features. The initial monthly payment is based on a "teaser" interest rate that is fixed for the first two years (for the 2/28) or three years (for the 3/27). Two important points are noteworthy about 2/28s and 3/27s. First, the fixed rate for the first two or three years, the teaser rate, was not particularly low compared to prime mortgages. For example, the national average rate on a 2006 subprime 2/28 mortgage was 8.5% and would reset on average to 6.1% over the benchmark LIBOR. (See Rosengren, 2007). These high initial rates are not surprising because most of these mortgages were refinanced or the homes were sold prior to the mortgage being reset.

As an example, on a 2/28 mortgage originated in 2006, the initial interest rate might have been 8.64%. After the initial period comes the rate "reset" (or step-up date), which is a higher interest rate, say LIBOR plus 6.22%. At the time of origination, LIBOR could have been 5.4%. So the new interest rate at the reset would have been 11.62%. This rate floats, so it changes if LIBOR changes. The interest rate is updated every six months, subject to limits called adjustment caps. There is a cap on each subsequent adjustment, called the "periodic cap," and a cap on the interest rate over the life of the loan, called the "lifetime cap." The reset rate is significantly higher, but potentially affordable.

The above discussion emphasizes why the reset date on a hybrid ARM is so important. The higher payment for the borrower at the reset date comes from the significantly higher monthly mortgage payment that occurs at reset. Borrowers, thus, have an incentive to refinance their mortgage before the reset date. This is what I meant above when I stated that subprime mortgages are designed to "essentially force" a refinancing.

Another important characteristic of subprime mortgages is the size and prevalence of the prepayment penalties. See, for example, Farris and Richardson (2004). Fannie Mae estimates that 80% of subprime mortgages have prepayment penalties, while only 2% of prime mortgages have prepayment penalties (see Zigas, Parry, and Weech, 2002). Further evidence for this comes from the prevalence of net interest margin securities (NIMs) in subprime securitizations. NIMs are securitizations of the early excess cash flows and prepayment penalties in subprime RMBS transactions. They are interest-only strips that derive their cash flow from the excess or residual cash flows, including significantly the prepayment penalties. See Bear Stearns (September 2006b), Frankel (2008), Zelmanovich et al. (2007) and McDermott, Albergo, and Abrams (2001). I discuss NIMs further below.

It is worth briefly contrasting a subprime mortgage with a standard, prime, 30-year fixed-rate mortgage. With a prime mortgage, the borrower repays principal over time, and the mortgage matures after 30 years. The borrower may prepay the mortgage, typically without penalty. The borrower may benefit from house price appreciation, but the lender does not (directly) benefit.

I now turn to a simple, stylized example to try to understand how the design of the subprime mortgage addressed the riskiness of the borrowers.

A Simple Stylized Example

The standard, prime mortgage is typically a fixed-rate 30-year loan. The usual way of thinking of mortgage design and pricing is to recognize the embedded optionality in these mortgages: the borrower has the right to prepay the mortgage (a call option to refinance) and the right to default (a put option).[21] That is, the mortgage can be purchased from the lender at par, via prepayment, which is a call option, depending on interest rates. Or the mortgage can be sold by the borrower to the lender for the value of the house, via default, amounting to a put option. The literature on this is voluminous. See Kau and Keenan (1995) for a review.

A subprime mortgage is very different. Of course, borrowers can always prepay (but subject to the prepayment penalty), and they can always default. But, as mentioned above, one important difference is that subprime mortgages typically have significantly higher prepayment penalties than prime mortgages (where it is typically zero). But that is not the only important difference. The following example is intended to illustrate that a subprime mortgage contains an implicit embedded option on house prices for the lender. To the extent that this option is valuable, lenders may be willing to lend to riskier borrowers.

The intuition is as follows. If house prices rise and borrowers build up equity in their homes, the borrowers will become less risky, ceteris paribus. But lenders are unwilling to speculate on house prices and borrower repayment behavior for long periods, so they want the right to end the mortgage early, because foreclosure is costly. If borrowers "extract equity" through refinancing after house prices have risen, then the plan of the lenders may not work. So lenders incorporate high prepayment fees to try to prevent this. I develop these ideas with the example below.

In my example, mortgages to prime borrowers would be made for two periods, but the candidate borrower that I will consider is rated "subprime," and so the lender is unwilling to make a traditional two-period mortgage. The prospective borrower has a given income, which perhaps cannot be documented, and lacks money for a down payment. So this mortgage, if made, would be to a borrower with no collateral. It is simply too risky to make a standard prime mortgage.

To see how a subprime mortgage works, consider a lender who operates in a competitive market and faces a financing cost of r_B per period. Let $r_{M,t}$ be the mortgage rate that the lender may offer for a subprime mortgage during period t. The amount of the mortgage is $L. Over period t, the probability of borrower default is p ($r_{M,ti}L$, LTV_t), where the probability of default is increasing in the mortgage payment, $r_{M,t}L$ (implicitly relative to the borrower's income) and in the loan-to-value (LTV_t) ratio, which measures the equity stake the borrower has in the home.[22] Borrowers work harder if they have an equity stake. To summarize, a higher mortgage payment and more debt relative to the home value increase the chance of defaulting. If there is a default, the recovery rate on the home value, V_t, at the end of period t is 50%, so for a mortgage of size \$L, the lender would recover $R_t = \min [\, 0.5V_t,\, L]$ if there is a default at the end of period t. Call R_t the "recovery amount" for period t.[23]

The subprime candidate borrower is applying for a mortgage of size \$L for a home worth \$L, so the LTV would be 100%. On a one-period mortgage, the lender breaks even if the mortgage rate, $r_{M,1}$, is such that:

$$(1 + r_{M,1})\, (1 - p\,(r_{M,1}L,\, LTV_1))\, L + R_1\, p\,(r_{M,1}L,\, LTV_1) - (1 + r_B)\, L = 0. \qquad (1)$$

Of course, there may be no mortgage rate that satisfies (1). The lender cannot simply increase the mortgage interest rate because this increases the likelihood of default as it becomes less likely that the borrower can make the higher mortgage payment. In any case, since by assumption the first period is rather short, realistically the borrower would have to refinance at the end of the first period or default would be certain to occur. But I have already ruled out granting long-term (two-period) mortgages to subprime borrowers as too risky.

Imagine a subprime mortgage, as follows. The lender offers to extend a mortgage loan for the full two periods (imagine that period 1 is two years and period 2 is 28 years, though I omit the technicalities of discounting, and so on), with an initial mortgage rate of $r_{M,1}$ for the first period. Assume that the mortgage rate for the second period (the "step-up" rate) is prohibitively high, so that the borrower must refinance the mortgage or default at that time. This is by design. Also, I will assume that the prepayment penalty is high.

Suppose now that during any period there is a γ% chance that house prices rise by Φ% and a 1 − γ% chance that they fall by Φ%. During the first period, house prices will either rise or fall. For simplicity, assume that the house price change occurs an instant before the end of the first period, so that it does not affect the initial loan-to-value ratio (LTV) or the probability of default during the first period. Then, at the start of the second period, if house prices have risen, the LTV will have fallen to LTV_D (the "D" subscript is for "down.") This corresponds to the borrower having positive equity in the home. On the other hand, if during the first period house prices have fallen, then the LTV will be higher, LTV_U ("U" is for "up"), corresponding to the borrower having a negative equity position in the home.

The assumed evolution of home prices affects the first-period outcome—default or refinance. The evolution of house prices does not affect the probability of default (by assumption), but it does affect the recovery amount. If there is a default at the end of the first period, then the value of the house is different in the two cases, depending on whether home price appreciation occurred or did

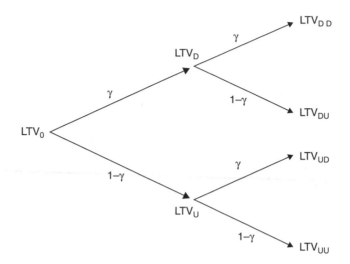

FIGURE 3.1 The Evolution of House Prices and the Loan-to-Value Ratio.

not. Following the notation shown in figure 3.1, the expected value of the first period mortgage, $E(L_1)$, is:

$$(1 + r_{M,1})(1 - p(r_{M,1}L, LTV_0)) L + \gamma R_{D,1} p(r_{M,1}L, LTV_0)$$
$$+ (1 - \gamma) R_{U,1} p(r_{M,1}L, LTV_0) - (1 + r_{B,1}) L$$

where $R_{D,1} = \min [0.5 (1 + \Phi) V_t, L]$, in the case of house prices rising and LTV going down, and $R_{U,1} = \min [0.5 (1 + \Phi) V_t, L]$; note that the subscripts on "R" refer to the LTV going down (D), since house prices went up and house prices rising corresponding to the LTV going up (U).

If house prices fall at the end of the first period, assume that the initial lender will not refinance the mortgage (and neither will any other lender). The borrower now has negative equity, and the likelihood of default going forward is (by assumption) too high for any lender. If home prices rise at the end of the first period, then the initial lender will be willing to refinance the mortgage.

A rise in home prices over the first period has two effects: (1) the borrower has positive equity in the house, which is collateral from the point of view of the lender; this makes the lender's recovery amount higher; (2) with a lower LTV going forward, the probability of default is lower, *ceteris paribus*, so the mortgage rate for the next period, $r_{M,2}$, may be lower, making the payment lower, which also reduces the default likelihood. (Of course, as I discuss below, the borrower may extract the equity for consumption.)

House prices may rise or fall over the second period. As before, I assume that house prices change an instant before the end of the period and so the change does not affect the probability of default during the period. It does affect the recovery amount at the end of the second period. The expected value of the second-period mortgage (conditional on it being made), E (L_2), is:

$$(1 + r_{M,2}) (1 - p (r_{M,2}L, LTV_D)) L + \gamma R_{DD,2} \, p (r_{M,2}L, LTV_D)$$
$$+ (1 - \gamma) R_{DU,2} \, p (r_{M,2}L, LTV_D) - (1 + r_{B,2}) L.$$

Note that the second-period mortgage rate, $r_{M,2}$ (and lender borrowing rate, $r_{B,2}$) may be different than the first-period rate, and that the loan-to-value ratio at the start of the period is now LTV_D as house prices have risen. At the end of the second period, if house prices fell and the borrower defaults, the bank will recover $R_{DU,2}$; the bank will recover $R_{DD,2}$ if house prices rose.

The expected payoff to the lender over the two periods (omitting discounting and the prepayment penalty) is: E $(L_1) + \gamma E (L_2)$. Note that the second-period mortgage is only made if prices have risen during the first period. This occurs with probability γ.

At the end of the first period, the borrower is in a difficult spot because he either defaults or must refinance. The lender faces a choice, which depends on house prices. If house prices have risen (LTV goes down), the lender chooses max $[R_{D,1}, E (L_2)] = E (L_2)$. If house prices have fallen (LTV goes up), the lender chooses max $[R_{U,1}, E (L_2)] = R_{U,1}$. In other words, the lender decides whether to refinance or take the recovery value. This is the optionality in the mortgage for the lender. It is an implicit option, as the strike price is the recovery amount, which depends on what house prices did over the second period.

The lender does not take into account costs to the borrower from defaulting, if there are such costs.

The example makes the following points:

1. The key design features of a subprime mortgage are: (1) it is short-term, making refinancing important; (2) there is a step-up mortgage rate that applies at the end of the first period, creating a strong incentive to refinance; and (3) there is a prepayment penalty, creating an incentive not to refinance early. If the step-up rate and the prepayment penalty are both sufficiently high so that without refinancing from the lender, the borrower will default, then the lender is in a position to decide what happens. The lender is exposed to house prices, more sensitively than with conventional mortgages.

2. In an important sense, the decision to default has effectively been transferred from the borrower to the lender. The step-up interest rate forces the borrower to come back to the lender after the first period, and the lender decides whether to extend another loan or not. Instead of the borrower having an option to default, the lender has an option to extend.

3. The design of the subprime mortgage creates the refinancing option. But the borrower can refinance at the reset date with any originator. It may be that the subprime market is competitive with respect to initial mortgages, but not with respect to refinancing; borrowers are largely tied to their initial lenders.[24] In that case, the original lender can benefit from any home price appreciation.

4. If $E(L_1) < 0$, i.e., the expected profit to the lender from the first-period loan is negative, then the refinancing must be tied to the original lender. The subprime mortgage, including the possible second-period refinancing, may be expected to be profitable if the probability of a house price increase, γ, is perceived to be sufficiently high. This happens if the borrower is tied to the original lender for refinancing. In fact, $r_{M,1}$, the first-period mortgage rate, may be set low (relative to the risk of loss due to default) as a teaser rate, making $E(L_1)$ negative, and still the overall loan may have a positive expected value if the probability of a house price increase, γ, is perceived to be sufficiently high. This may be viewed as "predatory" lending; the borrower is attracted to borrow, but may not understand that effectively it is the lender who makes the choice to refinance or not at the end of the first period.

Refinancing does not mean that the borrower receives a long-term mortgage. The borrower could be rolled into another subprime loan. In fact, a borrower could receive a sequence of subprime loans as house prices rise, each time building up equity and obtaining increasingly lower interest rates.[25] But in such a sequence, the lender effectively has the right to opt out by not refinancing and taking the recovery amount. In other words, a sequence of refinancings into subprime mortgages corresponds to a compound option for the lender.

The borrower always has the right to prepay the mortgage, but with the higher prepayment fee. So far, I have assumed that this was prohibitively high. But, in practice, we do observe prepayments. In prime mortgages, this is usually the result of mortgage rates going down. But here there is another motivation as well. The borrower may want to extract equity value if house prices have risen.

In my example above, one can imagine that this corresponds to the borrower and lender agreeing to refinance the loan at the end of period 1, but the new mortgage allows the borrower to extract equity in the process. At the end of the first period, the borrower owes $L to the bank. If house prices have risen, the house is now worth $(1+\Phi) L$. If the lender is willing to make the same subprime mortgage that was made at the start of period 1, then the borrower can extract $\Phi L. Such equity extraction is common in the prime market, but also very common—possibly more common, depending on the year—in the subprime market. In survey data, home equity extractions are often used for consumption. See Chomsisengphet and Pennington-Cross (2006, 2007) and Greenspan and Kennedy (2005, 2007). This is discussed further below.

Refinancing and Equity Extraction

Between 1998 and 2006, subprime mortgages worked as they were supposed to. During this period, house prices rose and prepayment speeds were high; at least half of these mortgages (of all types) were refinanced within five years, and up to 80% of some types were refinanced within five years. See Bhardwaj and Sengupta (2008a). In other words, the bulk of the "originations" in the subprime market were refinancings of existing mortgages.

Who got the benefit of the option on house prices? To the extent that lenders are willing to refinance the house even with equity extraction, there is a split of the capital gain. In that case, the borrower gets cash. Lenders only face a possibly safer borrower if equity is built up. Note that if $E(L_1) < 0$, then the lender will not want to allow equity extraction at the end of period 1 unless there is a large fee to compensate the lender for the foregone $\gamma E(L_2)$.

The benefits of refinancing were divided between lenders and borrowers, but we do not know the split. Greenspan and Kennedy (2007) estimate that during the period 1991–2005, $520 billion was extracted on average annually from all mortgages. Figure 3.2 shows the Greenspan and Kennedy estimates of net equity extraction and extraction as a percentage of personal disposable income.[26] These data do not distinguish between prime and subprime mortgage extractions; they just convey a sense of the magnitudes. Bhardwaj and Sengupta (2008B) report that the fraction of subprime refinancings that involved some equity extraction ranged from 51.3% to 58.6% over the period 1998–2007, with no trend.[27] Chomsisengphet and Pennington-Cross (2006) examine the early period of the subprime market, prior to 2002, and show that a higher proportion of subprime refinancing involve equity extraction, compared to prime refinancings.

Summary

To reiterate, no other consumer loan has the design feature in which the borrower's ability to repay is so sensitively linked to appreciation of an underlying asset. This sensitivity to the market price, the house price, will have far-reaching implications. But if this were the end of the story, there would not have been a

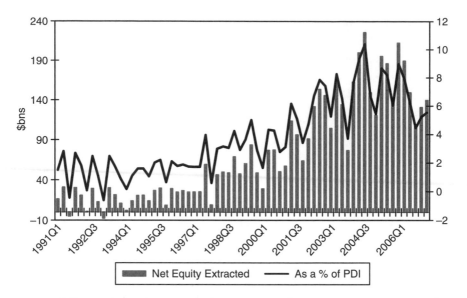

FIGURE 3.2 Net Equity Extraction and as a Percent of PDI. Source: Greenspan and Kennedy (2005, 2007).

systemic banking crisis (although obviously there would be the problem with foreclosures for many people).[28]

42-96

The Design and Complexity of Subprime RMBS Bonds

The next link in the chain concerns how the subprime mortgages were financed. This, too, will require a unique security design, quite different from traditional securitizations.[29]

The originators of subprime mortgages, including many of the names that later became well known, such as Countrywide Financial, New Century, Option One, and Ameriquest, were largely new entrants into mortgage lending. The main financing method for subprime originators was securitization. This will be important not only because the risk will be spread, but also because the structure of the securitization will have special features reflecting the design of the subprime mortgages. This latter point means that there will be additional complexity.

Financing Subprime Mortgages via Securitization

Table 3.5 shows the extent to which lenders relied on securitization for the financing of the mortgages. This table provides a snapshot of the quantitative

TABLE 3.5 Mortgage Originations and Subprime Securitization

	Total Mortgage Originations (Billions)	Subprime Originations (Billions)	Subprime Share in Total Originations (% of dollar value)	Subprime Mortgage Backed Securities (Billions)	Percent Subprime Securitized (% of dollar value)
2001	$2,215	$190	8.6%	$95	50.4%
2002	$2,885	$231	8.0%	$121	52.7%
2003	$3,945	$335	8.5%	$202	60.5%
2004	$2,920	$540	18.5%	$401	74.3%
2005	$3,120	$625	20.0%	$507	81.2%
2006	$2,980	$600	20.1%	$483	80.5%

Sources: Inside Mortgage Finance, The 2007 Mortgage Market Statistical Annual, Key Data (2006), Joint Economic Committee (October 2007).

importance of subprime securitizations. It shows that subprime mortgage origination in 2005 and 2006 was about $1.2 trillion, of which 80% was securitized.

The Design of Subprime Residential Mortgage-Backed Securities (Subprime RMBS)

Subprime RMBS bonds are quite different from other securitizations because of the unique features that differentiate subprime mortgages from other mortgages. Like other securitizations, subprime RMBS bonds of a given transaction differ by seniority, but unlike other securitizations, the amounts of credit enhancement for each tranche and the size of each tranche depend on the cash flow coming into the deal in a very significant way. The cash flow comes largely from prepayment of the underlying mortgages through refinancing. What happens to the cash coming into the deal depends on triggers which measure (prepayment and default) performance of the underlying pools of subprime mortgages. The triggers can potentially divert cash flows within the structure. In some cases, this can lead to a leakage of protection for higher rated tranches. Time tranching in subprime transactions is contingent on these triggers. The structure makes the degree of credit enhancement dynamic and dependent on the cash flows coming into the deal. In this section, I briefly explain the structural features of subprime bonds.

The credit risk of the underlying mortgages is one important factor to understand in assessing the relative value of a particular subprime RMBS. Later, I will focus on the characteristics of the mortgages themselves, but here I focus on the securitization structure. However, the credit risk of the borrowers is intimately linked to the structure of the bond and, indeed, the structure of the particular transaction to which the bond is a part. Figure 3.3 shows the basic structure of a subprime mortgage-backed security (MBS) transaction.[30]

Overwhelmingly, asset-backed securities (ABS) and mortgage-backed securities (MBS) use one or both of the following structures:

- A senior/subordinate shifting of interest structure ("senior/sub"), sometimes called the "six-pack" structure (because there are three mezzanine bonds and three subordinate bonds junior to the AAA bonds), or
- An excess spread/overcollateralization ("XS/OC") structure. Over-collateralization means that the collateral balance exceeds the bond balance; that is, deal assets exceed deal liabilities.

Because credit risk is the primary risk factor, subprime RMBS bonds have a senior/sub structure, like prime RMBS, but also have an additional layer of support that comes from the excess spread, i.e., the interest paid into the deal from the underlying mortgages minus the spread paid out on the RMBS bonds issued by the deal.[31] Another important feature is overcollateralization; that is, there are initially more assets (collateral) than liabilities (bonds). (The overcollateralization reverts to an equity claim if it remains at the end of the transaction.)

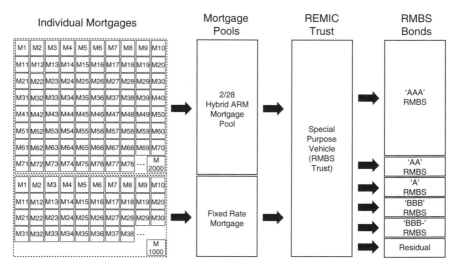

FIGURE 3.3 Sample Subprime MBS Structure. Source: Kevin Kendra, Fitch, "Tranche ABX and Basis Risk in Subprime RMBS Structured Portfolios," Feb. 20, 2007.

In a prime deal with a senior/sub structure, basically the total amount of credit enhancement that will ever be present is in place at the start of the deal. The tranche sizes are fixed. In this setting, assuming that defaults and losses are bunched near the start of the deal is conservative, as this erodes the credit enhancement early on, and it cannot be replaced. Because of sequential amortization, senior tranches are being paid down over time in this structure.

Subprime transactions are different because the XS/OC feature results in a buildup of credit enhancement from the collateral itself during the life of the transaction. The allocation of the credit enhancement over time depends on triggers that reflect the credit condition of the underlying portfolio. Excess spread is built up over time to reach a target level of credit enhancement. Once the OC target is reached, excess spread can be paid out of the transaction (to the residual holder) and is no longer available to cover losses. Later, I discuss the triggers in more detail.

There are several key features of RMBS structures to be mentioned. First, there is a lockout period. Mezzanine and subordinate bonds are locked out of receiving prepayments for a period of time after deal settlement. In other words, during the lockout period, amortization is sequential. The period of time of the lockout and other details differ, depending on the type of collateral in the deal. Second, there may be cross-collateralization. That is, some transactions contain multiple loan groups. After interest payments are made on bonds in one group, available remaining funds can be used to pay interest to bonds in another group.[32]

Figure 3.4 displays the two types of transaction structures: the senior/sub structure and the OC structure. These transactions are quite complicated, so as a prelude to discussing XS/OC structures, I will very briefly start with the typical prime and Alt-A deal structure. I emphasize that what follows is a brief overview only.

Prime and Alt-A Deals

Most prime jumbo and Alt-A transactions use a six-pack structure, and most subprime, and a few Alt-A deals, use the XS/OC structure. Choice of structure is mostly a function of the amount of excess spread in the deal. Excess spread is the difference between the weighted average coupon on the collateral and the weighted average bond coupons. In an XS/OC structure, the excess spread is typically between 300 and 400 basis points.

There is no overcollateralization in a six-pack structure. In a six-pack deal, the mortgage collateral is tranched into a senior (AAA) tranche, mezzanine tranches (AA, A, BBB), and subordinated tranches (BB, B, and unrated). The

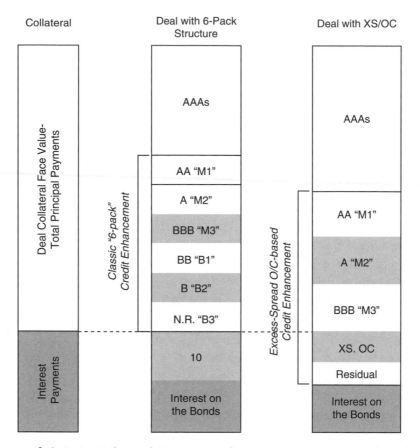

FIGURE 3.4 Senior/Sub 6-Pack Structure vs. the XS/OC Structure. Note: The scale in the figure does not accurately reflect relative sizes of bonds, IO, or interest flow. Source: UBS.

most junior bond, essentially equity, is unrated because it is the "first-loss" piece, meaning that it will absorb the first dollar of loss on the underlying pool of mortgages.

In a senior/sub, or six-pack, structure, the mezzanine ("mezz") bonds and subordinate bonds are tranched to be thick enough to absorb collateral losses to ensure that the senior bonds have a probability of loss sufficiently low to justify a triple-A rating. This is accomplished by reversing the order of the priority of cash flow payments and losses in the transaction. In the early years of the transaction, prepaid principal is allocated from top down ("sequential amortization"); that is, only the senior bonds are paid, while the mezz bonds and sub bonds are "locked out" from receiving prepaid principal. Losses are allocated from the bottom up; that is, the lowest rated class outstanding at the time will absorb any principal losses.

By using sequential amortization, the senior bonds are paid down first, and there is an increase in the percentage of the remaining collateral that is covered by the mezz and sub bonds. This continues during the lockout period, which may be the first five years in a fixed rate transaction, or for as long as 10 years in a prime ARM transaction.

In ARM deals, there may be triggers that allow for a reduction in the length of the lockout period if certain performance metrics are satisfied. The two most common metrics in prime ARM senior/sub structures are (1) a step-down test and (2) the double-down test. A step-down test refers to when prepaid principal switches from sequential pay to pro rata amortization. Typically, prepaid principal switches from sequential pay to pro rata for all outstanding classes if: (a) the senior credit enhancement ("CE") is twice the original percentage; and (b) the average 60+ day delinquency percentage for the prior six months is less than 50% of the current balance; and (c) cumulative losses are under a specified percentage of the original balance. The double-down test means that prior to the initial three-year period, 50% of prepaid principal can be allocated to the mezz and sub bonds, if the above three criteria (a)—(c) are satisfied.

Subprime Deals

XS/OC deals are much more complex than straight senior/sub deals (which I have only briefly described above). As an overview, in contrast to a six-pack deal in a, say, $600 million XS/OC transaction, the underlying mortgage pool might have collateral worth $612 million, a 2% overcollateralization. The $12 million of overcollateralization can be created in either of two ways: (1) it can be accumulated over time using excess spread; or (2), it is part of the deal from the beginning when the face value of the bonds issued is less than the notional amount of the collateral.

XS/OC structures involve the following features (see, e.g., Bear Stearns, September 2006a):

- Excess Spread: Like senior/sub deals, the excess spread is used to increase the overcollateralization (OC) by accelerating the payment of principal on senior bonds via sequential amortization; this process is called "turboing." Once the OC target has been reached, and subject to certain performance tests, excess spread can be released for other purposes, including payment to the residual holder.
- The OC Target: The OC target is set as a percent of the original balance and is designed to be in the second-loss position against collateral losses. The interest-only strip (IO) is first. Typically, the initial OC amount is less than 100% of the OC target, and it is then increased over time via the

excess spread until the target is reached. When the target is reached, the OC is said to be "fully funded." When the deal is fully funded, net interest margin securities (NIMs) can begin to receive cash flows from the deal. Subject to passing certain performance tests, OC can be released to the residual holder.

- Step-down date: The step-down date in an XS/OC deal is the later of a specified month (e.g., month 36) and the date at which the senior credit enhancement reaches a specified level (e.g., 51%). Prior to the step-down date, the senior bonds receive 100% of the principal prepayments. When the senior bonds are completely amortized away, prepaid principal continues to sequentially amortize, with the next class being the outstanding mezzanine bonds.

- Performance Triggers: Transactions are structured to include performance triggers that, under certain circumstances, will cause a reallocation of principal to protect or increase subordination levels. Generally speaking, there are two types of triggers: delinquency triggers and loss triggers. A trigger is said to "pass" if the collateral does not breach the specified conditions, and to "fail" if those conditions are hit or breached. If a trigger fails, principal payments to the mezzanine and subordinate bonds are delayed or stopped, preventing a reduction of credit enhancement for the senior bonds.[33] Loss triggers are target levels of cumulative losses as of specific dates after the deal start. For example, the loss trigger in months 1–48 might be 3.5%, rise to 5.25% in months 49–60, 6.75% in months 61–72 and stay flat at 7.75% thereafter.

- Available Funds Cap (AFC): Generally, bonds in XS/OC deals pay a floating coupon. The underlying mortgages typically pay a fixed rate until the reset date on hybrid ARMS. This creates the risk that the interest paid in to the deal from the underlying collateral is not sufficient to make the coupon payments to the deal bondholders—"available funds cap risk." To prevent this situation, the deal is subject to an AFC. Investors receive interest as the minimum of index (e.g., one-month LIBOR) plus margin or the weighted average AFC.

There are many nuances to these triggers. See, e.g., Moody's (November 22, 2002, May 30, 2003, September 26, 2006).

The structure can be summarized with a series of diagrams due to Fitch (2007). Then I will briefly present a sample transaction. Following that, I will show two other transactions to illustrate the cash flow dynamics and credit enhancement buildup.

As shown in figure 3.5, principal waterfalls are sequential-pay, typically, for the first three years. That is, all scheduled principal and prepayments go to repay the senior bondholders first, until they are paid in full. Then principal payments go to the next senior note holder, until they are paid in full, and so on. As discussed, after the first three years (scenario 1 in figure 3.6), credit enhancement (CE) "steps down" if certain performance tests have been met (scenario 2). For

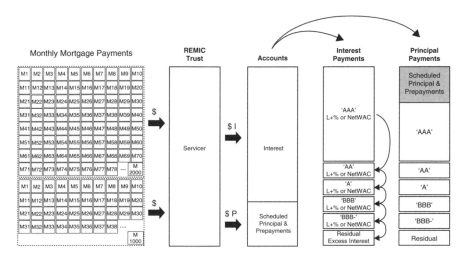

FIGURE 3.5 Sample Subprime RMBS Payments. Source: Kevin Kendra, Fitch, "Tranche ABX and Basis Risk in Subprime RMBS Structured Portfolios," Feb. 20, 2007.

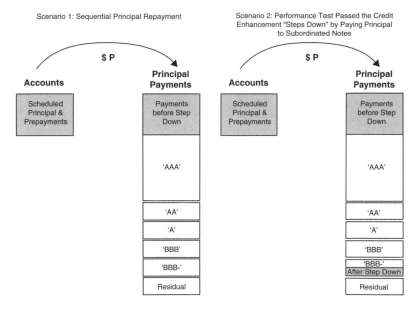

FIGURE 3.6 Sample RMBS Interest Waterfall. Source: Kevin Kendra, Fitch, "Tranche ABX and Basis Risk in Subprime RMBS Structured Portfolios," Feb. 20, 2007.

example, if overcollateralization (OC) targets have been met, the CE steps down by repaying subordinate bondholders. OC targets are set to double the original subordination. Interest waterfalls involve regular interest that is paid sequentially to bonds, capped at the weighted-average mortgage-rate net of expenses (net weighted average coupon or available funds cap, as discussed above).

"Excess interest" is the remaining interest (which goes into the interest collection account) after paying bondholders regular interest (see figure 3.7). Excess interest (or "excess spread") is first used to cover realized collateral losses. Second, excess interest is used to cover any interest shortfalls due to the Net WAC being lower than the stated bond coupon. Lastly, the remaining excess interest goes to the holder of the residual bond, typically the originator of the mortgages.

The lockout and step-down provisions are common structural features of subprime deals. To reiterate, the lockout provision locks out the subordinate bonds from receiving principal payments for a period of time. After the lockout period, deals are allowed to step down; that is, principal payments can be distributed to the subordinated bonds, provided that the credit-enhancement limits are twice the original levels, and the deal passes other performance tests, measured by triggers.

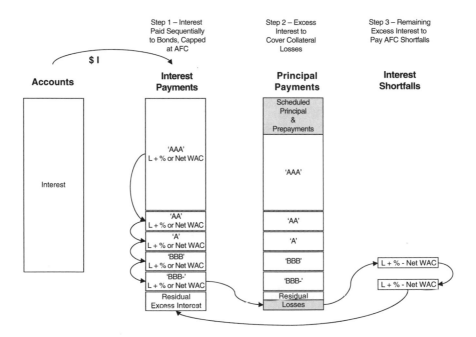

FIGURE 3.7 Allocation of Interest. Source: Kevin Kendra, Fitch, "Tranche ABX and Basis Risk in Subprime RMBS Structured Portfolios," Feb. 20, 2007.

Example of a Subprime RMBS Deal

As a typical example of a subprime mortgage securitization, I briefly look at the Structured Asset Investment Loan Trust 2005–6, issued in July 2005. The capital structure of the bond is shown below.[34] Note how much of this deal is rated investment-grade and how much is AAA. The certificates consist of the classes of certificates listed in table 3.6, together with the Class P, Class X, and Class R certificates. Only the classes of certificates listed in the tables were offered publicly by the prospectus supplement.

Note the structure of the transaction. There are four mortgage pools, with only limited cross-collateralization. Principal payments on the senior certificates will depend, for the most part, on collections on the mortgage loans in the related mortgage pool. However, the senior certificates will have the benefit of credit enhancement in the form of overcollateralization and subordination from each mortgage pool. That means that even if the loss rate on the mortgage pool related to any class of senior certificates is low, losses in the unrelated mortgage pools may reduce the loss protection for those certificates.

Note the thinness of the mezzanine tranches at inception; they are almost digital with respect to defaults, unless the amount of prepayment cash coming into the deal is quite significant in the early life of the transaction. For example, the M9 tranche thickness is only 50 basis points, and yet it is rated BBB-, an investment-grade rating. It is not that this rating is necessarily inaccurate, but that it assumes that the deal's cash flow mechanics have a reasonable chance of working.

Some of the characteristics of the pools are shown in table 3.7. The prospectus gives an overview of the triggers for this deal, as follows (italicized terms in original, which means they are defined elsewhere in the document):

> The manner of allocating payments of principal on the mortgage loans will differ, as described in this prospectus supplement, depending upon the occurrence of several different events or triggers:
>
> - whether a distribution date occurs before or on or after the "*step-down date*," which is the later of (1) the distribution date in July 2008 and (2) the first distribution date on which the ratio of (a) the total principal balance of the subordinate certificates plus any overcollateralization amount to (b) the total principal balance of the mortgage loans in the trust fund equals or exceeds the percentage specified in this prospectus supplement;
> - a "*cumulative loss trigger event*" occurs when cumulative losses on the mortgage loans are higher than certain levels specified in this prospectus supplement;

TABLE 3.6 Structured Asset Investment Loan Trust 2005–2006 Capital Structure

Class	Related Mortgage Pool(s)	Principal Type	Principal Amount	Tranche Thickness	Moody's	S&P	Fitch
A1	1	Senior*	455,596,000	20.18%	Aaa	AAA	AAA
A2	1	Senior*	50,622,000	2.24%	Aaa	AAA	AAA
A3	2	Senior	506,116,000	22.42%	Aaa	AAA	AAA
A4	3	Senior, Sequential Pay	96,977,000	4.30%	Aaa	AAA	AAA
A5	3	Senior, Sequential Pay	45,050,000	2.00%	Aaa	AAA	AAA
A6	3	Senior, Sequential Pay	23,226,000	1.03%	Aaa	AAA	AAA
A7	4	Senior, Sequential Pay	432,141,000	19.14%	Aaa	AAA	AAA
A8	4	Senior, Sequential Pay	209,009,000	9.26%	Aaa	AAA	AAA
A9	4	Senior, Sequential Pay	95,235,000	4.22%	Aaa	AAA	AAA
M1	1, 2, 3, 4,	Subordinated	68,073,000	3.02%	Aa1	AA+	AA+
M2	1, 2, 3, 4,	Subordinated	63,534,000	2.81%	Aa2	AA	AA
M3	1, 2, 3, 4,	Subordinated	38,574,000	1.71%	Aa3	AA−	AA−
M4	1, 2, 3, 4,	Subordinated	34,036,000	1.51%	A1	A+	A+
M5	1, 2, 3, 4,	Subordinated	34,036,000	1.51%	A2	A	A
M6	1, 2, 3, 4,	Subordinated	26,094,000	1.16%	A3	A−	A−
M7	1, 2, 3, 4,	Subordinated	34,036,000	1.51%	Baa2	BBB	BBB
M8	1, 2, 3, 4,	Subordinated	22,691,000	1.01%	Baa3	BBB−	BBB−
M9	1, 2, 3, 4,	Subordinated	11,346,000	0.50%	N/R	BBB−	BBB−
M10-A	1, 2, 3, 4,	Subordinated	5,673,000	0.25%	N/R	BBB−	BB+
M10-F	1, 2, 3, 4,	Subordinated	5,673,000	0.25%	N/R	BBB−	BB+

*The Class A1 and Class A2 Certificates will receive payments of principal concurrently, on a pro rata basis, unless cumulative realized losses or delinquencies on the mortgage loans exceed specified levels, in which case these classes will be treated as senior, sequential-pay classes.

TABLE 3.7 Summary of the Pools' Characteristics

	Pool 1	Pool 2	Pool 3	Pool 4
% First Lien	94.12%	98.88%	100.00%	93.96%
% 2/28 ARMS	59.79%	46.68%	75.42%	37.66%
% 3/27 ARMS	20.82%	19.14%	19.36%	9.96%
% Fixed Rate	13.00%	8.17%	2.16%	11.46%
% Full Doc	59.98%	56.74%	44.05%	35.46%
% Stated Doc	39.99%	37.47%	34.30%	33.17%
% Primary Residence	90.12%	90.12%	80.61%	82.59%
WA FICO	636	615	673	635

- a *"delinquency event"* occurs when the rate of delinquencies of the mortgage loans over any three-month period is higher than certain levels set forth in this prospectus supplement; and
- in the case of pool 1, a *"sequential trigger event"* occurs if (a) before the distribution date in July 2008, a cumulative loss trigger event occurs or (b) on or after the distribution date in July 2008, a cumulative loss trigger event or a delinquency event occurs (p. S-7, emphasis in original).

This is the structure that was discussed above.

How Subprime Bonds Work—Why Does the Detail Matter?

In this subsection, I briefly look at two subprime securitization deals; one is a 2005 transaction and the other is a 2006 transaction. The two examples are Ameriquest Mortgage Securities Inc. 2005-R2 (AMSI 2005-R2) and Structured Asset Investment Loan Trust 2006–2 (SAIL 2006–2). The point of the comparison is to show how these two transactions fared; one is 2005 vintage mortgages and the other is 2006 vintage mortgages. The 2006 vintage subprime mortgages have not fared well as house prices started to turn down, as discussed further below. The examples show how the refinancing or lack of refinancing of the underlying mortgages impacts these securitizations.

Both AMSI 2005-R2 and SAIL 2006–2 have the basic structures discussed above, with overcollateralization and various triggers determining the dynamics of credit enhancement. AMSI 2005-R2 consists of three portfolios. Both deals have overcollateralization.

The next two tables show the structure of each deal, what the deals looked like at inception with respect to tranche sizes and ratings, and then what the tranche sizes and ratings looked like in the first quarter of 2007. The BBB tranches are highlighted. Note the tranche sizes of the BBB tranches, as a percentage of collateral at inception. They are very thin, almost unbelievably thin. Normally, the rating agencies would not allow such thin tranches, but these tranches are expected to build up as the more senior tranches amortize due to refinancing and sequential amortization. Also, note the subordination percentages for the BBB tranches at inception. For example, the M9 tranche of AMSI 2005-R2 has only 1.1% of subordination, unbelievably small. But, again, the dynamics of the transaction mean that this should grow as time passes, amortization occurs, and credit enhancement builds up.

These features, the thin tranches and low initial subordination levels, are acceptable if the underlying mortgages refinance as expected. In that case, the deals shrink as amortization occurs. Credit enhancement will build up, and after the step-down date, the BBB tranches will look acceptable. Of course, this depends on house prices.

What happened? Looking at 2007Q1, things are very different for the two deals. AMSI 2005-R2 is, of course, older. By 2007Q1, AMSI 2005-R2 has passed its triggers. Note that the tranche thicknesses, measured as a percentage of collateral, have increased. And, very significantly, note that the subordination level percentages have built up. For example, initially M9 had 1.1% subordination. In 2007Q1, its subordination percent is 9.06%. (Still, Fitch—ever conservative—has downgraded the BBB tranches to B!!)

Things are much different for SAIL 2006–2. Being a 2006 deal, it is younger. But it is also a transaction that occurred during the period when house prices did not rise, and refinancing was harder to accomplish. Neither the tranche size nor the subordination has increased significantly. This deal is in trouble, as reflected in the ratings of the mezzanine tranches. Standard securitizations have fixed tranche sizes; that is, tranche thickness does not vary over time. To some extent, excess spread is used to create credit enhancement through reserve fund buildup, but this is not the main credit enhancement. See Gorton and Souleles (2007) for a description of standard securitization.

The foregoing examples of subprime securitization show a very different story. They are not at all like standard securitization transactions. In particular, the difference illustrates how the "option" on house prices implicitly embedded in the subprime mortgages has resulted in very house price-sensitive behavior of the subprime RMBS. Unlike standard securitization transactions, here the tranche thickness and the extent of credit enhancement depend on the cash flow coming into the deal from prepayments on the subprime mortgages via refinancing. This depends on house prices.

This point about the link to house prices is dramatically illustrated by these two bonds. The 2005 bond passed its triggers and has achieved the levels of credit enhancement and subordination envisioned by the original structure. It has benefited from the refinancing and prepayments of the underlying mortgages. The 2006 bond has not. In 2006, subprime borrowers had not built up enough equity to refinance. They could not prepay, and the 2006 bond has not been able to pass its triggers. (This does not mean that the 2006 bond would be a bad buy. At fire sale prices, it may well be a good buy.)

If this were the end of the story, it is not clear whether there would have been a systemic problem when the house price bubble burst. I suspect not, but, in any case, it is not the end of the story.

TABLE 3.8 Ameriquest Mortgage Securities Inc. 2005-R2 (AMSI 2005-R2)

| | At Issue in 2005 | | | | | 2007Q1 | | | |
	Size	Related Mortgage Pool(s)	Ratings (Fitch, Moody's, S&P)	% of Collateral	Sub-ordination	Size	Ratings (April 25, 2008)	% of Collateral	Subordination
Publicly Offered Certificates									
A-1A	258,089,000	I	AAA/Aaa/AAA	21.5%	35.48%	30,091,837	AAA/Aaa/AAA	8.3%	91.67%
A-1B	64,523,000	I	AAA/Aaa/NR	5.4%	19.35	7,523,047	AAA/Aaa/NA	2.1%	89.58%
A-2A	258,048,000	II	AAA/Aaa/AAA	21.5%	35.48%	43,208,414	AAA/Aaa/AAA	12.0%	77.62%
A-2B	64,511,000	II	AAA/Aaa/NR	5.4%	19.35%	10,801,936	AAA/Aaa/NR	3.0%	63.56%
A-3A	124,645,000	III	AAA/Aaa/AAA	10.4%	19.35%	-	PIF/WR/NR*	0.0%	63.56%
A-3B	139,369,000	III	AAA/Aaa/AAA	11.6%	19.35%	9,597,506	AAA/Aaa/AAA	2.7%	63.56%
A-3C	26,352,000	III	AAA/Aaa/AAA	2.2%	19.35%	26,352,000	AAA/Aaa/AAA	7.3%	63.56%
A-3D	32,263,000	III	AAA/Aaa/NR	2.7%	19.35%	3,994,403	AAA/Aaa/AAA	1.1%	63.56%
M1	31,200,000	I,II,III	AA+/Aa1/AA+	2.6%	16.75%	31,200,000	AA+/Aa1/AA+	8.6%	54.92%
M2	49,800,000	I,II,III	AA/Aa2/AA	4.1%	12.60%	49,800,000	AA/Aa2/AA	13.8%	41.13%
M3	16,800,000	I,II,III	AA-/Aa3/AA-	1.4%	11.20%	16,800,000	AA-/Aa3/AA-	4.7%	36.48%
M4	28,800,000	I,II,III	A+/A1/A+	2.4%	8.80%	28,800,000	A+/A1/A+	8.0%	28.50%
M5	16,800,000	I,II,III	A/A2/A	1.4%	7.40%	16,800,000	A/A2/A	4.7%	23.85%
M6	12,000,000	I,II,III	A-/A3/A-	1.0%	6.40%	12,000,000	BBB/A3/A-	3.3%	20.53%
M7	19,200,000	I,II,III	BBB+/Baa1/BBB+	1.6%	4.80%	19,200,000	B/Baa1/BBB+	5.3%	15.21%
M8	9,000,000	I,II,III	BBB/Baa2/BBB	0.7%	4.05%	9,000,000	B/Baa2/BBB	2.5%	12.72%
M9	13,200,000	I,II,III	BBB/Baa2/BBB-	1.1%	2.95%	13,200,000	B/Baa3/BBB-	3.7%	9.06%
Not Publicly Offered Certificates									
M10	7,800,000	I,II,III	BB+/Ba1/BB+	1.0%	1.30%	7,800,000	CCC/Ba1/BB+	2.2%	6.90%
M11	12,000,000	I,II,III	BB/Ba2/BB	1.3%	0.00%	12,000,000	CCC/Ba2/BB	3.3%	3.58%
CE	15,600,000		NR/NR/NR			12,928,188	NR/NR/NR	3.6%	0.00%
Total	1,200,000,000					361,097,331.00			
Collateral	1,200,000,147					361,097,430.00			

* PIF = tranche "paid-in-full"; WR = "withdrawn rating"; NR = "no rating."
Prospectus dated March 22, 2005. AMSI 2005-R2 closed March 24, 2005.

TABLE 3.9 Structured Asset Investment Loan Trust 2006-2 (SAIL 2006-2)

	At Issue 2006				2007Q1			
	Size	Rating+ (Moody's, S&P, Fitch)	% of Collateral	Subordination	Size	Rating (April 25, 2008)	% of Collateral	Subordination
Publicly Offered Certificates								
A1	607,391,000	Aaa/AAA/AAA	45.3%	16.75%	89,285,238	Aaa/AAA/AAA	11.0%	26.16%
A2	150,075,000	Aaa/AAA/AAA	11.2%	16.75%	150,075,000	Aaa/AAA/AAA	18.5%	26.16%
A3	244,580,000	Aaa/AAA/AAA	18.2%	16.75%	244,580,000	Aaa/AAA/AAA	30.2%	26.16%
A4	114,835,000	Aaa/AAA/AAA	8.6%	16.75%	114,835,000	Aaa/A/A	14.2%	26.16%
M1	84,875,000	Aa2/AA/AA	6.3%	10.42%	84,875,000	Ba3/CCC/B	10.5%	15.70%
M2	25,136,000	Aa3/AA-/AA-	1.9%	8.55%	25,136,000	B3/CCC/CCC	3.1%	12.60%
M3	20,124,000	A1/A+/A+	1.5%	7.05%	20,124,000	Caa2/CCC/CCC	2.5%	10.12%
M4	20,124,000	A2/A/A	1.5%	5.55%	20,124,000	Caa3/CC/CC	2.5%	7.63%
M5	15,428,000	A3/A-/A-	1.1%	4.40%	15,428,000	Ca/CC/CC	1.9%	5.73%
M6	15,428,000	Baa1/BBB+/BBB+	1.1%	3.25%	15,428,000	C/CC/CC	1.9%	3.83%
M7	11,404,000	Baa2/BBB/BBB	0.9%	2.40%	11,404,000	C/CC/C	1.4%	2.42%
M8	10,733,000	Baa3/BBB-/BBB-	0.8%	1.60%	10,733,000	C/D/C	1.3%	1.10%
Not Publicly Offered Certificates								
B1	7,379,000	Ba1/?/?	0.6%	1.05%	7,379,000	C/D/C	0.9%	0.19%
B2	7,379,000	Ba2/?/?	0.6%	0.50%	1,534,646	WR/NR/NR	0.2%	0.00%
CE	6,708,733				98		11.0%	88.99%
Total	1,341,599,733.00				810,940,982.00			

Prospectus dated September 26, 2005.

There are also Class P, Class X, Class LT-R and Class R certificates. The Class X Certificates will be entitled to Monthly Excess Cashflow, if any, remaining after required distributions are made to the Offered Certificates and the Class B1 and Class B2 Certificates and to pay certain expenses of the Trust Fund (including any payments to the Swap Counterparty) and, on and after the Distribution Date in April 2016, to deposit any Final Maturity Reserve Amount in the Final Maturity Reserve Account. The Class P Certificates will solely be entitled to receive all Prepayment Premiums received in respect of the Mortgage Loans and, accordingly, such amounts will not be available for distribution to the holders of the other classes of Certificates or to the Servicers as additional servicing compensation. The Class LT-R and Class R Certificates will represent the remaining interest in the assets of the Trust Fund after the required distributions are made to all other classes of Certificates and will evidence the residual interests in the REMICs.

Collateralized Debt Obligations (CDOs)   97- 108

The next link in the chain is collateralized debt obligations (CDOs), special-purpose vehicles that issue long-dated liabilities in the form of rated tranches in the capital markets and use the proceeds to purchase structured products for assets. In particular, ABS (asset-backed securities) CDOs purchased significant amounts of subprime RMBS bonds. This section proceeds as follows. I start with a very brief description of how cash CDOs work (as opposed to synthetic or hybrid CDOs). I then describe the amounts of CDOs issued before addressing the question of how much subprime RMBS went into CDOs. I then look at synthetic subprime risk before discussing the issue of the final location of the CDO tranches with subprime risk. This involves a discussion of some off-balance-sheet vehicles that purchased CDO tranches—another link in the chain.

The Design of CDOs

A cash CDO is a special-purpose vehicle that buys a portfolio of fixed income assets and finances the purchase of the portfolio via issuing different tranches of risk in the capital markets. These tranches are senior tranches, rated Aaa/AAA, mezzanine tranches, rated Aa/AA to Ba/BB, and equity tranches (unrated). Of particular interest are ABS CDOs, CDOs which have underlying portfolios consisting of asset-backed securities (ABS), including residential mortgage-backed securities (RMBS) and commercial mortgage-backed securities (CMBS).

CDO portfolios typically included tranches of subprime and Alt-A deals, sometimes quite significant amounts. The interlinking of subprime mortgages, the subprime RMBS and the CDOs is portrayed in figure 3.8 (due to UBS). To the left of the figure is a representation of the creation of a subprime RMBS deal. Some of the bonds issued in this subprime deal go into ABS CDOs. In particular, as shown on the right-hand side of the figure, RMBS bonds rated AAA, AA, and A form part of a "high-grade" CDO portfolio, so called because the portfolio bonds have these ratings. The BBB bonds from the RMBS deal go into a "mezz CDO," so named because its portfolio consists entirely, or almost entirely, of BBB-rated ABS and RMBS tranches.

If bonds issued by mezz CDOs are put into another CDO portfolio, then the new CDO—now holding mezz CDO tranches—is called a "CDO squared" or "CDO^2." There are some important features to ABS CDOs that make their design more complicated, in ways which play a role later. Perhaps most importantly, many cash ABS CDOs are managed, which means that there is a manager (a firm) that oversees the CDO portfolio. In particular, this manager is allowed to trade—buy and sell—bonds to a limited extent (say 10% of the

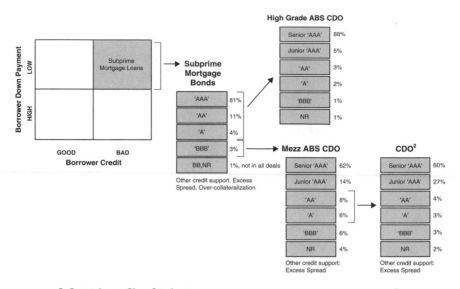

FIGURE 3.8 Risk Profile of Subprime Mortgage Loans. Source: UBS, "Market Commentary," December 13, 2007.

notional amount per year) over a limited period of time (say, the first three years of the transaction). The putative reason for this is that structured products amortize, so to achieve a longer maturity for the CDO, managers need to be allowed to reinvest. They can take cash that is paid to the CDO from amortization and reinvest it, and with limitations, as mentioned, they can sell bonds in the portfolio and buy other bonds. There are restrictions on the portfolio that must be maintained, however. CDO managers typically owned part or all of the CDO equity, so they would benefit from higher yielding assets for a given liability structure. Essentially, think of a managed fund with term financing and some constraints on the manager in terms of trading and the portfolio composition.

The restrictions on the portfolio composition would limit structured product asset categories to certain maximum amounts of the portfolio. Other restrictions would include maximums and minimums by rating category, restrictions on weighted average life (WAL), correlation factors, weighted average rating factor (WARF), numbers of obligors, etc.[35] Table 3.10 is a very simplified summary example. Portfolio restrictions are far from standardized.

Priority of cash flows in CDOs is first of all based on seniority, for allocating losses. Credit enhancement is also provided via other mechanisms such as sequential amortization. Finally, there are also coverage tests and triggers which divert cash flows from subordinate tranches, prevent reinvestment in

TABLE 3.10 Sample ABS CDO Portfolio Criteria

Correlation Factor/10-year WARF	23 max / 465 max
Collateral Items rated A3 or better	12.5% min
Collateral Items rated Baa3 or better	95.0% min
Collateral Items rated < Ba3	0.0%
Obligor Concentration Limit	1.5% max
Obligor Concentration of > 1.0% and ≤ 1.5%	15 obligors max
Number of Obligors	93 min
Obligations with WALs > 10 years	0.0%
Obligations with WALs of > 9.0 and ≤ 10.0 years	5.0% max, must be RMBS/CMBS
Obligations with WALs of > 6.5 and ≤ 10.0 years	25.0% max
Obligations with WALs of > 6.0 and ≤ 10.0 years	57.5% max
Obligations with WALs of > 5.5 and ≤ 10.0 years	70.0% max
Portfolio WAL in Years	5.65 max
CDO Securities	20.0% max
CLO Securities (subset of CDO Securities)	5.0% max

new assets, and cause amortization to be sequential, if the tests are not met. Two common tests are overcollateralization (OC) tests and interest coverage tests. Roughly speaking, an OC test is the ratio of CDO assets at par to the par value of the A tranche, the most senior tranche (in the Tranche A Overcollateralization Test): $\frac{CDO\ Assets\ at\ Par}{Tranche\ A\ Par\ Amount}$. The Tranche B OC test is similar: $\frac{CDO\ Assets\ at\ Par}{Tranche\ A\ and\ B\ Par\ Amount}$ and so on. There are also interest coverage tests. For example, the Tranche A Interest Coverage Test is a ratio: $\frac{CDO\ Assets'\ Coupon}{Tranche\ A\ Coupon}$, and other interest coverage ratios are analogous. If coverage tests are not met, cash is diverted, and trading limited, until the tests are passed. For our purposes here, I do not need to go into all the details of how CDOs work.

Many CDOs are structured to experience an event of default ("EOD") when a minimum overcollateralization ("OC") ratio for senior liabilities is not maintained. This means that if the par value of assets falls below the face value of senior liabilities, an EOD occurs, allowing the senior investors (the controlling class) to take control of the CDO. Senior investors may choose to liquidate the assets.[36] Also, many CDO transactions that have OC-linked EODs also include ratings-based par haircuts in the calculation of the aggregate outstanding par amount of the underlying assets. As a result, downgrades of underlying collateral assets, such as RMBS and ABS CDO tranches, trigger EODs.

In the EODs that have occurred to date, the CDO has tripped a trigger that is related to the failure to maintain a minimum ratio of overcollateralization (OC), namely, the ratio of the par value of assets to the face value of the CDO's senior obligations. The EODs that have occurred to date have not been due to the failure of the CDO to make payments to note holders. Rather, the OC-related EOD triggers have been hit because their calculation is affected by certain rating-related par "haircuts."[37]

When an EOD occurs, the senior controlling classes of the CDO are in a position to decide what to do. They may: (1) do nothing, and continue to receive payment of principal and interest; (2) accelerate the maturity date of their notes; (3) liquidate the assets of the CDO and use the proceeds to pay off the notes following the order of priority. Currently, some CDOs are liquidating, but it is not clear what will happen in the remaining cases.[38]

There is no standardization of triggers across CDOs. Some have sequential cash flow triggers, others do not. Some have OC trigger calculations based on ratings changes; others do not. There is no straightforward template. In fact, each ABS CDO must be separately modeled. The above discussion provides a much abbreviated glimpse at the structure that must be modeled. This will play a role later when I discuss the problems investors face when they attempt a valuation of CDO tranches.[39]

Why would CDOs buy subprime RMBS bonds? Not surprisingly, it was profitable. With regard to the lower rated tranches, the BBB tranches of subprime RMBS were difficult to sell. Perhaps this was because they were so thin when first issued (see the above examples), so that at first glance they seemed unreasonable. But this would not be so obvious if they were purchased by a CDO. By 2005, spreads on subprime BBB tranches appeared to be wider than other structured products with the same rating, creating an incentive to arbitrage the ratings between the ratings on the subprime and on the CDO tranches.[40] CDO portfolios increasingly were dominated by subprime, suggesting that the market was pricing this risk inconsistently with the ratings. This was not common knowledge.

Also, concerning the higher rated tranches, CDOs may have been motivated to buy large amounts of structured assets because their AAA tranches would be used as fodder for profitable negative-basis trades. This may have increased the appetite of CDOs and of dealer banks underwriting the CDOs. In a negative-basis trade, a bank buys the AAA-rated CDO tranche while simultaneously purchasing protection on the tranche under a physically settled credit default swap (CDS). From the bank's viewpoint, this is the simultaneous purchase and sale of a CDO security, which meant (for awhile) that the bank could book the NPV of the excess yield on the CDO tranche over the protection payment on the CDS.

If the CDS spread is less than the bond spread, the basis is negative. Here's an example. Suppose a bank borrows at LIBOR + 5 and buys a AAA-rated CDO tranche, which pays LIBOR + 30. Simultaneously, the bank buys protection (possibly from a monoline insurer) for 15 basis points. So the bank makes 25 bps over LIBOR net on the asset, and it has 15 bps in costs for protection, for a 10 bps profit.[41]

Note that a negative-basis trade swaps the risk of the AAA tranche to a CDS protection writer. Now, the subprime-related risk has been separated from the cash host. Consequently, even if we were able to locate the AAA CDO tranches, this would not be the same as finding out the location of the risk. We do not know the extent of negative-basis trades.[42]

CDO Issuance

Table 3.11 shows CDO issuance. The first column of the table shows total issuance of CDOs. The next column shows total issuance of structured finance CDOs (also called ABS CDOs, for asset-backed securities); these CDOs have RMBS, CMBS, CMOs, ABS, CDOs, CDS, and other securitized/structured products as collateral. This is the category of CDO that would include subprime mortgages.[43] Structured finance CDOs have consistently been the modal category.

Another way to divide CDOs is by their structure. Cash flow CDOs have assets and liabilities that are entirely cash instruments (i.e., physical bonds). Liabilities are paid with the interest and principal payments (cash flows) of the underlying cash collateral. Hybrid CDOs combine the funding structures of cash and synthetic CDOs. Synthetic CDOs sell credit protection via credit default swaps (CDS) rather than purchase cash assets.[44] The liability side is partially synthetic, in which case some protection is purchased from investors on the most senior tranches. Mezzanine tranches are not synthetic, but paid-in in cash which is deposited in an SPV and used to collateralize the SPV's credit-swap obligations, namely, potential losses resulting in writedowns of the issued notes. Note that synthetic funded CDOs would be the location of synthetic subprime risk in the form of credit protection written on a subprime index (the ABX index).[45]

Finally, we can think of categorizing CDOs by the motivation for the transaction. As the name suggests, Arbitrage CDOs are motivated by the spread difference between higher yielding assets and the lower yields paid as financing costs. This is often viewed as a rating agency-created arbitrage. Another motivation is regulatory bank capital relief or risk management. Balance sheet CDOs remove the risk of assets off the balance sheet of the originator, typically synthetically.

Looking at the table, the first point to note is that CDO issuance has been significant—and the bulk of it has been CDOs with structured products as

TABLE 3.11 Global CDO Issuance ($millions)

	Total Issuance	Structured Finance	Cash Flow and Hybrid	Synthetic Funded	Arbitrage	Balance Sheet
2004 Q1	24,982.5	NA	18,807.8	6,174.7	23,157.5	1,825.0
2004 Q2	42,864.6	NA	25,786.7	17,074.9	39,715.5	3,146.1
2004 Q3	42,086.6	NA	36,106.9	5,329.7	38,207.7	3,878.8
2004 Q4	47,487.8	NA	38,829.9	8,657.9	45,917.8	1,569.9
2004 Total	157,418.5	NA	119,531.3	37,237.2	146,998.5	10,419.8
% of Total			75.9%	23.7%	93.4%	6.6%
2005 Q1	49,610.2	28,177.1	40,843.9	8,766.3	43,758.8	5,851.4
2005 Q2	71,450.5	46,720.3	49,524.6	21,695.9	62,050.5	9,400.0
2005 Q3	52,007.2	34,517.5	44,253.1	7,754.1	49,636.7	2,370.5
2005 Q4	98,735.4	67,224.2	71,604.3	26,741.1	71,957.6	26,777.8
2005 Total	271,803.3	176,639.1	206,225.9	64,957.4	227,403.6	44,399.7
% of Total		65.0%	75.9%	23.9%	83.7%	16.3%
2006 Q1	108,012.7	66,220.2	83,790.1	24,222.6	101,153.6	6,859.1
2006 Q2	124,977.9	65,019.6	97,260.3,	24,808.4	102,564.6	22,413.3
2006 Q3	138,628.7	89,190.2	102,167.4	14,703.8	125,945.2	12,683.5
2006 Q4	180,090.3	93,663.2	131,525.1	25,307.9	142,534.3	37,556.0
2006 Total	551,709.6	314,093.2	414,742.9	89,042.7	472,197.7	79,511.9
% of Total		56.9%	75.2%	16.1%	85.6%	14.4%
2007 Q1	186,467.6	101,074.9	140,319.1	27,426.2	156,792.0	29,675.6
2007 Q2	175,939.4	98,744.1	135,021.4	8,403.0	153,385.4	22,554.0
2007 Q3	93,063.6	40,136.8	56,053.3	5,198.9	86,331.4	6,732.2
2007 Q4	47,508.2	23,500.1	31,257.9	5,202.3	39,593.7	7,914.5
2007 Total	502,978.8	263,455.9	362,651.7	46,230.4	436,102.5	66,876.3
% of Total		52.4%	72.1%	9.1%	86.8%	13.3%
2008 Q1	11,710.1	4,736.1	10,673.9	186.0	10,468.4	1,241.7
% of Total		40.4%	91.2%	1.6%	89.4%	10.6%

Source: Securities Industry and Financial Markets Association.

collateral. The issuance volume that involves synthetically creating risk is also significant. As noted, the motivation has primarily been arbitrage.

It is also notable what data are missing. There is no data on the amount of subprime exposure in CDOs, whether cash or synthetic. This is a glimpse of part of the information problem. To figure out the subprime exposure in a CDO requires a "look through" to the subprime RMBS bonds in the portfolio of the CDO and then looking through those bonds individually to determine what subprime mortgages are associated with each RMBS bond in the portfolio.

Subprime RMBS Bonds and ABS CDOs

Issuance of ABS CDOs roughly tripled over the period 2005–2007, and ABS CDO portfolios became increasingly concentrated in U.S. subprime RMBS. Table 3.12 shows estimates of the typical collateral composition of high-grade and mezzanine ABS CDOs. As the volumes of origination in the subprime mortgage market increased, subprime RMBS increased and so did CDO issuance.

How pervasive is subprime collateral in ABS CDOs? Looking through the CDO portfolios for a sample of CDOs provides a sense of how many real estate-related bonds are in the CDO portfolios. UBS undertook this exercise for a sample of 420 ABS CDOs. The results are shown in table 3.14. The important point of this analysis is that the amount of subprime RMBS bonds in ABS CDOs is very significant.

TABLE 3.12 Typical Collateral Composition of ABS CDOs (percent)

	High Grade ABS CDO	Mezzanine ABS CDO
Subprime RMBS Tranches	50%	77%
Other RMBS Tranches	25	12
CDO Tranches	19	6
Other	6	5

Source: Citigroup, cited by Basel Committee on Banking Supervision (BIS) (April 2008).

TABLE 3.13 Subprime-Related CDO Volumes

Vintage	Mezz ABS CDOs ($ billions)	High Grade ABS CDOs ($ billions)	All CDOs ($ billions)
2005	27	50	290
2006	50	100	468
Yr to 9/2007	30	70	330

Source: UBS, "Mortgage Strategist," November 13, 2007.

TABLE 3.14 Residential Mortgage Deals in 420 ABS CDOs

	Number of Deals by Vintage and Mortgage Loan Type				
Vintage	Subprime	Alt-A	Seconds	Prime	Total
2003	215	63	7	144	429
2004	371	252	25	188	836
2005	488	452	62	209	1,211
2006	522	487	69	142	1,220
2007	150	113	21	28	312
Total	1,746	1,367	184	711	4,008

Source: UBS, "Mortgage and ABS CDO Losses," December 13, 2007.

Synthetic Subprime Risk

Subprime risk can be traded via credit derivatives referencing individual sub-prime cash bonds or via an index linked to a basket of such bonds. Dealer banks launched the ABX.HE (ABX) index in January 2006. The ABX index is a credit derivative that references 20 equally weighted RMBS tranches. There are also indices comprising subindices linked to a basket of subprime bonds with specific ratings: AAA, AA, A BBB, and BBB-. Each subindex references 20 subprime RMBS bonds with the rating level of the subindex. Every six months, the indices are reconstituted based on a pre-identified set of rules. The index is overseen by Markit Partners. The dealers provide Markit Partners with daily and monthly marks.[46]

For our purposes here, the main point is that subprime risk can be traded synthetically with credit derivatives. Risk cannot be created on net because these are derivatives, but the identities of the longs and shorts are not known, as this market is over-the-counter. Table 3.15 shows approximations of the amount of BBB-rated subprime RMBS issuance over 2004–2007 and the expo-sures of mezzanine CDOs issued in 2005–2007 to those vintages of BBB-rated subprime RMBS. Note that the mezzanine CDOs issued in 2005–2007 used CDS to take on *significantly greater* exposure to the 2005 and 2006 vintages of subprime BBB-rated RMBS than were actually issued. This suggests that the demand for exposure to riskier tranches of subprime RMBS exceeded supply by a wide margin. The additional risk exposure was created synthetically. (Though on net, there is no new risk.)

In addition, synthetic CDOs relying completely on derivatives became increasingly important. Prior to 2005, the portfolios of ABS CDOs were mainly made up of cash securities. After 2005, CDO managers and underwriters began using CDS referencing individual ABS, creating synthetic exposures.

TABLE 3.15 BBB-Rated Subprime RMBS Issuance and Exposure in
Mezzanine ABS CDOs Issued in 2005–2007 to BBB-Rated Subprime RMBS
($ billions)

	2004	2005	2006	2007
BBB-rated Subprime RMBS Issuance	12.3	15.8	15.7	6.2
Exposure of Mezzanine ABS CDOs issued in 2005–2007	8.0	25.3	30.3	2.9
Exposure as a Percent of Issuance	65	160	193	48

Source: Federal Reserve calculations, cited by Basel Committee on Banking Supervision (BIS) (2008c).

"Synthetic CDOs" are CDOs with entirely synthetic portfolios; the portfolio of a "hybrid CDO" consists of a mix of cash positions and CDS. CDO managers and underwriters used synthetic exposures to meet the growing investor demand for ABS CDOs and to cater to investors' preferences to have particular exposures in the portfolio that may not have been available in the cash market. CDO managers and underwriters were able to use CDS to fill out an ABS CDO's portfolio when cash ABS, particularly mezzanine ABS CDO tranches, were difficult to obtain.

So far, the subprime mortgages have been securitized, and tranches of these securitizations have been sold, in large part, to CDOs, and tranches of the CDOs have been sold to investors. Additional subprime risk has been traded via derivatives.

I now turn to the question of the identity of the investors in these risks. Who were these investors? Where did the risk go?

Where Did the CDO Tranches Go?

The short answer is that we do not know for sure. Investors around the world purchased rated tranches of CDOs. Lehman Brothers had the following estimates of the location of the AAA-rated CDO tranches (see Figure 3.9). Investors in the AAA CDO tranche risk (synthetic, if not cash) include bond insurers, insurance companies, and other categories of institutional investors. The category labeled "ABCP/SIV" refers to asset-backed commercial paper conduits (ABCPs) and structured investment vehicles (SIVs), which I discuss briefly below.

The remaining category, "CDO CP put providers," refers to structures which transform long-dated CDO tranche paper into money market mutual fund-eligible investments. This is accomplished by shortening the maturity of the CDO tranche via a liquidity put provider, sometimes called a 2a-7 put, after the part of the Investment Company Act that restricts money market funds to instruments that are 365 days or less in maturity.[47] Longer term bonds are shortened by attaching a put option or tender feature allowing or requiring the investor to sell the security to the put provider, with a stated notice period. Rule 2a-7 allows the money market fund to treat the put notice period as being the maturity of the bond.

Note that in the crisis, money market funds exercised their puts, forcing put writers to buy the notes, putting further stress on their liquid resources.

One significant category of investors, shown in figure 3.9, consists of certain kinds of off-balance-sheet vehicles known as structured investment vehicles (SIVs), asset-backed commercial paper conduits (ABCPs), and SIV-Lites. The nuances of the differences among these vehicles do not concern us here (see Moody's, February 3, 2003; Moody's, January 25, 2002; Standard and Poor's, September 4, 2003). I provide the briefest of overviews to highlight one structural feature that is important.

An SIV is a limited-purpose operating company that undertakes arbitrage activities by purchasing mostly highly rated medium- and long-term fixed income assets and funding itself with cheaper, mostly short-term, highly rated CP and MTNs. An SIV is a leveraged investment company that raises capital by issuing capital market securities (capital notes and medium-term notes) as

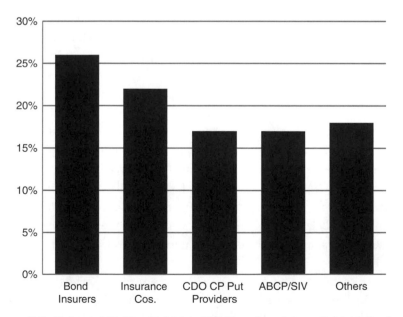

FIGURE 3.9 Estimated Holdings of AAA CDO Tranches. Source: Lehman Brothers estimates, as of November 13, 2007, based on the 10-Qs of AMBAC, MBIA, ACA, XLCA, FGIC and rating agency reports on bond insurers.

well as ABCP. ABCP typically comprises around 20% of the total liabilities for the biggest SIVs.[48] A variant of an SIV is a so-called SIV-lite. SIV-lites share some similarities with collateralized debt obligations (CDOs) in that they are closed-end investments. SIV-lites issue a greater proportion of their liabilities as ABCP than SIVs (around 80%–90%), are typically more highly leveraged, and seem to have invested almost exclusively in U.S. RMBS. As a consequence, several SIV-lites have restructured their liabilities following the recent turmoil in U.S. mortgage markets. Appendix B lists the larger SIVs and their outcomes. Unlike conduits that issue only ABCP, SIVs and SIV-lites tend not to have committed liquidity lines from banks that cover 100% of their ABCP. Rather, they use capital and liquidity models, approved by ratings agencies, to manage liquidity risk. The lack of a full, commercial bank guarantee has reportedly led to discrimination against SIV paper by ABCP investors.

The important point is that these vehicles are very different from the special-purpose vehicles (SPVs) used in securitization. Standard securitization SPVs are not managed; they are robot companies that are not marked-to-market; they simply follow a set of prespecified rules. See Gorton and Souleles (2007). Unlike securitization vehicles, these are managed, and they are market value vehicles. They raise funds by issuing commercial paper and medium-term notes, and they use the proceeds to buy high-grade assets to form diversified portfolios. They borrow short and purchase long assets. They are required by rating agencies to mark portfolios to market on a frequent basis (daily or weekly), and, based on the marks, they are allowed to lever more or required to delever. On SIVs, see Moody's (January 25, 2002), and on ABCPs, see Moody's (February 3, 2003).

Money market mutual funds apparently not only purchased various structured assets, via liquidity (or 2a-7) puts (as discussed above), but also sometimes invested in SIVs. Later, these money market mutual funds had to be bailed out by their sponsors to keep them from "breaking the buck." See the chronology in Appendix A.

Summary

Investors purchased CDO tranches based on ratings, portfolio criteria, and the identity of the CDO manager. Purchasers of CDO bonds receive trustee reports detailing the portfolio of the CDO, which changes over time as the manager trades. CDOs are not market-value structures.[49] It is literally not possible for a buyer of a CDO tranche to do the double look-through to determine, say, the extent of subprime exposure. That would require looking through each of the bonds in the CDO portfolio, and if the CDO owns other CDO tranches, looking through those as well. Imagine also an investor in an SIV. The SIV has a portfolio of structured assets, which may include CDO tranches. The investor cannot answer the question: is my SIV investment sensitive to 2006 subprime mortgages?

108-112

Complexity and the Loss of Information in the Current Crisis

Now we come to the first information issue. What is the loss of information? The information problem is that the location and extent of the (2006 and 2007 Q1–2 vintage) subprime risk is unknown to anyone. It is very hard to determine the location of the risk, partly because of the chain of interlinked securities, which does not allow the final resting place of the risk to be determined. But also, because of derivatives, it is even harder: negative-basis trades moved CDO risk, and credit derivatives created additional long exposure to subprime mortgages.

Determining the extent of the risk is also difficult, because the effects on expected losses depend on house prices as the first-order risk factor. Simulating the effects of that through the chain of interlinked securities is basically impossible. I will begin by illustrating this last point with a very simple description of the payoffs to the interlinked securities. I will then discuss the implications.

A Simple Stylized Example of the Interlinking of Security Designs

As before, I will give an extremely simplified example to attempt to convey the essence of the complexity problem and the loss of information. I will ignore the dynamic aspects of subprime RMBS transactions and consider extremely simple tranching: a subordinated (or, synonymously, junior or first-loss) tranche (called the "sub" tranche) and a senior tranche. The subprime RMBS deal will securitize a single subprime mortgage.

There are three financial instruments: (1) a subprime mortgage; (2) a senior/sub tranche RMBS securitization of the single subprime mortgage; (3) a senior/sub tranche CDO, which has purchased the senior tranche of the RMBS. I omit a fourth step, of an SIV buying the senior CDO tranche or a CDO tranche having a 2a-7 put attached, and so on. The transactions all last for one period, and all payoffs are at the end of the period. I will ignore discounting.

The mortgage has a face value of 100. At the end of the period, the mortgage has a step-up rate and will be refinanced or not. If it is not refinanced, then it defaults, in which case the lender will recover $R. So the loss is $100 - R \equiv$ Loss if there is a default. If it is refinanced, then the new mortgage is worth M (in expected value) to the lender.

Ignoring for a moment the dependence of R and M on home prices, the payoff to the lender at the end of the period on the current mortgage is: Max (R, M). If the new mortgage is worth less than the recovery value of the home, then the lender does not refinance (nor will any other lender), and the homeowner defaults.

The lender finances the mortgage by securitizing it. It is sold at par of 100. The lender retains the refinancing option as discussed above, and the securitization will either receive par or R at the end of the period.

The subprime RMBS transaction has two tranches: the first tranche attaches at 0 and detaches at $N; the second tranche attaches at $N (e.g., N = 30 means that the first $30 of loss is absorbed by the sub piece) and goes to the end, 100. The par value of the senior tranche is, therefore, 100 − N. In other words, the first $N of loss will be borne by the sub piece.

Looking at the senior tranche, the loss on this tranche at the end of the period, L_S, is given by:

$$L_S = Max\ [Loss - N,\ 0].$$

The payoff or redeemed amount, V, on this senior tranche at the end of the period is:

$$V = Min \begin{cases} Max\ [100 - N, 0], \\ 100 - N - L_S \end{cases}.$$

Since 100 − N is always greater than 0, Max [100 − N, 0] is always equal to 100 − N. L_S is always greater than or equal to 0, so 100 − N − L_S is always less than or equal to 100 − N. Therefore, $V = 100 - N - L_S$. Substituting in for L_S: $V = Min\ [100 - N, 100 - Loss]$.

So, for example, if Loss = 50 and N = 30, then if the mortgage is not refinanced and defaults, the senior tranche will have a $20 loss since the first-loss tranche only absorbs the first $30 of loss. The final value, V, of the senior tranche is $50.

The senior tranche of the subprime RMBS is sold to a CDO, which has two tranches: the first tranche attaches at 0 and detaches at N_{CDO}; the second tranche attaches at N_{CDO} and goes to the end, 100 − N. Note that the size of the CDO is 100 − N (= 70 in the example), since it only purchases the senior tranche of the subprime RMBS. Note that N_{CDO} will be less (in dollars) than N because the CDO portfolio is smaller; the sub tranche of the CDO may be larger in percentage terms, though.

Looking at the senior tranche, the loss on this tranche at the end of the period, L_{CDO}, is given by:

$$L_{CDO} = Max\ [Min\ (L_S,\ 100 - N) - N_{CDO},\ 0].$$

At the end of the period, the payoff on the senior tranche of the CDO, V_{CDO}, is given by:

$$V_{CDO} = Min \begin{cases} Max\,[(100 - N - N_{CDO}),0], \\ 100 - N - N_{CDO} - L_{CDO} \end{cases}.$$

Substituting for L_{CDO}:

$$V_{CDO} = Min \begin{cases} Max\,[(100 - N - N_{CDO}),0], \\ N - N_{CDO} - Max\,[Min(L_S,100 - N) - N_{CDO}, \end{cases}$$

and substituting now for L_S:

$$V_{CDO} = Min \begin{cases} Max[(100 - N - N_{CDO}),0] \\ N - N_{CDO} - Max[Min\,(Max[Min\,(100 - Loss,100) - N,0],100 - N) - N_{CDO},0] \end{cases}.$$

Looking at this final expression, we can see the dependence of the senior CDO tranche on the structure of the securitization (i.e., the tranching (N)) and on the underlying single subprime mortgage, namely, its loss. And keep in mind that loss depends on house price appreciation. Nowhere does M appear, because if the loan is refinanced at the end of the period, then it is paid off and there are no losses. M is the expected value of the new loan. In the simple formulation above, the dependence on house prices only appears in terms of the recovery value of the house if there is a default. In the real structure, the refinancing results in M being paid into the securitization, which is cash that would be allocated following the priority rules and the triggers, which determine the amortization. So that aspect is lost in the simplified example.

Here's a very simple numerical version of the above example. Assume that the subprime mortgage par amount is 100; assume the size of RMBS sub tranche is $20, so the size of the senior RMBS tranche is $80. The senior RMBS tranche is sold to a CDO, which only buys this tranche, so the size of the CDO is $80. The size of CDO sub tranche is $15, and so the senior tranche size is $65. I maintain these parameters and vary the recovery amount in table 3.16. The table shows the loss on the senior RMBS tranche, the payoff to the senior RMBS tranche, the loss on the senior CDO tranche, and the payoff on the senior CDO tranche—all at the end of the period.[50]

The example is not realistic because it is too simplified, but it does convey the intuition for a few points. What does the example show? First, the affects of tranching are apparent. The sub tranche of the RMBS absorbs the first loss. Since the "inner" RMBS tranche (i.e., the one in the CDO) is a senior tranche, the losses on the senior CDO tranche are always less than (or, in the extreme, equal to) the losses on the senior RMBS tranche.[51] However, conversely, if the

TABLE 3.16 A Simple Numerical Example of Losses on Subprime Tranches

	Parameters							
Recovery Amount ($)	90	70	60	50	40	30	20	10
	Outcomes							
Loss on Senior RMBS Tranche (L_S)	0	10	20	30	40	50	60	70
Payoff on Senior RMBS Tranche (V)	80	70	60	50	40	30	20	10
Payoff on Sr. Tranche as % of par	100%	87.5%	75%	62.5%	50%	37.5%	25%	12.5%
Loss on Senior CDO Tranche (L_{CDO})	0	0	5	15	25	35	45	55
Payoff on Senior CDO Tranche (V_{CDO})	65	65	60	50	40	30	20	10
Payoff on Sr. Tranche as % of par	100%	100%	92.3%	76.9%	61.5%	46.2%	30.8%	15.4%

CDO had purchased a mezzanine tranche, say, going from 10 to 20, then the example would be very different. A senior CDO tranche could easily be at risk of loss if the portfolio consisted of mezzanine RMBS tranches.

Obviously, the example could be extended to include an SIV which purchases the senior tranche of the CDO.

Discussion

Valuation of V_{CDO} requires mathematically integrating the above expression over a distribution of house prices. There are two practical problems with this. First, as a practical matter, the dependence on house prices creates a practical valuation problem—even if one takes a stand on the distribution of house prices. Imagine, for example, that the subprime securitization has four portfolios, each with thousands of mortgages, as in the above examples. The CDO has purchased 100 tranches of different securitizations, including, say, 20 senior subprime tranches from different deals. In principle, the issue is how to evaluate the senior CDO tranche (even ignoring all the OC tests and other complications of the CDO structure). Not only is that valuation very difficult to do, but even linking the three structures together in a meaningful way is nigh impossible. An investor who actually purchased a particular CDO tranche or a particular subprime RMBS tranche would receive trustee reports and would, therefore, know the underlying portfolio.[52] The subprime RMBS investor could, with some difficult look-through to the underlying mortgages, try to determine the value of his tranche.[53] The computational complexity is very high.

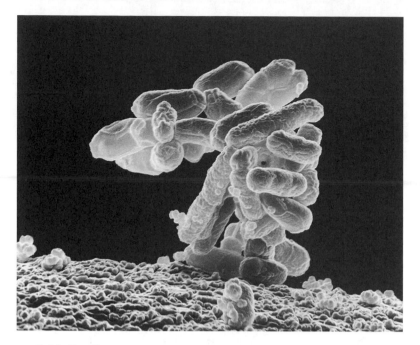

FIGURE 3.10 E. coli

The second problem is taking all of the structure into account. There are vendor-provided packages that model the structure of structured products, but the valuation is based on (point estimate) assumptions that are input by the user, rather than simulation of the performance of the underlying portfolios.

The Problem and the Panic

Normally, these details of the chain would not be of interest to many people. Securitized bonds provided collateral for repo, and the shadow banking system worked. But once subprime risk infected the system, the vulnerability to panic was increased. And if panic occurred, then the details would matter. I have described these details.

Subprime risk, even though not large by itself, has been spread inside and outside the banking system, globally and domestically, and no one knows where it is. No one knows which firms are exposed and have concentrations of this risk. Think of ground beef. Ground beef is made by grinding cow carcasses and then mixing the meat to obtain the desired fat content. (Americans apparently are very particular about this.) If E. coli is later discovered, perhaps from only one steer, it can still happen that millions of pounds of ground beef are recalled. Remarkably, it is possible to identify which ground beef to recall. Of course, the idea is that we have enough confidence in the system not to worry about this, and to eat hamburgers without fear. The problem we face today is that the subprime risks, the E. coli, have been spread around, but there is no fast way to recall the mortgages. Because the subprime risks are opaque and have been intertwined with ever more complicated securities and off-balance-sheet vehicles, there is the fear that all assets—all the beef—has gone bad. These fears have led to concerns about the liquidity of asset classes unrelated to subprime. And they have led to uncertainty about the value of these securities. Confidence in the information insensitivity of repo collateral has been called into question.

4

The Panic of 2007, Part 2

A bank is…a manufacturer of credit. The cornerstone of credit is confidence—confidence of men in men. A panic is a collapse of credit. It is an intensely human affair, and many of the determining influences are of a personal and confidential character, and very inadequately reflected in the cold figures of the bank statement.
—E.W. Kemmerer (1911)

The Panic

What triggered the Panic of 2007? How did it develop? In a panic, information-insensitive securities become risky because of a shock. Then it matters how the securities are constructed, in order to buy and sell them. I argued above that a complex chain of securities, derivatives, and special-purpose vehicles resulted in asymmetric information and a loss of information: the structurers understood the chain, but investors did not. The chain began to unravel when house prices did not rise and foreclosures began. Trade became difficult because buyers feared sellers were better informed, and the value of the distressed securities was hard to determine. In this section, I begin by briefly documenting these developments. Appendix A contains a brief chronology of the events of the panic.

House price declines and foreclosures do not explain the panic. I argue that the information story is more complicated. Dealer banks had the information about the subprime-related structures and about the placement of the various bonds. But there was no way to learn the consensus value of these bonds and structures or where the risk was located. There was no mechanism for the revelation and aggregation of diverse information about the effects of the house price decline and the foreclosures. This created a pivotal role for the ABX index, which started trading in early 2006 around the time that house prices began to fall. I review the role of this index in creating common knowledge that the situation of subprime borrowers was deteriorating quickly and that the value of subprime-related bonds and structures was going down. By 2007, the ABX indices had become the focal point of the crisis. I discuss the role of the ABX index in revealing information. This is followed by a brief discussion of the repo run and runs on SIVs—the panic itself. I devote little space to the repo market, which was covered above. Finally, I try to summarize the argument.

House Prices Do Not Rise

House prices were supposed to always go up. Between 2001 and 2005, home-owners enjoyed an average increase of 54.4% in the value of their houses, as measured by the Office of Federal Housing Enterprise Oversight (OFHEO).[1] In terms of the two-year fixed rate part of a 2/28 subprime mortgage, from January 1997 to July 2007, every rolling two-year period showed positive house

FIGURE 4.1 Politician: "I'll stop your horse, Sir." Bank Director: "Do it then, like a good fellow, but take care; see what I got for trying to stop him in my way." Harper's, October 24, 1857. Artist: Frank Bellew. (Provided courtesy HarpWeek, LCC)

price appreciation, according to the S&P/Case-Shiller (U.S. national) index. In fact, from March 1998 to March 2007, every rolling two-year period displayed double-digit house price appreciation. There was no appreciation or depreciation in August 2007, and starting in September 2007, house price appreciation has been negative. Figure 4.2 shows a plot of the lagging two-year house price appreciation.

But then house prices declined. In fact, the S&P/Case-Shiller (U.S. national) quarterly home price index declined by 4.5% in Q3 2007 versus Q3 2006—the largest drop since the index started recording data in 1988.[2] Home prices, as measured in the 20 U.S. metropolitan areas, declined by 4.9 %, the largest drop since the index was started in 2001, with 15 of the 20 cities showing year-on-year declines in prices. The two largest declines occurred in Tampa (−11.12% y-o-y) and Miami (−9.96% y-o-y). U.S. home prices declined 6.7% in October from a year earlier, a record drop for the 10-city S&P/Case-Shiller index.[3]

The ability of subprime and Alt-A borrowers to sustain their mortgage payments depends heavily on house price appreciation because of the need for refinancing. When house prices did not appreciate to the same extent as in the past—and in many areas they have recently gone down—the ability of borrowers to refinance has been reduced. In fact, because of the crisis, underwriting standards have become much tougher, and many lenders are in bankruptcy, meaning that the mortgage market for these borrowers to refinance has effectively closed.

Currently, almost all the major issuers of subprime mortgages are either out of business or have stopped making subprime loans unless they conform to GSE underwriting criteria. Problems in the Alt-A market are still mostly in the future, and it is likely that this market will also shut down. The unwillingness

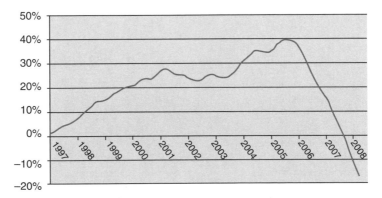

FIGURE 4.2 Lagging Two-Year House Price Appreciation (%). Source: S&P.

to originate subprime mortgages is significantly driven by the impossibility of a securitization takeout of the loans. This shutdown means that borrowers in the subprime and Alt-A mortgages will have a very difficult time refinancing when their hybrid ARMs are reset.

The shutdown of the subprime mortgage market is very important because of the number of borrowers who will soon reach their reset date, that is, the date at which the initial fixed teaser rate ends and the mortgage rate resets to a significantly higher floating rate. Evidence of the shutdown in the refinancing market comes from remittance data. Remittance data shows that the shutdown is dramatically reducing subprime prepayment speeds.[4] A decline in prepayment speed means that borrowers cannot refinance either because they no longer can find a lender or because they have no equity built up on their houses. Delinquencies and foreclosures are the result.

We now turn to the issue of how the information about house prices and delinquencies and foreclosures was linked to valuations of the various parts of the chain. Keep in mind that house price and mortgage performance information from indices arrives with a lag, not in real time.

TABLE 4.1 Delinquency Rates (%)

	Home Mortgage Delinquency Rate: Total (%)	Delinquency Rate: Prime Borrowers (%)	Delinquency Rate: Subprime Borrowers (%)
2003Q1	4.92	2.62	13.04
2003Q2	4.97	2.60	12.35
2003Q3	4.65	2.44	11.74
2003Q4	4.49	2.37	11.53
2004Q1	4.46	2.26	11.66
2004Q2	4.56	2.40	10.47
2004Q3	4.54	2.32	10.74
2004Q4	4.38	2.22	10.33
2005Q1	4.31	2.17	10.62
2005Q2	4.34	2.20	10.33
2005Q3	4.44	2.34	10.76
2005Q4	4.70	2.47	11.63
2006Q1	4.41	2.25	11.50
2006Q2	4.39	2.29	11.70
2006Q3	4.67	2.44	12.56
2006Q4	4.95	2.57	13.33
2007Q1	4.84	2.58	13.77
2007Q2	5.12	2.73	14.82
2007Q3	5.59	3.12	16.31
2007Q4	5.82	3.24	17.31

Source: Mortgage Bankers Association.

Information and Common Knowledge

It was widely understood that the structures along the chain were sensitive to house prices, that house prices were likely a "bubble." Not everyone had the same view on whether house prices would continue to rise, or if they were to stop rising, or when this would occur. Or what the effects would be. Different parties made different bets on this. But they did this without knowing the views of other participants. That is, there was a lack of common knowledge about the effects and timing of house price changes and about the appearance of increases in delinquencies. This explains why the interlinked chain of securities, structures, and derivatives did not unravel for awhile.

In an important way, this changed with the introduction of the ABX indices at the start of 2006. As mentioned above, the ABX index is a credit derivative that references 20 equally weighted RMBS transactions. There are also subindices, referencing the rated tranches of the same 20 transactions: AAA, AA, A BBB, and BBB-. Each subindex includes 20 subprime home equity bonds. The reference obligations in each subindex comprise bonds at the rating level of the subindex. Every six months, the indices are reconstituted based on a pre-identified set of rules. The ABX.HE indices that reference lower-rated RMBS tranches typically carry higher coupons than those referencing higher rated tranches due to the higher expected likelihood of default.

TABLE 4.2 ABX.HE Index Overview

	ABX.HE
Portfolio	20 deals in basket, with a new ABX.HE series expected to be launched approximately every 6 months
Credit Score	Each deal must have a maximum average FICO equal to 660
Age	Each tranche must have settled within 6 months of the roll date
Weighting	Reference obligations equally weighted by initial par amount, with subsequent weightings evolving as a function of prepayment and credit experience of underlying transactions
Lien Type	The pool must consist of at least 90% first lien loans
Diversification	–Limits same originator to 4 deals –Limits master servicer to 6 deals
Minimum Deal Size	$500mm
Average Life	Each tranche must have a weighted average life of 4-6 years as of the issuance date (except AAAs which must be greater than 5 years)
Credit Events	Failure to Pay Principal, Writedown
Settlement	Pay-as-you-go (PAUG)*

*PAUG is a form of settlement used in asset-backed credit default swaps. It allows two-way payments between the protection buyer and protection seller during the life of the contract. If the reference obligation is affected by interest shortfalls or principal writedowns, the protection buyer compensates the protection seller. These amounts are paid back to the protection buyer if the interest shortfalls or principal writedowns are reversed. The protection buyer has the option of physically settling the credit default swap if there is a principal write-down.

Figure 4.3 portrays the creation of a vintage of the ABX index and the sub-indices for the different ratings: AAA, AA, A BBB, and BBB-. Each subindex includes 20 subprime home equity bonds. The introduction of these indices is important for two reasons. First, they provided a transparent price of subprime risk, albeit with liquidity problems (see Gorton, 2009). Second, it allowed for efficient shorting of the subprime market. In addition to outright shorting, parties with long positions could hedge. The common knowledge problem concerning the value of subprime bonds may have been solved, but not the location problem. This is, of course, conjecture.[5]

As with credit default swaps (CDS) generally, entering into an ABX index contract is analogous to buying or selling insurance on a basket of the underlying RMBS tranches. An investor wanting to hedge an existing position or otherwise establish a short credit position using the index (known as the "protection buyer"), is required to pay a monthly coupon to the other party (the "protection seller"). The payment is calculated based on the outstanding notional amount of the index and the fixed coupon. In exchange for the payment, the protection buyer in an ABX index contract is compensated by the protection seller when any interest or principal shortfalls or writedowns on the underlying mortgages affect the constituent RMBS. Unlike with conventional "single-name" CDS, the index contract does not terminate when these credit events occur; rather, it continues with a reduced notional amount until maturity. If credit events are

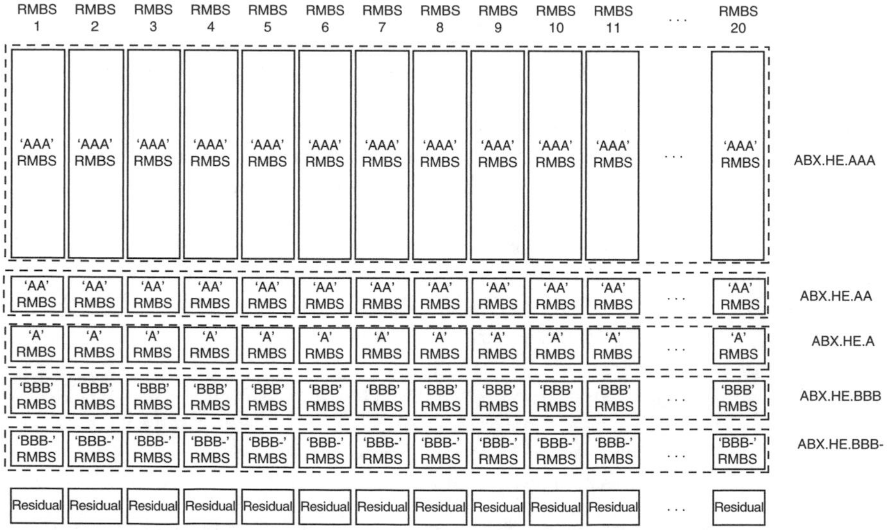

FIGURE 4.3 ABX.HE Indices. Source: Kevin Kendra, Fitch, "Tranche ABX and Basis Risk in Subprime RMBS Structured Portfolios," Feb. 20, 2007.

subsequently reversed—for example, a principal shortfall is made up—then the protection buyer reimburses the protection seller.

The ABX tranche coupon is determined on the initiation date. Subsequently, trades require an upfront exchange of premium/discount. In a typical transaction, a protection buyer pays the protection seller a fixed coupon at a monthly rate on an amount determined by the buyer. When a credit event occurs, the protection seller makes a payment to the protection buyer in an amount equal to the loss. Credit events include the shortfall of interest or principal as well as the writedown of the tranche due to losses on the underlying mortgage loans.

The initial coupon is determined at the launch of each ABX.HE index, based on an average quote from a survey of the market makers, the dealer banks. Knowledge about the structure of the subprime RMBS, CDOs, and off-balance-sheet vehicles is held by the dealer banks, which structure these transactions. They are the ones polled to determine the initial coupons on the ABX indices. The polling process works as follows:

> At or about 9:00 A.M. on the Business Day immediately prior to the Roll Date (the "Fixed Rate Determination Date"), the fixed rate for each sub-index for the new ABX.HE Index for purposes of the ABX Transactions Standard Terms Supplement will be determined by the Administrator by soliciting each ABX. HE Participant to submit an average mid-market spread for each sub-index (in increments of 1 basis point). The Administrator will re-solicit ABX.HE Participants until at least two-thirds of the ABX.HE Participants (rounded down) have submitted such spreads. The Administrator shall rank such submissions for each sub-index from lowest to highest spread and discard the top and bottom quartiles thereof (the number of submissions q in each discarded quartile will be given by $q=int(N_s/4)$ where N_s is the total number of submissions). The fixed rate for each sub-index shall be the lesser of (i) average of the remaining submissions for such sub-index (rounded up to the nearest basis point), as determined by the Administrator and (ii) 500 basis points. (Markit, *ABX Index Rules*)

The ABX.HE 06–1 (this is the official name for the 2006 first vintage) began trading on January 19, 2006. So, unfortunately, there are no observations on early index subprime product, such as the 2005–Q1 vintage. Moreover, the company administering the ABX, Markit, announced that the roll of the new ABX. HE, ABX.HE 08–1, would be postponed for three months from the date it was scheduled to launch, January 19, 2008. Markit said, "The decision to postpone its launch was taken following extensive consultation with the dealer community. It follows a lack of RMBS deals issued in the second half of 2007 and eligible for inclusion in the forthcoming Markit ABX.HE roll. The Markit ABX.HE 07–2 remains the on-the-run series until further notice" (see http://www.markit.com/ information/products/abx/contentParagraphs/04/document/20071219%20 Markit%20ABX.HE.pdf). No subsequent vintage has been issued. The graph in figure 4.4 shows the prices of the 2006–1, 2006–2, 2007–1, and 2007–2 vintages of the index for the BBB- tranche. These are the only vintages available. In three of the four cases, the index starts trading at par of 100. In the case of the 2007–2 index, it opened at a price significantly below par.[6]

The time pattern of prices in this graph is very interesting. The first vintage, ABX 2006–01, trades near par, as does the 2006–2 vintage initially. During 2006, there is little evidence of a major crisis. But the 2007–1 BBB- ABX nosedives upon issuance, and the 2007–2 vintage opens trading below 60. The dealers got the coupons badly wrong. One interpretation of this is that the fundamentals of subprime were weakening during 2006, as the ABX drifted down somewhat in the second half of 2006. But, starting in 2007, it seems clear that there were major problems. I view the ABX indices as revealing hitherto unknown information, namely, the aggregated view that subprime was worth significantly less. In fact, some of the dealer banks themselves, we now know, were shorting the index to hedge their long positions—of course, so was everyone else.[7]

The ABX indices also allow all parties (e.g., hedge funds) to express their views on the value of subprime RMBS bonds. Kiet Tran (no date) of Markit put it this way:

> The sub-prime debacle in the U.S. brought about a global credit crunch this summer with the ABX leading the charge. Subordinate tranches of the 06–2 and 07–1 series have lost over 75% of their value since the end

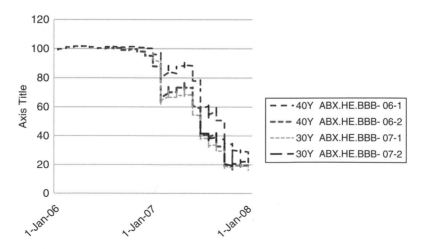

FIGURE 4.4 ABX BBB Prices.

of May. Even with the Fed rate cuts, the ABX free fall continues, particularly for the lower rated tranches. Early signals were seen in February 2007, a month where prices of the ABX BBB- tranches plunged more than 20%. Shareholder values of sub-prime mortgage lenders deteriorated in the following weeks, with the stock price of Accredited Home Lenders Holding Corporation dropping just over 80% between February month-end and the mid-March low.

ABX.HE acts as a vehicle for investors to hedge their sub-prime exposure and to express their views on the sub-prime market using a liquid and transparent instrument. The recent performance of the ABX does not bode well for the outlook for the sub-prime mortgage market but time will tell how far losses will extend. For the time being, the ABX.HE index is the acting weatherman of the sub-prime mortgage market, predicting a rough storm ahead.

It is not clear whether the housing price bubble was burst by the ability to short the subprime housing market or whether house prices were going down and the implications of this were aggregated and revealed by the ABX indices. As discussed below, the indices were the sole source of information for marking-to-market. It seems that the indices played a central informational role.

The Run on the SIVs

The runs began on ABCP conduits and SIVs. These vehicles were funded with short-maturity paper, and the "run" amounted to investors not rolling over the paper. Following the implicit (state-dependent) contract, discussed below, SIVs were absorbed back onto the balance sheet of their sponsors. The SIV sector essentially disappeared during the panic. See Appendix B.

As of December 2007, asset-backed commercial paper (ABCP) had declined by $404 billion from a peak of $1.2 trillion—a decline of about 34%. How much of this decline is due to SIVs unwinding? According to UBS:

> ...in August, SIV outstandings were $400 billion ($130 billion ABCP + $270 billion MTNs). Current SIV outstandings are $300 billion ($75 ABCP + $225 billion MTNs). This is, however, illusory; a large percentage of the $75 billion current outstanding SIV ABCP is no longer held by the intended investors (such as money market funds), but rather by bank sponsors themselves (which, of course, also ties up bank balance sheets), and to a lesser extent, by ABCP dealers and capital note holders. (UBS, "Mortgage Strategist," December 18, 2007, p. 10)

Appendix B describes the outcomes for the major SIVs. Concurrently with the run on these vehicles, prices of subprime-related bonds began to decline. Highly levered hedge funds that held these bonds began to incur writedowns and face margin calls. A number of hedge funds liquidated. Dealer banks began to announce writedowns.

Why were there runs on SIVs? Did they hold massive amounts of subprime-related paper? In August 2007, a few months prior to the runs, S&P reported on the portfolio composition of SIVs.

> We reviewed the portfolios specifically with an eye toward mortgage assets and CDO of ABS assets, which have recently experienced considerable pricing pressure in the markets. In the aggregate, SIV portfolios remain well diversified. Portfolio exposure to residential mortgage assets and CDOs of ABS average 24%. The exposure to subprime and home equity-backed RMBS assets forms a small proportion of the portfolios. Assets backed by prime RMBS form the largest proportion of the portfolios. On average, portfolios hold approximately 21% exposure to the U.S. RMBS prime markets, of which the vast majority is 'AAA' rated prime assets
>
> Two vehicles have significant above-average exposure to home equity and subprime assets. On Aug. 28, Standard & Poor's took a rating action on Cheyne. The other vehicle, Rhinebridge, recently received an infusion of capital. In aggregate, across the portfolios of all rated SIVs, the weighted averages of the portfolio-rating exposures are rounded to approximately 61% invested in AAA- rated assets, 27% invested in 'AA' rated assets, 12% invested in 'A' rated assets, and a residual of less than 1% in lower-rated assets. These numbers exclude Eaton Vance because it focuses on the non-investment-grade corporate market and has lower leverage guidelines. The financial sector comprises a weighted average of 41.5% of SIV portfolios.

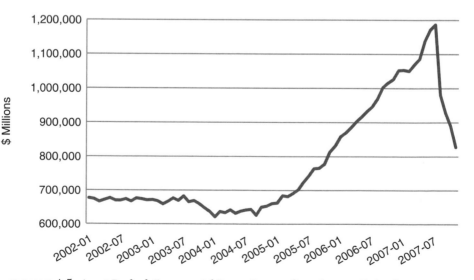

FIGURE 4.5 Asset-Backed Commercial Paper Outstanding. Source: Federal Reserve.

The chart in figure 4.6 shows the average asset distribution by sector across all SIV portfolios.

SIVs did not have significant exposure to subprime in aggregate. Home equity loans and subprime were 2.01%. CDOs of ABS amounted to 0.28%. Perhaps the problem was the exposure to the financial sector, 41.50%. The basic problem was that investors could not penetrate the portfolios far enough to make the determination. There was asymmetric information. The run on SIVs does resemble pre-Federal Reserve panics, and it is not surprising that the "super SIV" was a proposed solution. That resembled the 19th-century clearinghouses.[8]

Summary Overview

Looking into the chain of securities during the panic, information is "lost" due to complexity. That made trade hard. The table below may help organize what happened. Prior to the introduction of the ABX, there was no liquid, publicly visible market where subprime risk was directly priced. Individual transactions were priced, but these prices were not widely seen. Only the direct participants saw the prices. Moreover, parties wishing to hedge or short subprime had no easy way of doing this. To the extent that there was hedging and shorting, again the prices were not seen by a wider audience. The value of subprime mortgages and subprime-related instruments was not common knowledge. The ABX started trading in 2006 and started drifting downward in the second half of that year. In 2007, all the indices showed a distinctly negative view. This negative view became known, and it became known that everyone knew this.

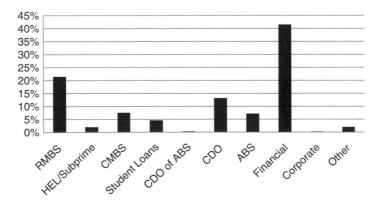

FIGURE 4.6 Composition of SIV Portfolios. Source: S&P (August 2007).

TABLE 4.3 Summary of the Chain of Subprime Risk

Step in the Chain	Information Created	Parties Involved
Origination of Mortgages	Underwriting Standards: Risk characteristics of mortgages	Mortgage Originators; brokers
Securitization of Mortgages	Portfolio of mortgages selected and RMBS Structured	Dealer Banks; Servicers; Rating agencies; Investors buy the deal
Securitization of ABS, RMBS, CMBs in CDOs of ABS	Portfolio of ABS selected; manager selected, and CDO Structured	Dealer Banks; CDO managers; Rating Agencies; Investors buy the deal
Possible transfer of CDO risk via CDS in Negative Basis Trade	CDO and tranche selected; counterparty risk introduced	Dealer Banks; Banks with balance sheets; CDO
Possible Sale of CDO tranches to SIVs and other such vehicles	CDO and tranche selected for SIV portfolio	SIV Manager; SIV Investors buy SIV liabilities
Possible investment in SIV liabilities by money market funds	Choice of SIV and seniority	Only the parties directly involved: buyer and seller
Possible sale of CDO tranches to money market funds via liquidity puts	CDO and tranche selected	Dealer Banks; Money Market funds; Put writer
Final resting place of the cash RMBS tranches, cash CDO tranches, and synthetic risk	Location of Risk	Only the parties directly involved: buyer and seller

Once the ABX indices started to drift downward, accountants required market participants to use these indices for mark-to-market purposes, which may have led to a feedback effect, discussed later.

"Asymmetric information" is a familiar term, referring simply to a situation where one side of a transaction knows more relevant information than the other side about the object being traded, potentially leading to well-known agency problems. Referring to table 4.3, investors purchased tranches of RMBS, CDOs, SIV liabilities, money market funds, and so on, and did so without knowing everything known by the structurers of the securities they were purchasing. These investors likely relied on repeated relationships with bankers and on ratings. Essentially, investors do not have the resources to individually analyze such complicated structures and, in the end, rely to a lesser extent on the information about the structure and the fundamentals and more on the relationship with the product seller. Agency relationships are substituted for the actual information. To emphasize, this is not surprising, and it is not unique to structured products.

But in this case the chain is quite long. Below I discuss whether incentives were aligned in these agency relationships along the chain.

No one knows where the subprime risk ultimately ended up, except that the final buyers and sellers of the risk of a particular transaction know. The final investor is invariably an agent acting as a delegated portfolio manager. Even if the final investor is a regulated entity, the entity may not report in a way which would make the risk clear to outsiders or regulators.

In economics, we often think of information as being exogenous payoff-relevant information, such as the distribution of payoffs or the type of a manager, which affects the distribution of payoffs. Economists think of information as a "signal" about the future payoff of a security. Agents obtain signals by expending resources. If they expend resources, they learn the signal plus noise. The costs of learning the signal are recovered by trading on this private information. In the process, the price aggregates the information. This is the gist of Grossman and Stiglitz's (1980) paper.

There is also information about the actions of other agents; that is, the strategies of other agents can affect payoffs, and so agents must form beliefs about what other agents are going to do. These are all familiar notions.

I have argued that one problem leading to the current crisis was the loss of information. What does it mean for information to be "lost" due to "complexity"? "Lost" implies that the information was known at one point, and then it became "lost." By "lost," I mean that for CDO investors and investors in other instruments that have CDO tranches in their portfolios, it is not possible to penetrate the chain backward and value the chain based on the underlying mortgages. The structure itself does not allow for valuation based on the underlying mortgages, as a practical matter. There are (at least) two layers of structured products in CDOs. Information is lost because of the difficulty of penetrating to the core assets. Nor is it possible for those at the start of the chain to use their information to value the chain upward, so to speak.

To be a bit more precise, the Grossman Stiglitz story is about secondary market security trading. But the securities and derivatives relevant to the subprime panic are not traded in secondary markets. The chain is a sequence of primary markets. In this chain, how are the signals propagated? The initial "signal" concerns the underwriting standards for the mortgages. At each step along the way, signals are somehow combined as different portfolios are formed, each requiring multiple signals. Economists simply have no theories about the aggregation and transmission of "signals" in this context. Essentially, incentive-compatible arrangements are substituted for the actual signals, which are too complex to be transmitted.

The Panic Continued: Liquidity, Accounting, and Collateral Calls

The panic was rooted in the fear of losses, the location and extent of which can't be determined. But there was also a virulent knock-on effect which is a significant force in its own right: liquidity dried up. With no liquidity and no market prices, the accounting practice of marking-to-market became highly problematic and resulted in massive writedowns based on fire-sale prices and estimates. Collateral calls, also based on marking-to-market, were massive, creating liquidity problems for some and windfall funding for others. Finally, there was an inability to raise cash because of a refusal to lend, especially in terms of repurchase (repo) agreements.[9] I review these issues in this section.

Liquidity

Aside from actual experiences of watching the repo market disappear, the evidence for the liquidity crisis is the sharp increase in spreads in important short-term funding markets, such as the interbank market. A number of observers point to

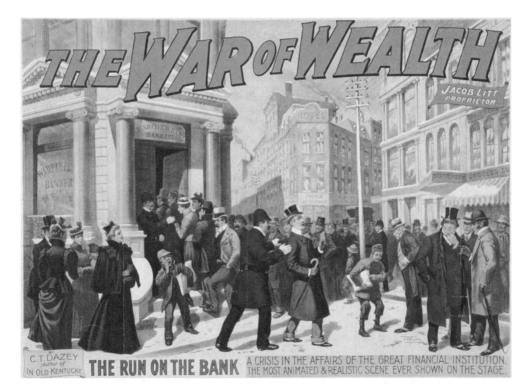

FIGURE 4.7 Theatrical poster for the 1895 play *The War of Wealth*. The play was written by Charles Turner Dazey, 1855–1938. (Library of Congress)

the spread between LIBOR and the overnight indexed swap (OIS) rate of the same maturity.[10] The OIS rate embeds the expectation of the overnight rate at that maturity, but does not reflect credit and liquidity risks, so the idea is that the spread takes account of interest-rate expectations. The increase in the spread is viewed as evidence of the stress in the interbank market, though whether it is "liquidity" or counterparty risk, to the extent that these are different, is less clear. See Mishkin (2008), Taylor and Williams (2008A, B), Michaud and Upper (2008).[11]

The three-month LIBOR-OIS spread is shown in figure 4.8. This spread had a multiyear average of 11 basis points and was 15 basis points on August 8, 2007. On August 10, it was over 50 basis points, and it was over 90 basis points by mid-September. This liquidity crisis was magnified by several factors, which I discuss next. The first is the accounting practice of marking-to-market. I briefly discuss this issue; a thorough discussion is beyond the scope of this paper.[12] A second factor in the liquidity crisis is collateral calls.[13]

Illiquidity causes mark-to-market losses to differ significantly from expected losses based on credit fundamentals. The difference is the liquidity premium. Of course, the problem is that we have no sure measure of the illiquidity discount, nor do we have a sure measure of the expected losses based on fundamentals. The Bank of England (2008) estimated, based on actuarial methods, that the realized subprime-related losses would eventually reach $170 billion. On the other hand, an estimate based on the usual market-value method gives an expected loss of $380 billion. See Bank of England (2008). This result is hardly unique: every comparison between market-price-based measures and actuarial measures gives the same result, namely, that writedowns calculated with market-price-based measures are significantly higher than expected losses

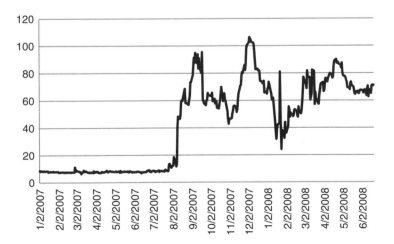

FIGURE 4.8 Three-Month LIBOR-OIS Spread (bps). Source: Bloomberg.

calculated using any other approach. This is no surprise—it is exactly the effect of illiquidity on prices.

The Impact of Accounting

The relevant accounting rule (in the United States) is the U.S. Financial Accounting Standards Board Rule 157, which was introduced in September 2006 to become effective for fiscal years that began after November 15, 2007. So the rule was coming into effect essentially in the middle of the panic.[14] The rule requires that (most) positions be marked-to-market under FASB 157.[15] The logic follows from the idea that if markets are efficient, that is, if prices aggregate the information and beliefs of market participants, then this is the best estimate of "value."[16] I leave aside the issue of whether "efficient markets" is an accurate description of any market other than perhaps stock markets. This accounting view creates an obvious problem during a banking panic, when market participants withdraw from markets, a problem which has been much commented on. See, for example, Fitch (2008), Euromoney (March 3, 2008), Norris (2007), and Standard and Poor's (2007, 2008), to name just a few.[17]

The accounting rules put the accountants at the forefront of decision making about the valuation of complex financial instruments. While the accounting outcome is basically negotiated, the rules put management at a bargaining disadvantage. As Pollock (2008) put it:

> There is no doubt that the move to FAS 157 and similar rules has resulted in a shift of power toward accounting firms and away from corporate management, a shift that only adds to the change put in place by Sarbanes-Oxley. At the same time, we have this perverse situation where the accountant has to opine on accounting treatment, but they cannot provide advice to the client because that would violate their "independence."

Accounting is supposed to produce information.[18] How can that happen in a panic? In a panic, no one wants to trade; there are no markets. And hence there are no market prices. Think of a 19th-century banking panic. In a 19th-century banking panic, the banking system was insolvent; the system could not honor depositor demands for withdrawal. There is no place to sell the assets of the banking system. Obviously, marking-to-market would confirm this. In the United States during the 19th century, this problem was solved by clearinghouses (something the short-lived "super SIV" attempted to imitate). During the 19th century, the institution of the clearinghouse evolved to the point where banks' response to panics was fairly effective. In the face of the insolvency of the banking system, the banks suspended convertibility and issued clearing-house loan certificates. Clearinghouse loan certificates created a market price, one which valued the assets of the banking system. These certificates traded at a discount to par initially. When the discount to par disappeared, correspond-ing to the market's view that the banking system was solvent, suspension was lifted. In other words, it took time for the asymmetric information to dissipate, and when it did, suspension was lifted. This system was abandoned with the founding of the Fed and the subsequent adoption of deposit insurance. These were institutions aimed at preventing a panic from happening. But they are not equipped to solve the information problem that arises if a panic does happen.

Clearinghouse loan certificates served an important function in produc-ing information about the aggregate banking system. There is no modern equivalent to clearinghouses. There is no information-producing mechanism that is implemented during panics. Accountants follow rules. So accountants enforced "marking." Accountants initially seized on the ABX indices as the

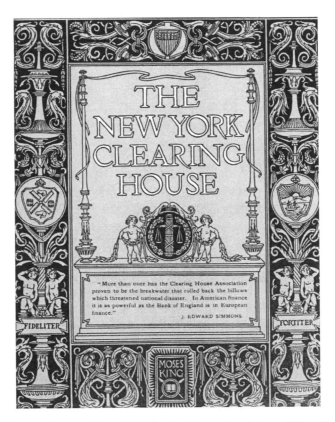

FIGURE 4.9 Front cover of *New York Clearing House Association, 1854–1905*, by William J. Gilpin and Henry E. Wallace.

"price," even for earlier vintages, but later were willing to recognize the difficulties of using the ABX indices.

Marking-to-market, however, implemented during a panic, has very
real effects because regulatory capital and capital for rating-agency purposes
is based on GAAP. There are no sizable platforms that can operate ignoring GAAP capital. In the current situation, partly as a result of GAAP capital declines, banks are selling assets or are attempting to sell assets—billions
of dollars of assets—to "clean up their balance sheets," raising cash and
de-levering. This pushes down prices, and another round of marking down
occurs, and so on. This downward spiral of prices—marking down, selling,
marking down again—is a problem when there is no other side of the market,
as has been often noted of late.[19]

The Scramble for Cash—Collateral Calls

A scramble for cash ensued, not just from de-levering and hoarding balance
sheets, but also from collateral calls.[20] For example, Bear Stearns Form 10-K,
November 30, 2007:

> investors lost confidence in commercial paper conduits and SIVs, causing
> concerns over large potential liquidations of AAA collateral. The lack of liquid-
> ity and transparency regarding the underlying assets in securitizations, CDOs
> and SIVs resulted in significant price declines across all mortgage-related
> products in fiscal 2007. Price declines were further driven by forced sales of
> assets in order to meet demands by investors for the return of their collateral
> and collateral calls by lenders. (p. 16)

Accredited home Lenders Holding Co. SEC filing Schedule 14D-9, June 19,
2007:[21]

> these events with the continued heavy repurchase demands from whole loan
> purchasers experienced during this period created a cycle beginning with
> a significant increase in the amount of distressed loans for sale in the market.
> This increase in loan supply reduced whole loan prices, providing a basis for
> warehouse line providers to mark down the collateral value of loans held in
> inventory and, as a result, to place margin calls on non-prime lenders. These
> increased margin calls resulted in more distressed sales which, in turn, put
> further downward pressure on whole loan sale prices, regenerating the cycle
> with escalating negative results. (p. 8)

There many examples like this.

Collateral usage in derivative transactions has increased significantly.
Collateral usage in derivative transactions is governed by the Credit Support

Annex (CSA) to the ISDA Master Agreement. A CSA provides credit protection by setting forth the rules governing the mutual posting of collateral. [22] The ISDA Margin Survey of 2007 estimates that the gross amount of collateral in use at the end of 2006 was $1.335 trillion, an increase of 0.4% over the previous year. The 2007 survey reported a 10% increase. The number of collateral agreements in 2007 was 133,000, compared with 110,000 in 2006. Cash is the most common kind of collateral.

In the credit derivatives market, buyers of protection can make collateral calls when spreads increase, that is, when marks suggest an increase in the likelihood that protection sellers will have to pay. (The mechanics of this are governed by the CSA.) Dealer banks, which have written and purchased protection, will both make collateral calls and face collateral calls. Collateral typically earns LIBOR, so a collateral call means paying LIBOR in an environment where the bank will have to pay much more than LIBOR to borrow. So there is a lot at stake in collateral calls.

This issue cannot be underestimated. The credit derivatives market is sizeable, indeed, and is based on collateral provisions in ISDA CSAs. The British Bankers Association 2006 survey estimated the total market notional at the end of 2006 to be $20.207 trillion. The ISDA mid-2007 survey estimated the size of the credit derivatives market to be $45.25 trillion. In the June 2007 survey, the U.S. Office of the Comptroller of the currency found that the total notional amount of credit derivatives held by U.S. commercial banks was $10.2 trillion. To put these numbers in a broader perspective, keep in mind that the U.S. corporate bond market is currently $5.7 trillion and that the U.S. Treasury market is currently $4.3 trillion.[23]

For the party calling for collateral, collateral becomes a form of funding. Because LIBOR is paid on collateral, firms receiving collateral can fund themselves at LIBOR, when issuing debt in the market would cost them much more. This is one reason that the scramble for cash in the form of collateral calls is very important. In fact, it is difficult to convey the ferocity of the fights over collateral.

Panic in the Repo Market

Aside from collateral calls creating a scramble for cash, the basic form of lending, repo, disappeared. The most important part of the panic occurred in the repo market. This was discussed in chapter 2, so it is only touched on here briefly.

Repos are essentially secured loans, so counterparty risk is not an issue. All general collateral (GC) repos have the same rate, the GC repo rates, or simply the repo rate. Typically, repos can be rolled over easily and indefinitely, though the repo rate may change. Repo is integral to intermediation by dealer banks because when assets are purchased for sale later, the assets are financed by repo.

Repo is likely one of the largest financial markets, though there are no official statistics on its size. Triparty repo was $2.5 trillion in 2007 (see Geithner, 2008).[24] Triparty repo is estimated to be about 15–20% of the repo market.[25] With respect to the financing activities of primary dealers reporting to the New York Fed, the average daily outstanding repo and reverse repo contracts totaled $7.06 trillion in the first quarter of 2008, a 21.5% increase over the same period in 2007. See the Securities Industry and Financial Markets Association (2008, p. 9). The Bond Market Association (renamed the Securities Industry and Financial Markets Association in 2005) conducted a dealer survey in September 2004 to determine the size of the repo market. As of June 30, 2004, the repo and securities lending market was $7.84 trillion. It is generally believed that this market has grown at around 10% per year, making it about $11.5 trillion today.

The repo market was shocked in August 2007 when haircuts rose above zero. This increase was disastrous. Repo depositors would not accept collateral without a haircut because they rightly believed that if the bank failed and they had to sell the collateral, there would be no market in which to sell it. This is due to the absence of prices. The amount lent depends on the perceived market value of the asset offered as security. If that value cannot be determined because there is no market—no liquidity—or there is the concern that if the asset is seized by the lender, it will not be saleable at all, then the lender will not engage in repo.

Why did the repo market disappear, if the problem was uncertainty about the valuation of subprime bonds? One can understand that dealers would not want to take subprime RMBS as collateral in repo, but what about ABS, RMBS, and CMBS generally? These asset classes are unrelated to subprime. The problem was that if a large bank failed or had to dump assets for other reasons (e.g., writedowns), then prices of these asset classes would fall. The uncertainty about what prices would be and about whether a bank would fail led to the very problem that was feared. With haircuts, banks were forced to de-lever, which meant selling assets and falling prices. Further, if no one would accept structured products for repo, then these bonds could not be traded—and then no one would want to accept them in a repo transaction. This externality is reminiscent of Pagano (1989).

With rising haircuts, there is less collateral. Without repo, assets cannot change hands, because the intermediaries cannot function. The only way to sell assets is at extremely low prices. But low prices than have a feedback effect, as they cause the mark-to-market value of all assets to fall, making it even less likely that repo can be done.

FIGURE 4.10 Keeping the money where it will do the most good. Uncle Sam: "Look out, boys, they say he's a Caesar (seiz-er)." (Provided courtesy HarpWeek, LCC)

Like repo, collateral calls, against credit derivative positions, for example, are also based on marks. That leads to fights over collateral due to disagreements about prices. (Such fights are ultimately governed by the Credit Support Annex.) The VCG Special Opportunities hedge fund, for example, sued Wachovia after the fund was asked to post $750,000 of collateral, but then was asked for an increase to $8.2 million. The fund refused the final call of $1.49 million, and Wachovia foreclosed on the fund (see WSJ, March 4, 2008, p. C1).

Explaining the Panic: A Competing Hypothesis

I have argued that subprime mortgages and subprime securitizations have a unique design in that they are particularly sensitive to declines in house prices, which led to an information problem for investors when the house price bubble burst, particularly due to the distribution methods, including CDOs, off-balance-sheet vehicles, and derivatives. In my view, it is precisely the particularity of the underlying subprime mortgage design and its transmission through the chain of structures that explains the problem. There is a specific sensitivity to house prices embedded in the design of these securities, structures, and derivatives. There are no such issues with securitization generally or with the use of off-balance-sheet vehicles for the securitization of those asset classes. Other securitizations are not so sensitive to the prices of the underlying assets, and so they are not so susceptible to bubbles. So my claim is that a very specific set of interlinked security designs made the chain susceptible to a house price decline. House prices stopped increasing in 2006, and the effects were revealed by ABX prices.

There is, however, another hypothesis about the panic, and in this section, I very briefly discuss this competing hypothesis.

The dominant explanation for the panic is the "originate-to-distribute" view, which is the idea that banking has changed in such a way that the incentives have been fundamentally altered as a general matter. It is argued that originators and underwriters of loans no longer have an incentive to pay attention to the risks of loans they originate, since they are not residual claimants on these loans. In this view, investors apparently do not understand this and have been fooled. (Fingers point to the rating agencies.)

The originate-to-distribute viewpoint has been described by the Joint Forum (which includes the Basel Committee on Banking Supervision, the International Organization of Securities Commissions, and the International Association of Insurance Supervisors) as follows:

> ...under the "originate-to-distribute" model, banks frequently no longer have significant retained exposures, nor have they necessarily retained the personnel specializing in workouts who can steer creditor negotiations. (*Credit Risk Transfer*, April 2008, p. 20)

> Since 2005, the growth of CRT [Credit Risk Transfer] continues to provide banks and securities firms with opportunities to profit from originating, structuring and underwriting CRT products. They can earn fees while not having to hold the associated credit risk or fund positions over an extended time period. This has been termed the "originate-to-distribute" model. (*Credit Risk Transfer*, April 2008, p. 41)

Here is a slightly fuller articulation of the view, by Mishkin (2008):

> The originate-to-distribute model, unfortunately, created some severe incentive problems, which are referred to as principal-agent problems, or more

simply as agency problems, in which the agent (the originator of the loans) did not have the incentives to act fully in the interest of the principal (the ultimate holder of the loan). Originators had every incentive to maintain origination volume, because that would allow them to earn substantial fees, but they had weak incentives to maintain loan quality....

All major bank regulators and central bankers appear to subscribe to this view, though their views have some differences and nuances.[26]

There is no question that banking has changed, and that these changes are very significant.[27] Figure 4.11 conveys a sense of the magnitudes of these changes. Issuance of asset-backed securities, excluding mortgage-backed securities, has exceeded the issuance of corporate debt in the United States in the past few years. Broadly, originate-to-distribute refers to this change. Twenty-five years ago, there were no asset-backed securities. In addition, banks sell loans. The syndicated loan market was $1.5 trillion in 2005 for nonfinancial corporations. Secondary loan trading in 2005 had a market volume of $176.3 billion. See Drucker and Puri (2007). Clearly, the old model of the bank, in which loans were held to maturity, does not exist as it used to.

The issue is whether these changes somehow explain the panic. Originate-to-distribute seems to refer to the general trend in banking that has been going on for at least 20 years, possibly starting with the junk bond market becoming a major competitor for bank loans.[28] In response to this and other competition, banks began selling loans and securitizing assets.[29] The originate-to-distribute view proposes nothing specific to explain why problems arose

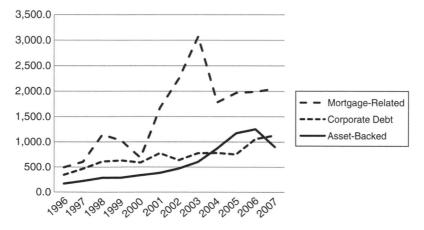

FIGURE 4.11   Issuance in U.S. Capital Markets ($Billion). Source: Securities Industry and Financial Markets Association.

with the securitization of subprime mortgages, as opposed to any other category of assets that are securitized. In fact, in securitization generally, there does not seem to have been the same problems as with subprime mortgages. The "severe incentive problems" and "principal-agent problems" would seem to be present in all securitizations.

Were Incentives Aligned?

The originate-to-distribute view argues that the risks of loans were passed along to investors, leaving the originators with no risk. But this can be immediately rejected. Significant losses have been suffered by many up and down the subprime chain. Originators, securitization structurers and underwriters—firms and individuals—have suffered. The subprime originators/underwriters that went bankrupt include Option One, Ameriquest, New Century, and the likes of Citibank, UBS, and Merrill Lynch, with billions of writedowns.[30] The following "agents" were fired: Chuck Prince, Ken Thompson, Marcel Ospel, James Cayne, Huw Jenkins, Stanley O'Neal, and a host of others. Thousands of other employees up and down the chain have lost their jobs. If these firms and individuals took excessive risk, they have realized losses. The fact that there have been losses on subprime mortgages is not ipso facto evidence of a lack of incentives.

How are interests aligned in securitization? There is direct exposure to the originated risk, and there are implicit contracts making the arrangements incentive-compatible. I very briefly review these points.

Originators of subprime mortgages face a number of direct risks. The mortgages must be warehoused by the originator prior to securitization. In other words, loans must be held before they are securitized. See Gordon (2008). When the pool of mortgages is large enough, they are transferred to the underwriter, who will assemble the securitization. The underwriters of the securitizations then must warehouse the RMBS tranches. In later stages, securitization tranches will be warehoused by the dealer banks, which underwrite the CDOs.

In 2006 and early 2007, some banks kept the most senior portions of CDOs on their balance sheets. Along this chain, these firms have significant risks in warehousing the different securities. Much of the writedowns by banks came from such warehousing. For example, the UBS "Shareholder Report on UBS's Write-Downs," April 18, 2008:

> UBS acquired its exposure to CDO Warehouse positions through its CDO origination and underwriting business. In the initial stage of a CDO

securitization, the desk would typically enter into an agreement with a collateral manager. UBS sourced residential mortgage backed securities ("RMBS") and other securities on behalf of the manager. These positions were held in a CDO Warehouse in anticipation of securitization into CDOs. Generally, while in the Warehouse, these positions would be on UBS's books with exposure to market risk. Upon completion of the Warehouse, the securities were transferred to a CDO special-purpose vehicle, and structured into tranches.... The CDO Warehouse was a significant contributor to Value at Risk ("VaR") and Stress limits applicable to this business relative to other parts of the CDO securitization process and warehoused collateral was identified as one of the main sources of market risk in reviews by IB Market Risk Control ("MRC") conducted in Q4 2005 and again in Q3 2006. (p. 13)

Similarly, the CFO of Bear Stearns, during the Earnings Conference Call of December 20, 2007: "...of the $1.9 billion in writedowns...about $1 billion of that came from the writedowns of CDOs and the unwinding of the CDO warehouse."

Warehousing is not the only risk. Originators of mortgages retain significant interests in the mortgages they originate due to servicing rights and retained interests. Mortgage servicing rights are valuable, and retained interests are also significant. When loans are sold in the secondary market, the mortgage servicing rights that are created are typically not sold.[31] An example of the value of mortgage servicing rights is provided by Countrywide. Countrywide Form 10-K, December 31, 2007:

When we sell or securitize mortgage loans, we generally retain the rights to service these loans. In servicing mortgage loans, we collect and remit loan payments, respond to customer inquiries, account for principal and interest, hold custodial (impound) funds for payment of property taxes and insurance premiums, counsel delinquent mortgagors and supervise foreclosures and property dispositions. We receive servicing fees and other remuneration in return for performing these functions. (p. 7)

In October 2007, Countrywide recorded writedowns of $830.9 million in the value of mortgage servicing rights. As of March 31, 2008, Countrywide had an estimated value of mortgage servicing rights of $17 billion and total assets of $199 billion, about 9% of total assets (see SEC Form 10-K, April 29, 2008).

More formally, Kohlbeck and Warfield (2002) calculate the present value of mortgage servicing rights for a sample of banks and show its relation to abnormal earnings. They find that the present value of mortgage servicing rights as a percentage of equity ranges from 2.7% to 3.5%.

Other financial interests are often retained, as well, including, for example, interest-only securities, principal-only securities, and residual securities. These retained financial interests are also significant. Missal (2008): "New Century's residual interests were large assets of the Company (worth hundreds of millions of dollars)....." (p. 234). The overcollateralization gives the sponsor a Credit Enhancement Security—a claim on the OC. These could be securitized in NIMs. Then the sponsor of the NIMs would retain a residual interest in the NIMs trust, which would remain on the balance sheet.

Perhaps a more detailed example can summarize this point. The information and table that follow are from page 35 of the 2007 Merrill Lynch annual report:

> Residuals: We retain and purchase mortgage residual interests which represent the subordinated classes and equity/first-loss tranche from our residential mortgage-backed securitization activity. We have retained residuals from the securitizations of third-party whole loans we have purchased as well as from our First Franklin loan originations.....
>
> Residential mortgage-backed securities ("RMBS"): We retain and purchase securities from the securitizations of loans, including sub-prime residential mortgages...
>
> Warehouse lending: Warehouse loans represent collateralized revolving loan facilities to originators of financial assets, such as sub-prime residential mortgages. These mortgages typically serve as collateral for the facility...
>
> The following table provides a summary of our residential mortgage-related net exposures and losses, excluding net exposures to residential mortgage-backed securities held in our U.S. banks for investment purposes....

Note the sizes of "Warehouse Lending," "Residuals," and "Mortgage Servicing Rights." (The numbers are in millions of dollars.) The losses are clearly significant.[32]

All along the chain, from originators to underwriters, there are very significant risks involved in creating and maintaining securitized products.

There are also implicit contractual arrangements in securitization, between the investors in the securitized assets—buyers of tranches—and the sponsors of the deals.[33] Gorton and Souleles (2007) argue that there is an implicit contract between the sponsor and investors in the liabilities of the special-purpose vehicles used for securitization. The implicit contract exists precisely to address the agency problems that could arise when assets are sold; essentially, the sponsor of the securitization guarantees it.

TABLE 4.4 Residential Mortgage-Related Net Exposures and Losses ($ millions)

	Net Exposure as of Dec. 29, 2007	Net Losses for the Year ended Dec. 28, 2007
U.S. Subprime		
Warehouse Lending	$137	$(31)
Whole Loans	994	(1,243)
Residuals	855	(1,582)
Residential MBS	723	(332)
Total U.S. Subprime	2,709	$(3,188)
U.S. Alt-A	2,687	(542)
U.S. Prime	28,189	N/A
Non-U.S.	9,582	(465)
Mortgage Servicing Rights	389	N/A
Total	$43,556	$(4,195)

Source: Merrill Lynch Annual Report, 2007, p. 357.

How do we know that such implicit contracts exist? Gorton and Souleles, empirically analyzing credit card securitizations, argue that this implicit contract is understood by investors and provide evidence that it is priced. Implicit contractual arrangements have also been argued to explain loan sales. Loan sales are not supposed to happen according to the traditional theories of banking, but following the advent of the junk bond market, banks began to sell loans. Although not required to retain part of the loan, banks in fact do retain pieces, more so for riskier borrowers. Also, loan covenants are tighter for riskier borrowers, whose loans are sold. See, for example, Gorton and Pennacchi (1995, 1989), Calomiris and Mason (2004), Drucker and Puri (2007), and Chen, Liu and Ryan (2007). Jiangli and Pritsker (2008) "find that banks use mortgage securitization to reduce insolvency risk."

With respect to subprime specifically, the implicit contractual arrangement between SIV sponsors and investors led sponsoring banks to take the off-balance-sheet SIVs back onto their balance sheets, when there was no explicit obligation to do so, consistent with the arguments of Gorton and Souleles (2007). See Appendix B.

Did Underwriting Standards Decline?

The evidence cited for the alleged originate-to-distribute agency problems is the deterioration of the 2006 and early 2007 subprime mortgages. Subprime performance during the period 2001–2005 was good by historical (subprime) standards. While delinquency and foreclosure rates for subprime mortgages were higher than for prime mortgages, their experience was as expected, i.e., delinquencies and foreclosures rose during the recession of the early 2000s. But the 2006 vintage of subprime mortgages is much worse.

The extreme deterioration of the 2006 vintage has been attributed to a decline in underwriting standards and to outright fraud. For example, the President's Working Group on Financial Markets (March, 2008) concluded that, "The turmoil in financial markets was triggered by *a dramatic weakening of underwriting standards for U.S. subprime mortgages, beginning* in late 2004, and extending into early 2007" (p. 1; emphasis in original). Or, another example, according to Fitch (2007):

> Fitch attributes a significant portion of this [2006] early default performance to the rapid growth of high-risk "affordability" features in subprime mortgages... In addition to the inherent risk of these products, evidence is mounting that in many instances these risks were not controlled through sound underwriting practices. Moreover, in the absence of effective underwriting, products such as "no money down" and "stated income" mortgages appear to have become vehicles for misrepresentation or fraud... (p. 1)

The evidence often cited is statistics like those in table 4.5, which shows the time profile of some subprime mortgage characteristics. Looking separately at these characteristics, it seems that standards were lowered. Note, for example, the increase in the percentage of mortgages with less than full documentation. But such statements are problematic because there are many dimensions to borrower risk, and there are tradeoffs between them. For a given aggregation of risk, there is a tradeoff between risk and return. So it seems difficult to define a "decline in lending standards."

Bhardwaj and Sengupta (2008B) attempt to address the multidimensional nature of lending standards. Before getting to econometric tests, however, they point out the difficulties of casual observation. For example, "borrowers with lower documentation have on average higher FICO scores" (p. 12) Bhardwaj

TABLE 4.5 Underwriting Standards for Subprime Mortgages

	ARM Share	Interest Only Share	Low/No Doc Share	Debt-to-Income Ratio	Average Loan-to-Value Ratio
2001	73.%	0.0%	28.5%	39.7	84.0
2002	80.0%	2.3%	38.6%	40.1	84.4
2003	80.1%	8.6%	42.8%	40.5	86.1
2004	89.4%	27.2%	45.2%	41.2	84.7
2005	93.3%	37.8%	50.7%	41.8	83.2
2006	91.3%	22.8%	50.8%	42.4	83.4

Source: Freddie Mac; see Joint Economic Committee (October 2007).

and Sengupta (2008b). Or, "For a given vintage, mortgages with a smaller LTV have a lower FICO score on average" (p. 14). FICO scores trend gradually up over the period 1998–2006 (see Bhardwaj and Sengupta (2008b)). Their final conclusion is: "Noticeably, there is little to suggest anything particularly remarkable about underwriting standards for mortgages of 2005–2007 vintages…" (p. 16).

So what does explain the performance of the post-2005 vintage subprime mortgages? House price appreciation (HPA) or, more specifically, depreciation, is the biggest single factor explaining defaults. For example, according to UBS: "…HPA alone is able to explain ~60% of the credit performance variance across states. Combined with combined LTV and percentage Full Doc, the three variables account for ~74% of credit performance variance. Also, interestingly, FICO score is statistically insignificant in interpreting the credit performance." See UBS, "Mortgage Strategist," Nov. 13, 2007, p. 33. The conclusion that HPA is the most important factor explaining default and loan severity is confirmed with econometric evidence. For example, according to Bharwaj and Sengupta (2007a):

> Using a competing risk hazard model, we show that an appreciation in house price had a positive and significant effect on the likelihood of prepayment but a negative and significant effect on the likelihood of default. In a regime of rising house prices, a financially distressed borrower could avoid default by prepaying the loan (either through a refinance or a property sale). Conversely, a sudden reversal in prices increased default in this market because it made this prepayment exit option cost-prohibitive.

The conclusion that HPA is the most important factor explaining default and loan severity is evidenced by Demyanyk and Van Hemert (2007).

If underwriting standards were declining, then "first-payment default" mortgages would increase. These are mortgages where the borrower defaults right away, missing the very first monthly payments. But most securitization contracts stipulate that if there is an early payment default, or some other defect in the mortgage (e.g., incorrect documentation), then the mortgage originator must repurchase the mortgage from the special-purpose vehicle. Because it is a defective mortgage, its value declines, so the originator incurs a realized loss; it has repurchased a loan for the same amount at which it was sold to the special-purpose vehicle, but has received back a mortgage worth less. It is difficult to see how a dramatic decline in underwriting would not result in a large number of first-payment defaults that the originators would have to absorb. Since the originators would, in fact, absorb these mortgages, they have no incentive to make them in the first place.

Finally, it is worth noting that evidence of a decline in lending standards is only a piece of the puzzle. The argument must be that, if this did occur, it was not reflected in the structure of the RMBS bonds. Somehow, the structurers would have to have been fooled into not increasing the credit enhancement to reflect this decline. This has never been systematically examined.

Summary

Securitization is an efficient, incentive-compatible response to bankruptcy costs and capital requirements. Although there are only a few studies, the evidence to date is consistent with the experience of a quarter century of securitization working very well. The assertions of the originate-to-distribute view simply are not consistent with what we know.

The idea that there is a moral hazard due to the alleged ability of originators to sell loans without fear of recourse, and with no residual risk, also assumes that the buyers of these loans are irrational. That may be, but the irrationality, it turns out, had to do with the belief that house prices would not fall.

Concluding Remarks

It might very properly be urged that the present is too early a date for us to draw wise conclusions from the lessons of the recent financial crisis. Indeed, one can hardly speak of it, as I did just now, as the recent crisis. It is the present crisis.... Domestic exchanges are still seriously disorganized. After the most heroic measures for relief, taken by the Treasury and by banks generally, we continue to be surrounded by abnormal conditions, and the day is somewhere in the future when we can look back with anything like academic interests and comment with intelligence on the true lessons which have been taught by this extraordinary financial event. (Frank Vanderlip, vice president, National City Bank, New York, speaking of the Panic of 1907; see Vanderlip, 1908, p. 2)[34]

When I read the numberless projects for our financial well being that fill the newspapers, our book shelves, and the Congressional Record, I ask myself on what do these men base their plans, on observation or actual contact and familiarity with the subject they talk about, and I must conclude that much of it is spun out of their inner consciences. (William Nash, 1908, p. 61, speaking of the Panic of 1907)

The Panic of 1907 led to the founding of the Federal Reserve System. In 1908, Congress passed the Aldrich-Vreeland Act, which, among other things, created the National Monetary Commission. This commission published a voluminous report that served as the major impetus for the founding of the Fed. (See Weston, 1922, for a review.) The Federal Reserve Act passed in December 1913. But it was then followed by a panic in 1914. (See Sprague, 1915 and Silber, 2007b). And, of course, the Great Depression came later, followed by large institutional changes, with the advent of deposit insurance being foremost among them.

A century after the Panic of 1907, we again contemplate the causes of a panic. Identifying the causes of the Panic of 2007 will in large part determine the policy response to the crisis. I have argued that the subprime crisis was caused by information problems related to declining house prices, which prevent subprime mortgages from being refinanced. The design of subprime mortgages is unique in that they are linked to house price appreciation. The securitization of subprime mortgages is also unique. Because subprime mortgages are financed through a chain of securities and structures, investors could not easily determine the location and extent of the risk. Information was lost. The house price declines led to a fear of losses that could not be measured because the subprime risk had been spread around the globe opaquely. The available information was on the side of the market that produced the chain of structures; outside investors know much less. The problem is that the magnitude of the structures, and their impenetrability by outsiders, was not completely understood; it was not common knowledge. The introduction of the ABX indices created a set of market prices that aggregated and revealed that subprime-related securities were worth a lot less than had been thought. The ability to short subprime risk may have burst the bubble and, in any case, resulted in the market crowding on the short side to hedge, driving ABX prices very low. The panic was then on.

There is much work to be done to understand the ongoing panic, to formally test my (sometimes admittedly vague) conjectures, and it will be surely be some time before researchers can sort through the events. As Mr. Vanderlip wrote, the lessons to be learned are likely only going to be known when there is more distance from the events. But, since panics are rare, it may be that we never have the ability to formally test in the way that is acceptable to academic economists. The scholars who studied panics before us, many of whom I have quoted, described the events with narratives. Perhaps that is the best we can do.

I have tried to convey the richness of the information and agency setting in which the crisis is taking place. During a panic, securities that used to be information insensitive become uncertain in price. Their internal workings, where the complexity is revealed, need to be examined. At this point, a few tentative conclusions can be drawn.

- Subprime mortgages were a financial innovation designed to be profitable by serving a constituency that had previously not had access to mortgage financing and hence could not own homes. This point is very important because the future regulatory response to the crisis will have implications for whether this constituency's needs will be met in the future or not. The reregulation of the financial system is intertwined with national housing policy, and this should be recognized. The current situation with Fannie Mae and Freddie Mac also stresses this point.

- The crisis was caused by house prices not rising and then falling. The introduction of the ABX index revealed that the values of subprime bonds (of the 2006 and 2007 vintage) were falling rapidly in value. But it was not possible to know where the risk resided, and without this information, market participants rationally worried about the solvency of their counterparties. This led to a general freeze of intrabank markets, writedowns, and a spiral downward of the prices of structured products as banks were forced to dump assets.

- The crisis illustrates and emphasizes the extent to which the traditional banking system is no longer as central to the savings-investment process as it once was. The capital markets, through the sale of intermediary-originated loans via securitization and the distribution of risk through derivatives, highlight the centrality of capital markets and illustrate the flexibility of structured products. This evolution has been going on for at least 25 years and should be viewed favorably.

- Securitization generally is not the problem currently. It is not the cause of the crisis. Securitization is an efficient form of financing, and there is no evidence that there is a systematic agency problem in its functioning. Rather, the particular form of the design of subprime mortgages is at root the problem. It was highly sensitive to house prices, and this sensitivity was passed through to a variety of other financial structures.

- Structured products and derivatives allow for the distribution of risks globally in a way which is opaque. In principle, this is not different than in, say, the 19th-century U.S. banking system, in which the particular loans that banks held were also opaque. Opaqueness and innovation probably go together, and there is a danger that innovation will be squelched if we do not recognize that there is likely a tradeoff here. The lesson, perhaps, is that we should be looking at the sectors that are very opaque, such as the hedge fund world, more closely.

- At the heart of many academic analyses of the functioning of capital markets and crises is the notion of "collateralizable" wealth, roughly, the amount of verifiably riskless assets or bonds that an economic agent has available to borrow against. The current crisis shows that in the case of financial collateral, it can be the case that portfolios thought to be safe, collateralizable wealth in all states of the world *ex ante*, turn out not to be collateralizable in the crisis. In my nomenclature, they become information sensitive. Even agency bonds, for example, were not acceptable as collateral in the repo market in August 2007.

- The crisis also illustrates that "states of the world" may best be viewed as endogenous. The chain of securities and structures created a "state of the world" that many agents did not recognize as existing *ex ante*. So the notion of "incomplete markets" may be more complicated than we generally recognize.

- Accounting is widely recognized as having a great deal of difficulty measuring firm value in a world of derivatives. The crisis also reveals that marking-to-market, based on the notion of "efficient markets," is flawed and needs to be rethought. At some point, double-entry bookkeeping as a paradigm will be recognized as inappropriate for financial firms, which are already moving aggressively to risk management as a replacement. Risk management, of course, is not perfect by any means, but looking at firms' behavior, the revealed preference of managements is that this is a more informative way of looking at firms.

- As Merton Miller (1986) pointed out over 20 years ago, financial innovation is largely driven by regulation and taxes. Regulation means constraints and costs. Imposing capital requirements on banks, for example, that are not consistent with their competitive environment accelerates disintermediation (see Gorton and Winton, 2000). Imposing costs, such as Sarbanes-Oxley, may have led to a competitive disadvantage for U.S. capital markets. See, for example, Zingales (2007). Entrepreneurs will take risks in some form, somewhere. In a global environment, one where capital is extremely fluid and risk can be moved quickly with derivatives, it will be difficult for national regulators to constrain entrepreneurs. The trends are already clear. Talent is increasingly moving to the least regulated platform: hedge funds. See, for example, Hester and Burton (June 19, 2008) and Guerrera and Brewster (April 30, 2008).

Postscript (Written October 4, 2008)

Since the above was written, the panic has continued almost out of control, and the economy has noticeably deteriorated. Lending has stopped almost completely. There is no doubt that we are now in a recession. The financial landscape has been completely altered by failures, mergers, and de facto nationalization. The "Emergency Economic Stabilization Act of 2008" has been passed. The logic of the plan seems to be that by buying distressed assets from banks, the uncertainty about the value of the banks will be removed, possibly enticing new investors to recapitalize the banks. The success or failure will depend on the exact details of how this is implemented. If the money allocated to the Troubled Asset Relief Program is used to try to shore up the weakest bank, the government may quickly use up the money allocated by Congress. That is the danger. If the money shores up banks that are stronger, it may be possible to entice lending again.

APPENDIX A: A BRIEF CHRONOLOGY OF THE EVENTS OF THE PANIC OF 2007

Date	Event
Dec. 2006	Ownit Mortgage Solutions files for bankruptcy.
March 13	Mortgage Bankers Association data for the last three months of 2006 shows late or missed payments on mortgages rose to 4.95%, rising to 13.3% in the subprime market. Subprime lender Accredited Home Lenders loses 65% of its value, having lost 28% a day earlier.
April 2	Mortgage originator New Century Financial Corporation files for bankruptcy.
April 18	Ellington Capital Management, a large hedge fund, buys $2.9 billion of nonprime mortgage loans from Fremont General Corp.
May 3	UBS closes its hedge fund Dillon Read Capital Management.
June 10–12	Moody's downgrades the ratings of $5 billion worth of subprime RMBS bonds and places 184 CDO tranches on review for downgrade. S&P places $7.3 billion of 2006 vintage RMBS bonds on negative watch and announces a review of CDO deals exposed to subprime RMBS bonds.
June 20	News reports suggest that two Bear Stearns-managed hedge funds invested in securities backed by subprime mortgage loans are close to being shut down.
June 22	One of the troubled hedge funds is bailed out through an injection of $3.2 billion in loans.

July10   S&P places $7.3 billion worth of 2006 vintage ABS
            backed by residential mortgage loans on negative
            ratings watch and announces a review of CDO deals
            exposed to such collateral; Moody's downgrades
            $5 billion worth of subprime mortgage bonds.

July 11   Moody's places 184 mortgage-backed CDO tranches on
            downgrade review; further reviews and downgrades are
            announced by all major rating agencies in the following
            days.

July 24   U.S. home loan lender Countrywide Financial Corp.
            reports a drop in earnings and warns of difficult
            conditions ahead.

July 26   The NAHB index indicates that new home sales slid by
            6.6% year-on-year in June; D.R. Horton, the largest
            homebuilder in the United States, reports an
            April–June quarter loss.

July 30   Germany's IKB warns of losses related to the fallout in
            the U.S. subprime mortgage market. Its main
            shareholder, Kreditanstalt für Wiederaufbau (KfW),
            assumes its financial obligations from liquidity facilities
            provided to an asset-backed commercial paper (ABCP)
            conduit exposed to subprime loans.

July 31   American Home Mortgage Investment Corp. announces
            its inability to fund lending obligations; Moody's reports
            that the loss expectations feeding into the ratings for
            securitizations backed by Alt-A loans will be adjusted.
            Hedge fund Sowood Capital informs investors it will
            shut down after losing 57% during the month (Sowood
            Alpha Fund). Sowood went from $3 billion to $1.5
            billion in less than four weeks.

August 1   Further losses exposed at IKB lead to a €3.5 billion
            rescue fund being put together by KfW and a group
            of public and private sector banks.

August 3–10 Massive deleveraging causes quantitative hedge funds
            to suffer losses.

August 6   American Home Mortgage Investment Corp. files for
            Chapter 11 bankruptcy, leading to a term extension
            on outstanding ABCP by one of its funding
            conduits.

August 9   BNP Paribas freezes redemptions for three investment
                funds, citing an inability to appropriately value them
                in the current market environment; the ECB injects
                €95 billion of liquidity into the interbank market;
                other central banks take similar steps.

August 13   Coventree, the largest nonbank sponsor of Canada's
                asset-backed commercial paper market, announces
                that it is unable to place any asset-backed
                commercial paper on behalf of its conduits, including
                Aurora, Comet, Gemini, Planet, Rocket, Slate, SAT,
                and SIT II.

August 16   Countrywide draws its entire $11.5 billion credit line.

August 17   The Federal Reserve Open Market Committee issues a
                statement observing that the downside risks to
                growth have increased appreciably; the Federal
                Reserve Board approves a 50-basis-point reduction in
                the discount rate and announces that term financing
                will be provided for up to 30 days.

August 17   Run on Countrywide: "Anxious customers jammed the
                phone lines and website of Countrywide Bank and
                crowded its branch offices to pull out their savings
                because of concerns about the financial problems of
                the mortgage lender that owns the bank" *Los Angeles
                Times,* August 17, 2007.

August 23   Countrywide gets $2 billion cash injection from
                Bank of America.

September 4   Overnight LIBOR reaches 6.7975%, the highest level
                since the LTCM crisis. Bank of China reveals
                $9 billion in subprime losses.

September 5   Cheyne Finance SIV goes into receivership, the first
                SIV to do so.

September 9   Run on Northern Rock; see Telegraph.co.uk,
                September 14, 2007. See http//www.telegraph.co.
                uk/finance/markets/2815684/Northern-
                Rock-shares-plunge-on-lending-crisis.html.

September 15   There is a run on British bank Northern Rock, the first
                in 150 years; £1 billion, amounting to 4–5% of retail
                deposits, are withdrawn (see BBC News
                http//news.bbc.co.uk/2/hi/business/
                6996136.stm).

September 18– November	Repeated large writedowns by major financial firms, leading to several high-profile CEOs to leave their positions.
October 15	Citigroup writes down additional $5.9 billion.
October 18	Rhinebridge Plc, the IKB SIV, suffers a "mandatory acceleration event" after IKB determines that the SIV may be unable to repay its debt.
November 13	Bank of America, Legg Mason, SEI Investments, and SunTrust Banks step in to prop up their money market funds against possible losses to debt issued by SIVs.
November 26	HSBC takes $41 billion in SIV assets onto its balance sheet.
November 27	Citigroup agrees to sell shares worth $7.5 billion to an investment fund owned by Abu Dhabi.
November 29	E-Trade, the online brokerage that was teetering at the edge of the subprime mortgage abyss, received a $2.55 billion bailout package led by Citadel Investment Group, a large hedge fund.
December 3	West LB and HSH Nordbank bail out $15 billion of their SIVs.
December 10	UBS announces a further $10 billion writedown. Bank of America announces it is shutting a $12 billion money market mutual fund after losses on subprime-related instruments, including investments in SIVs.
December 15	Citibank says it will take its seven SIVs back onto its balance sheet, $49 billion.
December 19	Morgan Stanley writes off $9.4 billion. ACA, a financial guarantor rated A, is downgraded to CCC by S&P, triggering collateral calls from its counterparties.
January 3	Peloton Partners, a $3 billion hedge fund, forced to liquidate.
January 15	Citigroup announces a fourth-quarter loss, partly due to $18 billion of additional writedowns on mortgage-related exposure.
February 27	Hedge fund Sailfish Capital Partners announces it is liquidating. Sailfish had managed $1.9 billion in the previous year.

March 3	Thornburg Mortgage Asset Corp. announces that it could not meet margin calls.
March 7–16	Fed announces an increase of $40 billion in the size of its new Term Auction Facility and then expands its securities lending activities through a $200 billion Term Securities Lending Facility that lends treasuries against a range of eligible assets.
March 14	Failure to roll repos causes a liquidity crisis at Bear Stearns. Bear Stearns announces $30 billion in funding provided by J.P. Morgan and backstopped by the government.
March 17	JPMorgan announces purchase of Bear Stearns for $2 a share, a little more than $236 million.
April 2	New Century files for bankruptcy.
June 5	MBIA and Ambac lose their triple-A ratings from S&P.
June 9	Lehman says it expects to lose $2.8 billion in the quarter ending May 31.
June 30	Legg Mason announces another $240 million in capital contributions to support three money market funds.
July 11	IndyMac Bank, a large mortgage lender, is seized by federal regulators. The cost to the Federal Deposit Insurance Corporation is estimated to be between $4 billion and $8 billion, potentially a loss of 10% of the FDIC's insurance fund for banks. Freddie Mac and Fannie Mae lost half their value in the week ending July 11. Moody's and S&P affirm that the United States would retain its AAA rating even if forced to rescue Fannie Mae and Freddie Mac.
July 14	Federal Reserve Board grants authority to the New York Fed to lend to Fannie Mae and Freddie Mac, should the need arise.

Sources: Various, including Fender and Hördahl (2007), BIS Annual Report 2007–2008, Bloomberg; *Financial Times; The Wall Street Journal;* BBC (http://news.bbc.co.uk/2/hi/business/7096845.stm), company press releases.

APPENDIX B

TABLE 4.6 Main SIV Outcomes

SIV	Manager/adviser	Initial rating date	Senior debt (mil. $)*	Current Status	Source
Beta Finance Corp.	Citibank International PLC	Sept. 8, 1989	20,175.95	Back on Balance Sheet	Citi Press Release 12/13/07
Sigma Finance Corp.	Gordian Knot Ltd.	Feb. 2, 1995	52,641.87	Must refinance $20 bil. by Sept.; S&P and Moody's downgrade	Bloomberg 4/8/08
Orion Finance Corp.	Eiger Capital Management	May 31, 1996	2,298.43	Defaulted	Reuters 1/16/08
Centauri Corp.	Citibank International PLC	Sept. 9, 1996	21,838.84	Back on Balance Sheet	Citi Press Release 12/13/07
Dorada Corp.	Citibank International PLC	Sept. 17, 1998	12,484.15	Back on Balance Sheet	Citi Press Release 12/13/07
K2 Corp.	Dresdner Kleinwort	Feb. 1, 1999	29,056.47	Back on Balance Sheet	Reuters 2/21/08
Links Finance Corp.	Bank of Montreal	June 18, 1999	22,301.10	Back on Balance Sheet	SEC 6-K 2/20/08
Five Finance Corp.	Citibank International PLC	Nov. 15, 1999	12,843.06	Back on Balance Sheet	Citi Press Release 12/13/07
Abacas Investments Ltd.	N.S.M. Capital Management/ Emirates Bank	Dec. 8, 1999	1,007.95	S&P affirms ratings	Reuters 6/17/08
Parkland Finance Corp.	Bank of Montreal	Sept. 7, 2001	3,414.43	Back on Balance Sheet	SEC 6-K 2/20/08
Harrier Finance Funding Ltd.	WestLB	Jan. 11, 2002	12,343.37	Back on Balance Sheet	Reuters 6/17/08
White Pine Corp. Ltd. (merged with Whistlejacket Capital Ltd.)	Standard Chartered Bank	Feb. 4, 2002	7,854.63	See below under Whistlejacket	
Victoria Finance Ltd.	Ceres Capital Partners	July 10, 2002	13,243.95	Chapter 11 in April 08	Reuters 6/17/08
Premier Asset Collateralized Entity Ltd.	Societe Generale	July 10, 2002	4,312.70	Moody's threatens downgrade: S&P affirms	Reuters 6/17/08
Whistlejacket Capital Ltd.	Standard Chartered Bank	July 24, 2002	8,844.63	Insolvent Feb 15, 08	Reuters 6/17/08
Tango Finance Corp.	Rabobank International	Nov. 26, 2002	14,039.75	Back on Balance Sheet	Reuters 6/17/08
Sedna Finance Corp.	Citibank International PLC	June 22, 2004	14,415.28	Back on Balance Sheet	Citi Press Release 12/13/07
Cullinan Finance Ltd.	HSBC Bank PLC	July 18, 2005	35,142.00	Back on Balance Sheet	Reuters 6/17/08

(continued)

TABLE 4.6 Continued

SIV	Manager/adviser	Initial rating date	Senior debt (mil. $)*	Current Status	Source
Cheyne Finance PLC	Cheyne Capital Management Ltd.	Aug. 3, 2005	9,726.18	Goldman leads restructuring	Reuters 6/17/08
Eaton Vance Variable Leveraged Fund	Eaton Vance	Sept. 23 2005	542.76	Moody's cuts ratings	Reuters 6/17/08
Carrera Capital Finance Ltd.	HSH Nordbank	June 30. 2006	4,283.48	Restructured	Reuters 6/17/08
Kestrel Funding PLC	WestLB/Brightwater Capital	Aug. 2, 2006	3,315.86	Back on Balance Sheet	Reuters 6/17/08
Zela Finance Corp.	Citibank International PLC	Sept. 18, 2006	4,188.70	Back on Balance Sheet	Citi Press Release 12/13/07
Cortland Capital Ltd.	IXIS/Ontario Teachers	Nov. 1, 2006	1,344.19	S&P affirmed ratings in Feb.; now on negative watch	Reuters 6/17/08
Vetra Finance Corp.	Citibank International PLC	Nov. 15, 2006	2,616.94	Back on Balance Sheet	Citi Press Release 12/13/07
Hudson-Thames Capital Ltd.	MBIA	Dec. 5, 2006	1,767.33	Ceased Operations Dec. 07	Reuters 6/17/08
Nightingale Finance Ltd.	Banque AIG	March 15, 2007	2,330.23	Back on Balance Sheet	Reuters 6/17/08
Axon Financial Funding Ltd.	Axon Asset Management Inc.	March 30, 2007	11,193.76	S&P cuts rating to default	Reuters 6/17/08
Rhinebridge PLC	IKB Credit Asset Management GmbH	April 13, 2007	2,199.63	Defaulted Oct. 07	Reuters 6/17/08
Asscher Finance Ltd.	HSBC Bank PLC	May 11, 2007	7,330.00	Back on Balance Sheet	Reuters 6/17/08
Total			$274,896.99		

* As of July 13, 2007, S&P.

5

Bank Regulation When "Banks" and "Banking" Are Not the Same

IN ALMOST ALL DEVELOPED COUNTRIES, COMPETITION FOR BANKS HAS come from the opening of debt markets and markets for mutual funds, and also from entry by foreign banks and nonbanks. A few examples will suffice to recall this well-known scenario to mind. In Japan, in 1975, 90% of the corporate debt of public companies was bank debt, but by 1992 it was less than 50% (Hoshi et al., 1993). In the case of Germany, the Deutsche Bundesbank (1987) reported that, "In the last few years, financing through securities has increasingly taken the place of conventional bank credit." Later, the Bundesbank (1992) reported that over the period 1978–1989, the stock of liabilities of large corporations to banks decreased from 13.7 to 7.6 as a percentage of total assets. In the United States, the bank share of short-term (nonfinancial) corporate debt fell from about 70% in the late 1970s to less than 60% by the late 1980s. Consistent with direct competition from the junk bond market, large U.S. banks' stocks showed an abnormally positive return upon announcement of the demise of Drexel Burnham Lambert (see Benveniste et al., 1993). In addition to competition from debt markets, foreign banks have become important in many countries' domestic banking markets. For example, foreign banks held 16.8% of U.S. banking assets in 1982, but by 1989 this had reached 26%. Japan's percentage share of U.S. domestic banking assets was 15% in 1989, up from 6.4% in 1982. There is also competition from nonbanks. Nonbank subsidiaries of General Electric, Westinghouse, IBM, and Weyerhaeuser, together with Heller and Transamerica, accounted for $58 billion of commercial loans in 1987. Ten large U.S. insurance companies accounted for $119 billion worth of commercial loans in 1987.[1]

Originally published 1994

Banks around the world have responded to these trends by engaging in new activities. For example, off-balance-sheet products, such as foreign-exchange forward contracts and options, interest-rate derivatives, such as swaps, swaptions, and captions, and currency trading are increasingly important bank activities. These activities, which have come under intense scrutiny because of possible risks to the world's banking systems, are not unique to banks.[2] They are often undertaken by nonbanks, sometimes the same firms that are now engaging in corporate lending. This raises the important question of whether the new activities are "banking," and if so, then which firms are "banks."

These trends, of nonbanks entering corporate lending, of the replacement of commercial loans with traded bonds, and of banks undertaking activities which are not necessarily "banking," clearly raise questions for bank regulators. In the past, "banks" were firms which engaged in "banking," namely, they issued demand deposits to finance loans (and did little else). Banks have been regulated because these activities, historically, led to banking panics. But the overlap between the activities which were the source of public policy concern and the set of firms known as "banks" is less clear today. One point of this article is to identify some of the difficulties that arise for bank regulation when it is not clear which firms are banks and which are not.[3] In addition, it is not clear whether many of the new activities that banks engage in are "banking" activities in the sense that they have important synergies with deposit taking and corporate lending; are the new activities cause for public policy concern?

Another point of this article concerns the proper conceptual framework for thinking about these issues. I argue that bank regulation is fundamentally based on creating incentives for banks to limit risk taking. In the past, this incentive was based on the value created for banks by limitations on entry into banking. Restricted entry, whether formal or informal, creates value to being deemed a "bank" by the government. This value, called "charter value," referring to the bank charter required from the government, is part of bank capital because it is a title to future monopoly profits. But it is lost if the bank fails. Thus, charter value creates an incentive for bank owners to avoid risk which would jeopardize their charter. In this way, charter value helps align the banks' private propensities for risk taking with the social goal of a stable banking system.

Entry into banking by competitors must change the way banks are regulated because bank regulation depends on restricting entry into the banking industry. Entry by competitors reduces charter value, since banks no longer have a monopoly on an important source of firm finance. Entrants underprice loans or debt in order to capture market share in financing corporations. Incumbent banks must then lower the interest rates they charge on loans, resulting in reduced profitability. But there are two further effects. First, in attempts to maintain profitability, banks enter new activities which are not necessarily a source of public policy concern per se, but become entwined with traditional banking activities and, hence, a source of concern. Second, and most important, with a less valuable charter, banks will engage in riskier activities. Without the incentive effects of a valuable charter, the level of bank risk taking should increase.

Bank regulators cannot easily respond to these recent changes by raising new entry barriers because the traditional activities of "banking," the activities which motivate bank regulation to start with, are not contained within any clearly delineated set of firms which can be called 'banks.' Without limited entry into banking, restrictions, such as capital requirements, will not be acceptable to market participants who must supply the capital to banks. After all, non-banks can engage in most of the same activities as banks and avoid the costs associated with regulatory restrictions. Consequently, the threat of exit from the regulated banking sector limits the ability of regulators to threaten banks.

If it is not clear what firms are "banks," then it is not "banks" which will be regulated, but certain specified "banking" activities, namely, any activity that "banks" engage in (since there is the further problem of trying to decide what is "banking"). From this point of view, regulation inevitably will be based on a universal banking model, since many nonbanks engage in the same activities as banks and so will also be regulated. Thus, there is a tendency for the regulatory framework to expand by creating an ever-increasing set of rules, regulations, and "fire walls" which rely on regulators for enforcement rather than on the creation of incentives for limiting risk taking. Limiting risk taking by creating incentives for banks to limit risk, via charter-value creation, is very different from attempting to limit risk taking more directly. With a high charter value, regulators rely on the understanding of the banks themselves to limit risk in, say, the derivatives business. With low charter value, limiting risk taking relies on training bank examiners to understand the derivatives business so that they can try to limit risk by enforcing strict rules in a world where banks have an incentive to take on more risk (since charter value is low).

It seems clear that bank regulation needs to be reconsidered. The important issues concern the definition of "banking" and "banks." In this article, I discuss these issues in more detail. In the next section, the historic rationale for bank regulation is reviewed and the basis of bank regulation, creating charter value through limiting entry, is discussed. Charter values decline when there is entry by nonbank competitors and by foreign banks. I then briefly provide some new evidence that the loss of market share by U.S. banks in financing

U.S. corporations is due to underpricing by competitors. Because of the costs
of setting up a bank relationship, underpricing by entrants reduces the profitability of the share of the corporate lending market that banks do not lose. Next,
I discuss the implications of these changes for bank regulation.

The Historical Bank Regulatory Framework

Banks are regulated because of the social costs of banking panics. In this section, I briefly review the origins of bank regulation. This discussion is important
because subsequently it will be necessary to evaluate new "banking" activities
in light of the social objective of avoiding costly banking panics.

The Rationale for Bank Regulation

Governments throughout the world regulate banks because the combination of
loans financed by demand deposits has, historically, been a volatile mix, leading
to costly banking panics.[4] If the banking system becomes insolvent, potentially
large costs are borne because the payments system is disrupted, borrowers
become illiquid, and information about borrowers is possibly lost.[5] Banking
system insolvency is caused by a banking panic, an event in which bank depositors en masse demand cash in exchange for their deposits. Banks cannot honor
these demands because markets for bank loans are not sufficiently developed.
Markets for loans do not exist because of the expense of producing information
about the riskiness of borrowers and the incentive problems of inducing banks
to monitor borrowers if the bank has nothing at stake (having sold the loan).[6]
In general, were banks to sell loans in private markets during a panic, it would
be at such discounts that banks would be unable to honor their debts. However,
if banks did not have to honor their debts immediately, then they might be
able to honor them over time, as their loans were repaid. In this sense, there is
a distinction between the market value of the bank when depositors demand
cash and when they do not demand cash.

The combination of lending financed by demand deposits is the source of
the problem of banking panics.[7] The trouble is that lack of information about
the value of bank loan portfolios can cause rational depositors to fear for the
value of their investments in banks, causing them to want to reallocate their
resources by withdrawing from banks based on macroeconomic information
or rumors. Banks which would otherwise be solvent can face withdrawals
because of the possibility that there exist banks which are not solvent. Without

FIGURE 5.1 Hugh McCulloch, First U.S. Comptroller of the Currency. (From *The Romance and Tragedy of Banking, Problems and Incidents of Governmental Supervision of National Banks* by Thomas P. Kane, Published in 1922, Bankers Pub. Co., New York)

information about which banks are insolvent and which are not, depositors may seek to withdraw their funds from all banks. The possible presence of insolvent banks creates an externality for other banks, since risk taking by a single bank can have consequences for the banking system.

Deposit insurance (possibly implicit) has been the (nearly) universal regulatory response to the possibility of banking panics because it eliminates the motivation for depositors to demand cash in exchange for deposits.[8] But it is only the beginning of bank regulation. Deposit insurance subsidizes risk taking, since it allows banks to borrow at the risk-free rate. Of course, if the insurance premium could be properly priced to reflect the risk, then this would not be true. But this obvious fact overlooks the equally obvious fact that if it were possible to price the risk of bank loan portfolios, then banking panics would not be an issue to begin with, because banks could sell their loans. So there is an issue of risk taking when deposit insurance (explicitly or implicitly) exists.

The decision to engage in banking, and the level of risk to accept, are decisions made by private agents, bank equity holders, or bank managers, based on a calculation of the expected benefits of engaging in banking relative to other opportunities. In making these decisions, private agents weigh the costs and benefits, but they do not take account of the external effects on other banks and on the economy due to the possible failure of their own bank. The bank regulator makes a different calculation since the regulator takes into account the social value of a stable banking system. On the one hand, the bank regulator is concerned that the level of risk that is privately chosen by a bank may be higher than socially desirable, in the sense that the likelihood of failure would impose costs on the economy that are best avoided. Thus, because of deposit insurance, one goal of the bank regulator is to limit the level of risk in the banking system. On the other hand, the regulator is also concerned about the size of the banking system. Limiting risk in banks must be consistent with private demands for the provision of banking services. For example, bank regulators are often concerned with the provision of loans to small business, the efficiency of the payments system, the availability of banking services in poor communities, etc. Meeting these perceived needs requires the existence of a banking system of the appropriate size. The two goals are difficult to meet simultaneously. For example, a requirement that banks hold 100% reserves clearly limits the riskiness of banks, but it also eliminates bank loans if loans can only be produced by firms that issue demand deposits.[9]

The bank regulator must balance the two social goals of limiting risk in the banking system while allowing for the production of the desired level of loans and deposits. This can be difficult because, in limiting risk, the regulator cannot force private agents to abide by bank regulations because private agents can always choose not to participate as equity holders in banks. In other words, regulations which make the cost of capital in banking too high will result in a banking system which is too small; regulations which are too lax result in a larger banking system, but possibly one which is too risky.

Limiting Entry: The Basis of Bank Regulation

How can bank regulators affect the risk-taking propensities of banks when deposit insurance exists? Regulators have at their disposal two instruments: restrictions (which are, in effect, taxes) and subsidies. The restrictions include (non-interest-bearing) reserve requirements, capital requirements, limitations on asset holdings and trading activities, prohibition of some kinds of activities, reporting requirements, and so on. The subsidies are in the form of under-priced deposit insurance, (explicit or implicit) limitations on entry into banking, interest-rate ceilings on liabilities, some freedom from bankruptcy constraints (i.e., the ability to continue in business for some time after insolvency), and other benefits of being in a "club" with the central bank (e.g., discount window access).[10]

The effectiveness of both restrictions and subsidies depends on limiting entry into banking. Restrictions on banks, such as capital requirements and the requirement that banks hold non-interest-bearing reserves, are forms of taxa-tion. This is most clear in the case of required non-interest-bearing reserves, since these resources are idle. But capital requirements, to the extent that they are binding, are also costly. These taxes, however, while a distortion from the point of view of the bank, can serve the social function of altering the private incentives of the bank to take risk. This serves the public policy goal of a less risky banking system. Who bears the burden of these taxes? In the past, bank borrowers have borne this burden (see Fama, 1985; James, 1987). In other words, the demand for bank loans has been fairly inelastic. This is because in the past, bank loans did not have good substitutes, so borrowers were willing to bear these costs.[11] Imposing restrictions depends on an inelastic demand for loans or, in other words, limited entry into banking. Without this, banks would exit the regulated banking industry, becoming nonbanks providing the same services, but avoiding the costly restrictions. As substitutes for bank loans developed and as nonbanks entered the industry, these restrictions become increasingly costly; that is, the demand for loans becomes increasingly elastic, at least for large firms (though see Becketti and Morris, 1992 for a discussion of this).

The basic form of subsidizing banks has been to create charter value through restrictions on entry into banking and price ceilings on liabilities. A bank charter is an official or unofficial license to engage in the business of banking; it is an intangible asset which is forfeited if the bank becomes insol-vent (Marcus, 1990).[12] Entry into banking is sometimes formally limited by the requirement that a license be obtained to engage in the activities deemed banking (deposit taking and commercial lending). In addition, informally, large banks are members of a "club" with the central bank. The central bank, serving as lender of last resort and sometimes overseer of the banking system, protects its members not only in the sense of creating a market for loans via the discount window, but also in keeping troublesome competitors at bay and offering special privileges to large banks.

There is a great deal of evidence to suggest that banks rationally calculate the costs and benefits of charters and that regulatory changes (i.e., alterations of the balance of subsidies and taxes) affect bank value and, hence, bank decisions. A natural environment in which to study such questions is the United States, since there are numerous banks and regulatory systems there. For example, during the post-Second World War period in the United States, the percentage of banks in the Federal Reserve System decreased from 49.1% in 1945 to 39.3% in 1976, as banks changed from federal charters to state charters. Gilbert (1977) and Frodin (1980) show that U.S. banks' decisions were based on the costs and benefits of Federal Reserve System membership during this period. A second example is Black et al. (1990), who find that state statutes allowing interstate banking negatively affected the value of money-center banks, which were not allowed to enter these markets, but increased the value of large regional banks, which were allowed to enter other states. These examples concern regulatory arbitrage, that is, the choice of bank regulators based on an assessment of the costs and benefits of the different regulatory systems, but the point is that charter value is rationally assessed.

In the past, charter value created an incentive for banks to limit risk taking owing to their fear of losing the charter through insolvency. By creating charter value for banks, regulations acted to align the private goals of bank owners with the public goal of stability of the banking system. But creating charter value by limiting entry requires defining a set of activities called "banking," which only firms with charters are allowed to engage in. In the past, defining the activities which constituted banking was quite straightforward because private markets had created firms which took deposits and produced loans. It was these firms which were sometimes subject to panic and collapse. In some countries, the definition was further clarified by restricting the firms engaged in these activities from engaging in other activities not related to deposit taking and loan production.

Entry, Price Wars, and Market Share in Banking

Bank regulation depends on limiting entry, but recently banks in many countries have seen competitors enter banking. In some countries, money market mutual funds have become successful competitors for resources that previously became bank deposits. Also, new debt markets have opened, nonbanks have entered corporate lending, and foreign banks compete in domestic markets. A key issue concerns how entry by competitors leads to less profitable and riskier banks. After all, if more efficient providers of lending or investment services enter, banks should shrink or engage in new activities. I focus on entry into commercial lending in the next section. I discuss how corporate lending will be less profitable than before, whether banks lose market share or not. Entry by rivals is only successful if rivals can bid customers away with lower prices (lower interest rates on loans). This process forces banks to lower interest rates. Some evidence of underpricing by rivals is presented below. The point of this section is to provide some sense of the loss to U.S. banks caused by entry by competitors. The example, of foreign bank entry into the U.S. commercial lending market, illustrates the order of magnitude of the charter value decline. If you imagine that the private level of risk taking in 1980 was aligned with the socially acceptable level for the banking system, then the size of the decline in charter value will provide some sense of the current gap.

Bank Relationships and Switching Costs

It is not immediately obvious why entry from nonbank competitors should cause banks to display long periods of weak profitability and high risk. Entry by competitors means that the competitors have been successful in luring bank customers away from banks, but why should this cause banks to become riskier? In this subsection, I discuss this entry process in more detail as a first step to answering this question. The next subsection examines some evidence.

When a firm borrows from a bank, the bank learns information about the borrower which is not publicly available. This is why loans are hard to sell: the bank is better informed about the borrower's credit risk than are prospective loan buyers. The process of information acquisition about borrowers by banks is sometimes described as developing a "bank relationship." The development of a bank relationship means that switching to another bank or funding source is costly for a borrower since the new financing source does not know the information and time and resources are required to learn it. Some evidence on the magnitude of these costs comes from Slovin et al. (1993), who study the effects of the failure of Continental Illinois on borrowers. They found that when Continental failed, there were large negative wealth effects for firms that were Continental borrowers. This suggests that sizeable costs must be borne to establish a relationship with a new bank (or that Continental was systematically underpricing loans).

What happens when there are switching costs and entry occurs in an industry? New entrants seek to capture market share by inducing borrowers to switch from their current bank to another lender (a foreign bank or nonbank) or to a debt market. Borrowers must be induced to switch by the offer of a lower interest rate on the loan or debt. Faced with such new competition, banks must lower the interest rates they charge or face the loss of their customers. Roughly speaking, a price war occurs as banks and entrants lower prices to attract business, hoping to maintain market share. Note that because of the switching cost, it may be rational to maximize market share. Once customers have been lured away to a new entrant, they will not switch back unless there is another round of interest rate reductions. A price war is not profitable for banks; either they retain borrowers, but at lower interest rates, or they lose customers.

Underpricing by Entrants into Banking

Is there evidence of price wars in banking? Some suggestive evidence can be found by examining the interest rates that entrants in the U.S. corporate lending market charged in the 1980s compared to the rate charged by a U.S. bank, holding the risk of the borrower constant. The evidence presented below is restricted to foreign banks entering the U.S. market, but this is only because evidence about nonbank entrants and the effects of debt markets is not available.

The empirical procedure is, briefly, as follows. All U.S. firms that issue debt publicly must file with the U.S. Securities and Exchange Commission. The population studied consists of information on roughly 11,000 loans taken (by Loan Pricing Corporation) from these filings over the period mid-1987 to 1992. From the underlying population of 11,000, three samples were created consisting of: (i) all loans made by Japanese banks to U.S. firms; (ii) all loans made by non-Japanese foreign banks that entered the U.S. market during the 1980s (called "New Foreign"); (iii) all non-Japanese foreign banks that had a presence in the United States prior to 1980 (called "Old Foreign").

The sample of Japanese banks and the sample of New Foreign (but non-Japanese) banks are groups which entered the U.S. corporate lending market during the 1980s. The first sample, Japanese banks, is examined separately, since these banks lent heavily to U.S. firms during the 1980s, and there may be special reasons for this. In 1982, Japanese banks' percentage share of U.S. domestic banking assets was 6.4%, but had risen to 14.9% by 1989. See Rose (1991) for a discussion of the reasons for this trend.

The second sample, New Foreign (but non-Japanese) banks, are banks that established a presence in the U.S. during the 1980s. The third sample, Old Foreign (non-Japanese), had a presence in the U.S. before 1980. This group was already present in the United States It is, therefore, not clear that they increased their business by underpricing relative to U.S. banks.

Each sample consists of information on loans to U.S. firms. For each sample, a matching U.S. firm is found by matching firms on the basis of: (i) type of loan (term loan, revolving credit, letter of credit, etc); (ii) four-digit SIC code; (iii) whether the loan is secured or not; (iv) the maturity of the loan;

(v) the purpose of the loan (takeover financing, general corporate purposes, real estate purchase, etc); (vi) the size of the loan; (vii) the size of the firm. The idea is to match the foreign loan with a loan by an American bank to a firm of the same risk. The choice of characteristics to match on is dictated by the available information. In many cases, no suitable match can be found. All the loans in the matched samples are floating rate loans.[13]

The matched samples allow us to ask whether new entrants, in this case foreign banks, underprice to enter the U.S. lending market. The interest rate (including fees amortized over the loan life) on the U.S. loan is compared with the interest rate on the foreign bank's loan, holding risk constant by comparing with the matched firm. The mean difference between the U.S. rate and the foreign rate, in basis points, is shown in table 5.1. For each sample of foreign banks, there are three sets of results. The first set is exact matches. These are cases where both the foreign bank and the U.S. bank are making exactly the same type of loan (same contract, same maturity, same purpose, etc) to the same firm at the same time. These loans may or may not be secured. The second sample matches on all of the above characteristics and, in addition, on the fact that the loans are secured loans. Finally, exact matches and secured matches are combined.[14]

Japanese banks underpriced to enter the U.S. lending markets. The most dramatic result is the case of the exact matches. Lending to the exact same firms as the U.S. banks, Japanese banks charged 61.5 basis points less than the U.S. banks, on average. Non-Japanese banks also underpriced to obtain market share, though they were not willing to underprice to obtain a share of exact matches. Old Foreign banks possibly did not need to underprice in the case of exact matches. New Foreign banks made few loans in the exact-match case.

TABLE 5.1 Underpricing by Foreign Bank Entrants in the U.S. Lending Market

Match type		Japanese banks	New foreign banks (non-Japanese)	Old foreign banks (non-Japanese)
Exact	mean difference	61.50	38.34	5.34
	no. of observations	13	3	37
	t-statistic	3.17	0.63	0.65
Secured	mean difference	91.54	64.08	75.54
	no. of observations	22	33	51
	t-statistic	2.52	2.93	3.78
Secured	mean difference	80.38	59.84	73.18
and exact	no. of observations	35	34	53
	t-statistic	3.38	2.77	3.79

Source: Gorton (1994).

The Effects of Underpricing on U.S. Banks

The results in table 5.1 are, perhaps, not surprising given that we know that foreign banks have increased their market share at the expense of U.S banks. This observation must imply that these competitors reduced prices to attract customers away from U.S. banks. But this is not the point. It is not just that U.S. banks lost business. That fact would not, in itself, make U.S. banks riskier, though it can explain reduced profitability. In order for U.S. banks to maintain any market share, the interest rates to borrowers who did not switch to a foreign lender must have been decreased to induce them not to switch. The losses for U.S. banks then were enormous (as were the gains to U.S. borrowers). Note the size of the underpricing; for the cases where it is significant, it is always above 50 basis points and reaches a high of about 90 basis points. So the loss to U.S. banks would be on the order of 0.5% on the total of U.S. commercial lending. These losses are a rough indication of declines in charter values owing to entry by competitors. It is this decline in charter value which is most important, since it alters the degree of risk that banks will accept.

It is important to stress that U.S. firms benefited from entry by new competitors into U.S. corporate lending. Also, from the point of view of public policy, the problem with entry is not that U.S. banks suffered losses (though that is clearly a problem from the point of view of U.S. banks). Rather the problem is how banks can be regulated when entry is not limited, and the regulated group appears to be weak and prone to engaging in activities which are too risky from the point of view of maintaining a stable banking system.

Bank Regulation When Charter Values Are Declining

Limiting entry into banking creates capital in the form of a valuable charter. Entry into banking by nonbanks, i.e., firms which from the point of view of the government are not "banks," or by new debt markets, causes charter values to fall. The difficulties for bank regulation with such a situation are enormous. When charter values are declining due to entry, there is a difference between the privately optimal and socially optimal levels of risk in the banking system. Without charter value, banks engage in new activities which are risky and, possibly, difficult to assess. These activities may trigger panic because they are intertwined with lending and deposit taking. To the extent that nonbanks engage in banking, they may also be subject to runs.[15] The first scenario would occur, for example, if a bank were subject to a run because of defaults on its derivatives book. The second scenario would occur, for example, if a money market mutual fund were subject to large withdrawals because of publicized declines in the value of money market instruments. In both cases, the problem is that activities which are not related to lending and deposit taking become informationally intertwined with banking in the eyes of the public.[16] It is not only that banks may engage in new activities which are risky, they may also engage in old activities which are riskier than in the past, such as commercial real estate construction and development loans.

In this section, I briefly consider the current regulatory responses to this situation. I argue that they are basically unworkable at addressing the problem.

Capital Requirements

One basic regulatory response to the problem of entry by nonbanks has been capital requirements.[17] It should be emphasized that this represents a shift of policy focus. It was only in 1982 that U.S. bank regulators first began enforcing explicit capital adequacy requirements. Since then, there has been increasing attention devoted to capital requirements in the U.S. (See Baer and McElravey, 1992). The same emphasis on capital levels characterizes international bank regulation. The 1988 Basel Capital Accord established capital adequacy standards for international banks. The focus on capital requirements appears to coincide with the decline in charter values. The implicit logic appears to be that if capital cannot be created by limiting entry, then perhaps banks can be forced to produce it from private equity markets.

Can capital requirements substitute for the creation of capital via entry limitations? To see that such restrictions will not work, consider the response of private agents to an increase in capital requirements when charter value has declined. When capital requirements are raised, the existing bank equity holders must decide whether to meet the capital requirements, whether to shrink the size of the bank, or exit banking altogether (by giving up their charter but continuing in "banking"). The decision will be based on the cost of capital which, in turn, depends on the alternative uses of capital. Bank regulators cannot set the cost of capital; they set the capital requirement and then market participants decide whether or not to buy new bank equity, should it be offered.

When banks have high charter values, those values will be capitalized into the price of any new equity issued by the bank. When charter value is declining due to competition, that too will be priced. In the latter case, there are two possible responses to an increase in capital requirements. First, it may be that it is profitable to invest more equity in banks so that the capital requirement is met. Since charter value is declining, this must mean that banks have found profitable new activities. But, in this case, the capital requirement was not binding, and it is not clear why the additional capital was not in the banks in the first place. Second, the cost of capital may be such that banks choose not to issue equity (since nobody would buy the equity at a price the issuing banks found profitable). In this case, banks are unprofitable relative to alternatives, even with new activities. Hence, the capital requirement can only be met through reducing the size of banks. The increase in the capital requirement then serves the purpose of reducing the size of the official banking sector. After all, if charter values are declining, the "bank" can give up its bank charter and, by doing so, it can avoid the capital requirement but engage in the same activities, since entry is not limited. If that was the goal of the regulator, then it was accomplished.

Suppose the regulator wishes to reduce the level of risk in the official banking sector, while maintaining the existing size of the banking sector. Recall the regulator's two goals: maintain a stable banking system while ensuring that the size of the banking system is consistent with the desired level of banking services for the economy. Clearly, when charter values are declining, these goals cannot both be accomplished by capital requirements. The market will have already determined the capital ratio, and a regulatory increase above this level will result in a decline in the size of the official banking system. If regulators do not wish to force shrinkage of the system, then risk cannot be reduced via capital requirements. It may be that capital requirements are conceived of as a way to force the banking sector to shrink, but this is not the logic articulated by proponents of capital requirements.

There is an additional complication concerning reconciling the two regulatory goals discussed above. The difficulty is that entry into banking by non-banks may have occurred more on the asset side of bank balance sheets than on the liability side. In most countries, banks still have a monopoly on demand deposits and the payments system, even if they have lost market share in lending. This means that banks have access to an enormous pool of resources, but not necessarily any place to invest unless they engage in riskier activities. Regulators may want to reduce the amount of risky investments, perhaps via capital requirements, but seem unwilling to do so if it means shrinking the banking system's supply of media of exchange. Regulators cannot shrink one side of the balance sheet without shrinking the other. As a result, whatever the stated goal of capital requirements, the practical effect is not to shrink the banking system.

The banking system does not shrink when capital requirements are raised because bank regulators do not enforce capital requirements when they become binding. Japan is the best recent example of this. But it is important to stress that capital requirements should *not* be enforced if the effect would be to shrink the supply of needed bank services (on the liability side). If not enforcing capital requirements is for the best when weighing public policy goals, then clearly capital requirements do not constitute an workable way of creating a stable banking system. The fact that regulators renege on capital requirements when they become binding explains, in part, why banking systems seem not to be shrinking in the face of nonbank entry into banking.[18]

The same argument about the uselessness of capital requirements applies to any restriction imposed on banks in an environment where entry is not limited. That is, since bank equity holders can choose to exit banking if the restriction is too costly, regulators will not impose binding restrictions if they do not want the official banking sector to shrink. Note that if entry into banking can be limited, then restrictions can be imposed, because bank customers cannot obtain bank services elsewhere; the demand for bank services is then inelastic and customers are willing to bear the burden of the costly restrictions. Restrictions, such as capital requirements, cannot hold when there are substitutes for bank loans available (such as loans from nonbanks).

Increased Subsidies to Banks

When charter values are falling, capital requirements cannot, by themselves, result in a safer banking system of the same size. But there has been another regulatory response as well: an attempt to increase charter values, not by limiting entry, but by increasing the subsidies to banks. This has been done by increasing deposit insurance coverage, allowing insolvent banks to continue in operation for a period of time, directly transferring resources to banks which are insolvent, and so on.

The most direct evidence for the increase in subsidies comes from the U.S., where the "too big to fail" policy increased the value of being a large bank by broadening the range of liabilities which are effectively insured. O'Hara and Shaw (1990) found that the large U.S. banks covered by this policy did, in fact, increase in value in response to the U.S. Comptroller of the Currency's announcement of the policy. In other countries, there is no statistical evidence (partly because bank regulators typically do not announce "too big to fail" policies, even when they are in effect), though there is plenty of evidence of government bailouts of banks, e.g., Banesto in Spain and Credit Lyonnaise in France, and favorable treatment of troubled banks, as in Japan.

There is a problem with increasing subsidies to banks when entry is not limited. When banking is less profitable and riskier than before, the only way that the loss in value can be made up when entry is not limited is by directly transferring resources to banks, that is, by subsidizing their attempts to remain as large and as profitable as they were prior to entry by competitors. The subsidies are counterproductive because they do not result in a valuable asset which is lost if the bank becomes insolvent, like the charter. Rather than creating an incentive to limit risk, the subsidies are increased when the bank becomes insolvent, creating an incentive to engage in risk taking. The defense of these policies is that they are needed to protect the provision of banking services. For example, it is argued that the loss of information produced in the course of developing bank relationships would be sizeable if the particular bank were allowed to fail. (The Slovin et al., 1993, study is consistent with this.) Sprague (1986), the former chairman and director of the U.S. Federal Deposit Insurance Corporation, is fairly explicit about this rationale.

While it is true that there may be sizable costs to bank failure, the policy is fundamentally confused. In the current situation of reduced charter values, such policies can only increase the likelihood of the very events, risk taking, and failure that they are supposed reduce. These policies subsidize bank risk taking in an environment where banks can be expected to increase risk.

The Need to Redefine "Banking"

Entry into banking by competitors is of two distinct sorts. Were entry only coming from foreign banks, the problem would be quite different from the case of entry from nonbanks, debt markets, and money market mutual funds. I am primarily concerned with the latter case because it means that the activities of corporate lending and deposit taking can be separated or unbundled to a significant extent. I have focused on two implications of this trend. The first is that this unbundling of banking makes defining a "bank" much more difficult. In addition, when banks engage in new activities which nonbanks are also engaged in, the issue arises of whether these activities are "banking" in any meaningful sense. Without a definition of a "bank," it is impossible to create barriers to entry. As a result, bank charter value declines. This leads to the second implication, namely, that the decline in charter value associated with entry by competitors means that banks will rationally choose to become riskier. This raises the specter that the new activities that banks engage in are attractive primarily because they are riskier (in which case, the fact that banks are primarily engaged in them is not obviously evidence that they are "banking" activities).

These trends do not mean the end of banking. Even by the traditional definition of banking, i.e., financing loans by issuing deposits, banks are of fundamental importance for virtually every economy. Nevertheless, the demand for "banking" of the traditional sort has declined. Firms called "banks" may eventually find other activities which are profitable and transform themselves into viable entities which compete with other firms called "nonbanks." But the combination of the two trends in banking discussed above, new activities, and increased risk taking puts bank regulators in a difficult position. For example, bank regulators in the United States have complained that banks are making loans which are too risky (presumably relative to the level of risk that banks would have found acceptable when charter values were higher).[19] But, clearly, complaining about the dangers of this level of risk cannot change the fact that without valuable charters, rational banks should choose to become riskier. The same problem arises in discussions of derivatives in banking. That is, aside from whether derivatives are really "banking" or not, or whether they are really risky or not, the question arises of whether banks are willing to accept levels of risk which regulators find unacceptable from the point of view of public policy. If the risks are unacceptable, then, without raising charter value, regulators are forced into the position of having to attempt to limit risk taking by use of the "stick," rather than the "carrot."

What is important for public policy is the creation of confidence in a system which produces riskless demand deposits and a sufficient quantity of loans. How can this be achieved? I have argued that, at least historically, public policy goals have been achieved by subsidizing banking via limiting entry. This creates incentives for banks to limit their risk taking. This regulatory framework is superior to a system in which banks would prefer levels of risk which are higher than socially acceptable, and regulators must directly intervene in attempts to limit risk. Without some workable definition of banking, every activity undertaken by banks, and hence by nonbanks undertaking the same activity, must be regulated, a kind of de facto universal banking. Compared with a system where banks have incentives to limit risks themselves, this outcome, which relies on regulatory intervention, seems undesirable. Thus, my basic conclusion is that the best approach is to define a set of activities which constitute "banking," and then limit these activities to firms which receive charters.

In order to accomplish this goal, "banking" needs to be redefined to the extent that demand deposits are claims on new types of risky assets which are hard for market participants to evaluate. In order to have a workable definition of "banking," it may help to review why, historically, commercial loans have been financed by issuing demand deposits. There are two reasons for this combination to have been pervasive in history. First, consumers have a demand for an interest-bearing transactions medium that is riskless, or near riskless. The reason is that riskless securities have easily computable prices so that there is no loss to better-informed traders when less-informed traders must make purchases (or sales). The intuition for this is the same for understanding why "fire sales" of assets generally result in a loss for the seller. When consumers want to purchase goods, they do not want to be in the position of having to sell a highly illiquid asset for cash in order to use the cash to buy goods. Rather, they would prefer to have a very liquid asset which can be used to buy goods. But "liquidity" refers to the degree to which the asset value is not known. Very liquid assets have a low variance around their true value. Demand deposits are a leading example of liquid assets.

Liquid securities are generally thought of as government liabilities. How can private firms create liquidity? Banks are in a unique position in this regard because they are firms which hold diversified portfolios of loans (compared with nonfinancial firms, which are not diversified). By issuing debt claims on these diversified portfolios, banks come close to creating a riskless, interest-bearing transactions medium. This argument is developed by Gorton and Pennacchi (1990a, 1993a). Note the link between the creation of demand deposits and loans. Historically, banks were the only firms which held diversified portfolios, because of the nature of bank loans and, hence, it was natural for them to be the firms which issued transactions media.

The second (nonmutually exclusive) reason concerns the nature of the assets produced by banks. Loans are (at least, historically) not traded and difficult to value, as discussed above. Since information is difficult to produce about loans, there is the possibility that bank managers are not properly performing their jobs (of monitoring borrowers and producing information about borrowers). But, by structuring bank debt as puttable (i.e., demand deposits can be redeemed on demand), there is an incentive created for some depositors to produce information. Those that produce information will be first in line at the bank to withdraw when they discover bad news; they will, consequently, receive more than latecomers, compensating them for having produced information. Calomiris and Kahn (1991) develop this argument.

These two arguments explain the connections between the production of information-intensive assets and demand deposits. I take "banking" to refer to these two interrelationships, bank assets, and liabilities. Financial innovation has weakened these connections. But banks have also become engaged in many new activities. In order to make a decision about the direction bank regulation should take, it is necessary to decide whether these new activities are banking, that is, inherently connected to the process of producing demand deposits and loans. In other words, in the absence of deposit insurance, would we observe firms which combined these new activities with demand deposits? For many activities, the answer to this question must clearly be no, because there are many firms that have nothing to do with demand deposits, which are also engaged in these activities.[20]

From this point of view, it is difficult to view most derivative activity as banking. It does not primarily involve assessment of credit risk (interest rate risk or currency risk are the primary considerations); it is information-intensive only in the sense that firms can alter their positions very quickly.[21] But, even if many new activities that banks are engaged in do not seem to be banking in the sense of one of the above arguments, not all new bank activities can be so easily dismissed as not constituting "banking." Some off-balance-sheet activities, such as standby letters of credit or loan commitments, appear to be information-intensive in the same sense that commercial loans are, and hence, might well be related to the production of demand deposits.

While I view many of these issues as open questions, it does not seem so difficult to make these kinds of distinctions (though clearly there is some arbitrariness). These distinctions must be made in order for restricted entry to create charter value.

6

A Note to Those Reading
This in 2107

IF YOU ARE READING THIS IN 2107, IT IS LIKELY BECAUSE YOU ARE experiencing a banking panic in some futuristic banking system. (I wish I were there to see this new banking system.) You think to yourself that you never thought you would see a banking panic; aren't they things of the past, you say? How can a modern economy in 2107 have a banking panic? Are they still showing *It's a Wonderful Life* around Christmas, with its bank run on the Bedford Falls Savings and Loan? Maybe by 2107 there's a new movie that has a banking panic in it. Did your grandparents tell you about the Panic of 2007, like mine told me about the Great Depression?

Perhaps you are writing about the Panic of 2107, and you are thinking that you should refer to our rich history of panics, so you want to read the historical writings about the panics of 2007, 1907, and others. Maybe you already read these authors' articles and books when you were in graduate school. Perhaps you will read Ben Bernanke's papers on the Great Depression.[1] Perhaps Ben Bernanke has a memoir of the events of the Panic of 2007 seen from the point of view of the central bank. You think that when you write something you can quote from these writings to give your readers a sense of history—you think that "the earlier history offers important clues about how to think about what a 'systemic event' is and to what happened in the current crisis." You hope that you can "explain what happened...from the viewpoint that the details matter..." But you worry that no one really will care about the details.

If that is what is happening to you, Mr. Doppelgänger, then we in 2009, who lived through the Panic of 2007, have failed. Maybe we lacked imagination or political will, or maybe we just didn't get it, didn't understand what happened. Maybe the reregulation and the new legislation passed after the Panic of

2007 were aimed at the wrong issues. Maybe it had unintended consequences. Or maybe, in a better outcome, we designed a panic-proof banking system that lasted at least until 2107, and we can claim partial success—a one-hundred-year Quiet Period. But, as with our predecessors, the grand schemes we designed and claimed victory for failed—if you are reading this during the Panic of 2107. We didn't end banking panics forever, and maybe that is impossible. As for this book, I think of Walter Bagehot, whose book *Lombard Street: A Description of the Money Market* (1877) is the classic of central bank operations; he wrote: "I know it will be said that in this work I have pointed out a deep malady, and only suggested a superficial remedy" (chapter XIII: conclusion, p. 129). Like Bagehot, I too surely have no deep words of wisdom for you about remedies, but I offer three small pieces of advice.

First, measure correctly and often. Or, to repeat what Deep Throat told Bob Woodward in *All the President's Men* (a 1976 movie about the Watergate break-in): "Follow the money." Here's an example of what I mean. On March 23, 2006, the board of governors of the Federal Reserve System ceased publication of the M3 monetary aggregate, which among other things included repurchase agreements (repos). This was not viewed as a momentous event, but as esoteric and arcane. There were two reasons for discontinuing M3. First, it was highly correlated with the narrower monetary aggregate, M2. And secondly, the role of monetary aggregates has changed dramatically in recent decades: "nowadays monetary aggregates play little role in monetary policy deliberations at most central banks" (Woodford, 2007). For monetary theorists focusing on inflation, the issue is whether tracking monetary aggregates is informative for policy (about inflation). The details of this debate are important, but not for our purposes here. The point is only that no one thought that M3 should be calculated in a different way. This was not an issue that anyone raised.

The repos included in the old money measure of M3 were narrowly those done only by the limited number of primary dealers that are approved to do business with the Fed.[2] The repo market that has been much discussed in this book was much broader and was not included in M3 or indeed measured at all. If this broader repo market had been included, presumably M3 would have been on a steep upward trajectory that would have been noticed and questioned. But this did not happen. Instead, about a year and half after the calculation and publication of M3 ceased, the Panic of 2007 erupted in the much broader repo market. In other words, the shadow banking system was so far off the radar screen that instead of increasing the coverage of the repo counted for M3, the calculation was discontinued. The point is not to blame the Fed. But, you ask, how could this have happened? Is there something like this in 2107?

FEDERAL RESERVE statistical release

For release at 4:30 p.m. Eastern Time

March 16, 2006
H.6 (508)

Discontinuance of M3

As announced on November 10, 2005, the Board of Governors will cease publication of the M3
monetary aggregate on March 23, 2006. The Board will also cease publishing the following
components: large-denomination time deposits, repurchase agreements (RPs), and Eurodollars.
The Board will continue to publish institutional money market mutual funds as a memorandum
item in this release.

Measures of large-denomination time deposits will continue to be published by the Board in the
Flow of Funds Accounts (Z.1 release) on a quarterly basis and in the H.8 release on a weekly
basis (for commercial banks).

M3 does not appear to convey any additional information about economic activity that is not
already embodied in M2 and has not played a role in the monetary policy process for many
years. Consequently, the Board judged that the costs of collecting the underlying data and
publishing M3 outweigh the benefits.

On March 23, 2006, the Board will publish a final set of historical data on M3 and its
components. The Board will publish historical data on M1, M2, M3, and their components in
the current format for the last time today (www.federalreserve.gov/releases/h6/hist/). Beginning
March 9, 2006, each week the Board will publish historical data on M1, M2, and their
components (www.federalreserve.gov/releases/h6/hist/newformat.htm).

FIGURE 6.1   Federal Reserve Statistical Release

There are other ramifications of eliminating M3 besides broadening the
definition of repo for the purpose of M3. It is not only that M3 did not capture
the right measure of money because it did not measure the full extent of the
repo market, it is also that currently we do not know what the money supply
really is either. To see the problem, let's first review the money multiplier.
The money multiplier refers to how much money can be created based on
a given amount of cash ("base money" supplied by the government). Here,
to simplify things, think of "money" as checking accounts and government
currency. When you deposit your cash in a bank, the bank holds some of the
cash and lends the rest out. The amount lent out gets deposited in a bank
somewhere, and that bank holds some of it and lends the rest out, and so
on. So how much money in the form of demand deposits has been created
out of the cash? Say the cash in the economy is $1 and banks hold 10%
back as reserves when they receive a dollar in deposits. So they only lend

out 90 cents the first time. If you are mathematically minded, you can write down the infinite series of these transactions. You will see that the money multiplier is 1/r where r was 10% in our example. So the money multiplier is 10, and the maximum amount of money in circulation (cash and demand deposits) is 1 × 10, or $10.

Note that the explanation given above assumes that banks want to make loans, and that someone wants to borrow. Otherwise the money expansion process described by the money multiplier does not occur. Indeed, as of May 20, 2009, the money multiplier was *below* 1, meaning that banks are hoarding cash or there is no demand for loans.[3] In other words, currently, every dollar the central bank adds to the money supply results in the money supply increasing by about 95 cents.

In a panic, the money multiplier process works in reverse, causing the money supply to shrink. Again, as we have done throughout this book, let's think of the panics during the 19th century. These panics involved a collapse of the money supply. When individuals withdraw their currency from banks in exchange for their demand deposits, the money supply contracts. To meet these depositor demands for cash, banks call in loans, which in turn causes those borrowers to try to withdraw cash from their demand deposit accounts to repay the loan. But then that bank must call in its loans, and so on. However, in a 19th-century panic, convertibility was suspended, so this process was truncated. The loans did not have to be called in, nor did they have to be sold. But the money supply still shrank suddenly. The problem was that then no one knew what banks' checks were really worth, and so they were not acceptable as a medium of exchange. They ceased being "money" altogether. The money supply unexpectedly and quickly ended up being only the cash part. This was the currency famine.

In M3, some repo was counted, but all repo is money (not just repo done by primary security dealers that transaction with the Federal Reserve) in the same sense that demand deposits are money. In the repo market, there is also a money multiplier, although there is no reserve requirement, r. The counterpart to the reserve requirement is the repo haircut. But, prior to the panic, this was zero (at least in the interbank market), so a bond received as collateral could be "spent" completely; that is, it could be completely posted as collateral in some other transaction (rehypothecation). While in principle this would mean that the money supply could be infinite, there are some costs to this process which would keep it finite, and there must be a demand for all this money. We don't know how fast collateral was rehypothecated (the speed with which money circulates is called money velocity), so we don't know what the money supply was when the panic broke out.

In the repo panic, as we have seen, the depositors withdrew from the banks by forcing banks to accept haircuts on collateral. This causes the money supply to fall, but we don't know by how much. Subsequent to the panic, it is hard for us to know whether the Fed's actions have really increased the money supply or not. We know how much new money has been created, but we do not know how much was destroyed in the panic. Measurement is the root of the problem. But knowing what to measure requires curiosity. Curiosity and measurement—in other words, science.

The second lesson: confidence is somewhat fragile; it must be created and sustained. The problem is that we don't know how to create confidence, especially once it has been lost. We would like confidence in a banking system so that there are no panics. But, if there is a panic, we would like to re-establish confidence. The problem is that confidence cannot be dictated, ordered, legislated, or required. Confidence is a delicate social construct. The government is in the unique position to simply guarantee things (since it alone can tax), within reason, and that may create confidence. We may, for example, have confidence that the government can tax in the future to provide for social security, Medicare, and so on. But, short of such blanket guarantees, confidence is difficult to create.

Confidence that what we eat is healthy is a good example of the difficulties. The Food and Drug Administration and the U.S. Department of Agriculture here play the role of the bank regulators. Generally, people want to be able to buy food and have confidence that the food they buy is safe to eat. No one really wants to engage in testing food themselves. But the system is not infallible. Take one example (of many). In the fall of 2006, the government announced the recall of bagged spinach, which was potentially contaminated with E. coli bacteria. At that time, at least 114 people were sickened in 21 states; 16 had kidney damage and one had died (see *Washington Post*, September 19, 2006; p. HE06). Between September 14–22, 2006, the Food and Drug Administration promoted the message that all fresh spinach should be discarded. Later, it was reported that:

> September's national spinach recall has shaken consumer confidence in the safety of leafy green vegetables, according to a new national survey.
> Consumers are still avoiding greens and questioning safety issues, months after spinach contaminated with E. coli bacteria killed three people and sickened nearly 200.
> Plummeting spinach sales have also prompted the produce industry to seek federal oversight to assure buyers that fresh produce is safe. (See Lorin (2007)).

Based on a Rutgers University survey about this incident, more than 75% of the respondents with spinach in their home threw it out. See Cuite et al. (2007). How serious was the loss of confidence? Uncertainty about the source of the E. coli caused confusion. Nearly one-fifth of those aware of the recall stopped buying other bagged produce as a result of the spinach recall. Sales of pack-aged salad *without spinach* dropped 10%. There was also a reluctance to return to eating spinach. Reluctance to resume eating spinach "may have been rein-forced by the lack of a definitive statement by the government indicating that spinach was now '*safe*' to eat" (emphasis in original). Instead, the FDA issued a press release on September 22, 2006, indicating that "the public can be confi-dent that spinach grown in the non-implicated areas can be consumed."

The government oversight of food quality is generally sufficient to create confidence among American consumers that they can eat safely. And, when there is a problem, the food can be traced and recalled (unlike subprime mort-gages). For example, Thomas E. Stenzel, president and CEO of United Fresh Produce Association, offered this analysis:

> Let me turn specifically to a discussion of traceability in our industry. As con-text, let me suggest that an individually packaged food item with a UPC [bar] code and lot number provides about the most complete traceability possible. You simply punch in that code and the company can tell you when the item was packed, in what facility, and usually even whether it was packed on the morning or afternoon shift. Ironically, that's the specific case with the E. coli outbreak associated with spinach two years ago. The only contaminated spin-ach ever in the marketplace was bagged on one shift, on one day, in one pro-cessing plant, with the same lot code appearing on every bag. (Stenzel, 2008).

But, when there is an outbreak of E. coli or salmonella, there can be a reaction which, in retrospect, appears to be an overreaction. And sometimes the changes in food consumption appear to be permanent, as with mad cow disease, which led to widespread changes in eating habits. See Shell (1998).

Food is not so different from banking. In normal times, everyone needs to have confidence that transactions can be conducted with a medium of exchange that is immune to gaming. No one wants a lot of information. Like eating, we just want to trade without being harmed. Market participants must be confi-dent that the securities used for transactions, demand deposits, or collateral are information insensitive. Securities must be designed so that there is no information to announce, about which there is more below. But, in a panic, this confidence disappears and the issue for the central bank is how to create confidence. A panic is somewhat akin to a large recall of food—imagine if all food was recalled!

There is one difference between eating and trading that is important, namely, market participants can produce their own information about the value of their checks or their bonds. But, paradoxically, that shouldn't be necessary; we want them to have confidence that this is not necessary. To see this, suppose you inherit a stock portfolio from your rich uncle. And now you want to sell some of the stock to pay off your mortgage. But let's also imagine that you wake up that morning magically knowing the future about stock prices; you know which stock prices will go up and which will go down. And, further, let's suppose that everyone knew you knew this, or suspected you had this sudden knowledge. Would your knowledge lead to untold riches? No, you would not become rich, because no one would trade with you. You would be better off without the magical knowledge, but you would also need others to know that you did not have this magical knowledge. Even if you did not have the knowledge, if others thought you did, they would not trade with you.

Transactions in the economy depend on debt in the same way. You don't want to magically know things, and you don't what other people to know things either. And, you don't want people to think you know secrets. No one should want to study magic. Securities and institutions need to be designed so no one finds this in their interest. Debt is designed to be immune from most information; when it is traded people don't have to do a lot of due diligence. Demand deposits and AAA securities are the leading examples. Collateral for repo must have this property. Repo trading has been likened—by repo traders—to speed chess; that is, there is no time to do due diligence on the collateral offered and indeed almost none is done. What is needed is only the general knowledge that the collateral is high-grade, that there is no real point to doing due diligence because nothing will be found out. And both sides to the transaction understand this. (This is why credit ratings are *general* indicators.)

So, in normal times, liquidity depends on confidence that no one trading knows a magical secret about the security used to trade. Debt and the institutions associated with debt, like banks, the repo market, clearing systems, collateral, and so on, have the feature that they are like electricity, recalling the analogy from the introduction (and moving away from E. coli). That is, it is almost always the case that no one need be really concerned with electricity because it is designed to function without constant attention by most people. There is no reason for every person to check the electricity each time before throwing the light switch. People can have confidence in the system. They can turn their lights on and off—write checks, engage in repo, invest in AAA securitized products—and not have to spend a lot of time or money becoming electricians. The economy couldn't really function if everyone had to be an electrician.

FIGURE 6.2　Electrical Transmission Lines Part of the Electrical System (http://
en.wikipedia.org/wiki/File:Electric_transmission_lines.jpg)

The "deep malady" Bagehot refers to is the fact that the lights can go out.
It is not just that an investment-grade company can fail. It is the systemic event
in which all the lights go out at the same time. In a banking panic, the trigger is
a shock, some economic news that causes doubt about bank solvency, the value
of debt, and whether other people will buy the debt. Then, the inner workings
suddenly matter. And it turns out that, like the electrical system, the inner
workings are very complicated. And people are angry that there is no light and
that it is complicated. They have lost confidence in the electrical system.

What is to be done when the lights go out? The central bank faces a terrible
task in a panic because the problem is to eliminate the doubt and restore confidence when market participants are painfully sensitive to information and also
to the lack of information. Not surprisingly, a Gallup poll taken in June 2008
found that the percentage of Americans saying they had a "great deal" or "quite
a lot" of confidence in U.S. banks fell to 32%, matching the 32% of March 1991
(the trough of the last recession, which had its peak in July 1990) and near the
three-decade low of 30% in October 1991 (see Jacobe, 2008).[4] In a panic, the
central bank can buy bonds and lend through the discount window, but that
does not per se address the information problem that is at the root of the panic.
The central bank is in the difficult position of having rather primitive tools at
its disposal to address information problems.

How can confidence be restored? Here the 19th-century experience of clearinghouses is not much help. As I have mentioned above, one thing the clearinghouses did was to prevent the publication of bank-specific information once convertibility had been suspended. In normal times, the clearinghouse required that banks (individually) publish certain specified accounting information. But, during the panic, the banks banded together, diversifying the risk faced by depositors of individual banks. The clearinghouse was, in effect, saying "the banking system is in this together." The clearinghouse loan certificates that were issued started out at a discount, which then shrank over time, as if the passage of time was itself information that the banking system will survive.

In the modern era, the central bank can try to make debt more information insensitive by recapitalizing banks or by issuing blanket guarantees, but the first is difficult to get right, because banks are different, and the central bank may not know how they differ or how much is needed to eliminate the information sensitivity. Blanket guarantees may work if the central bank is credible, but are potentially very costly (see Laeven and Classens, 2008). Also, it is one thing to have a blanket guarantee on demand deposits *ex ante* and another to issue a blanket guarantee during a crisis, when it is less clear what to guarantee. To try to create confidence, the Fed undertook the bank stress tests in the spring of 2009.[5] It did not issue a blanket guarantee. That was never considered, perhaps because it was not clear what to guarantee. Such a guarantee of a floor on the value of subprime mortgages might have been effective had it come in the fall of 2007 or perhaps early in 2008.

Part of the problem is that confidence in the central bank is initially shaken, just because the panic happened at all. So the first step of the central bank must be bold to address that issue before the question of restoring the banking system can be addressed. But the reality is that we want a system where the Fed does not face this problem. We want a system that is not prone to panics, or, better yet, a system that does not have panics, a system where losing confidence does not happen: another Quiet Period. We want the electricity to always work. We want no E. coli, ever. The problem for you in 2107 is like the one we faced in the aftermath of the Panic of 2007: how can such a system be designed? That leads to the final point.

The final advice: try to clearly articulate the narrative of the panic. As George Orwell put it in *1984*: "He who controls the past, controls the future."[6] I mentioned this in the introduction and reiterate it here. The future of the financial system is a function of the explanation of the past, so the narrative of what happened in the crisis is very important. This will be hard because all banking, when it matters, ultimately resolves into politics. This is one of the messages of Bray Hammond's book *Banks and Politics in America from the*

FIGURE 6.3 The Federal Reserve Building, Washington, D.C. (Dan Smith)

Revolution to the Civil War (1957), which won the Pulitzer Prize in history in 1958 (and is a great book); it is more about politics than economics.[7] But the magnitude and importance of the Panic of 2007 force us to eschew personalities per se and focus on banking and economics. That is what I have tried to do, and I recommend that you do the same in 2107. The problem in 2107 may well be, as it was in the Panic of 2007, that the crisis is very hard to understand because the causal events were invisible to most people. The crisis itself is no doubt complicated. Probably there have been all sorts of financial innovations since 2007. Maybe things were not measured correctly, and possibly there are no data to display to really convince people of your explanation. Many of the explanations that will be proposed will be short-lived; after awhile, their explanatory power will be weakened as they are revealed to be superficial, thin gruel for the hungry, bread and circuses (*panem et circenses*). But you have little time. So tell the story.

Notes

1. One need only recall the narrative that was put forth to justify invading Iraq to understand the importance of a narrative for policy.

2. Abram Piatt Andrew (1873–June 1936) was a Harvard professor and later assistant secretary of the treasury. He wrote frequently about panics.

3. I studied the Free Banking Era (see Gorton, 1996, 1999). While private money markets were efficient, in the sense that the discount from par (that is, a ten-dollar bill issued by a New Haven bank might be worth only \$9.80 in Boston) did reflect the transportation costs of going from Boston to New Haven, it was still hard to transact.

4. In their monumental *Monetary History of the United States, 1867–1960* (1971), Milton Friedman and Anna Schwartz wrote that, "Federal insurance of bank deposits was the most important structural change to result from the 1933 panic, and, indeed, in our view, the structural change most conducive to monetary stability since state bank notes were taxed out of existence after the Civil War" (p. 434).

5. Address to the U.S. Chamber of Commerce, May 4, 1933. Quoted by Senator Murphy (D-Iowa) in the *Congressional Record* (1933), p. 3008; and quoted by Flood (1992).

6. "Clearing" refers to the institutional process of changing ownership of a security in exchange for cash.

7. Hypothecation means the pledging of securities to secure a loan. Rehypothecation is not permitted in some jurisdictions, but it is common in the United States.

8. M3 also included institutional money-market mutual funds, large-denomination certificates of deposit, and Eurodollars. M3 has been discontinued, as of March 23, 2006, because it "does not appear to convey any additional information about economic activity that is not already embodied in M2" (see http://www.federalreserve.gov/Releases/h6/discm3.htm).

9. Noyes wrote books and articles about banking and finance. See his memoir, *The Market Place: Reminiscences of a Financial Editor* (Little, Brown and Company, 1938).

10. Edwin W. Kemmerer, an economist at Princeton, was another important writer on panics and banking, as well as an important figure in the founding of the Federal Reserve System.

11. See http://www.kc.frb.org/home/subwebnav.cfm?level=3&theID=10979&SubWeb=10660.

12. A firm may be financed by issuing securities that are claims on the general credit of the corporation; that is, they are backed by the assets of the company, or the firm can finance itself by segregating specified cash flows and selling claims specifically linked to these specified cash flows. The latter strategy is accomplished by setting up another company, called a Special Purpose Vehicle (SPV) or Special Purpose Entity (SPE), and then selling the specified cash flows to this company; the SPV, in turn, issues securities into the capital market to finance the purchase of the cash flows from the company (called the "sponsor"). The sponsor services the cash flows, that is, makes sure that the cash flows are arriving, etc. The SPV is not an operating company in the usual sense. It is more of a robot company in that it is a set of rules. It has no employees or physical location. As we will see, an SPV has some special properties that make it different in other ways, as well. The latter process is called securitization.

13. See http://www.kc.frb.org/home/subwebnav.cfm?level=3&theID=10976&SubWeb=10660 for Bernanke's Jackson Hole speech.

14. See http://www.kc.frb.org/home/subwebnav.cfm?level=3&theID=10976&SubWeb=10660 for Bernanke's Jekyll Island speech.

CHAPTER 2

1. Famously due to Adam Smith, *The Wealth of Nations*, Book IV, Ch. II (Modern Library, New York, 2000).

2. In this well-known movie starring Jimmy Stewart, there is a run on the local savings bank in the fictional town of Bedford Falls. It is not a systemic event, but it seems to correspond to most people's idea of a "banking panic."

3. The savings and loan crisis was costly, 2% of GDP, but was not a systemic event since it was confined to a particular group of institutions facing the same regulations.

4. The figure shows the number of bank failures, rather than total assets of failed banks or fraction of banks failing. This is due to data limitations. The Panic of 1893 is visible in the figure, and also the recession starting in July 1990.

5. There is a large literature on "The Great Moderation." For a survey of some of the empirical evidence, see Summers (2005). For a survey of the literature, see Stock and Watson (2002). Gali and Gambetti (2008) is a recent paper.

6. The most common explanations for the Great Moderation fall into one of three categories: better monetary policy, changes in inventory management, and good luck. Ironically, the idea that the Great Moderation might have something to do with the financial system is not something even contemplated by economists, despite the evidence that banking shocks have significant effects on economic growth. See, for

example, Bernanke (1983), Boyd, Kwak, and Smith (2005), Cerra and Saxena (2008), Valencia (2008), and Levintal (2008).

7. Adverse selection refers to the potential for an informed party in the transaction to take advantage of a less informed party. See Gorton and Pennacchi (1990a), Holmström (2008) and Dang, Gorton and Holmström (2009).

8. To understand that this was an issue historically, one need recall the Free Banking Era; see Gorton (1996, 1999).

9. More formally, a sale and repurchase agreement (repo) is a sale of a security combined with an agreement to repurchase the same security at a specified price at the end of the contract term, usually very short. Legally, a repo is a secured or collateralized loan, that is, a loan of cash against a security as collateral. The right to use such collateral pledged to them in another unrelated transaction is referred to as the "right of rehypothecation." See Johnson (1997).

10. A "derivative" security is a contractual arrangement where the payoffs to the parties depend on the movement in prices. No cash changes hands initially; when the price subsequently moves, the contract becomes an asset for one party and a liability for the other party. For example, a call option on the stock becomes an asset to the holder of the call when the stock price goes above the strike price.

11. "Securitized" debt refers to the financing of loans off-balance sheet. The cash flows from a pool, or a portfolio of loans, are segregated and sold to a special purpose vehicle (a legal entity with a limited purpose) and financed by selling securities specifically linked to these specified cash flows. The securities are differentiated based on seniority and are called "tranches." This is discussed further later in the main text.

12. Though prior to the run on repo, there was the run on structured investment vehicles (SIVs); this is discussed in chapter 4.

13. For example, Noyes (1909): "There is a general run of depositors on the banks, with one day (October 24) of almost complete suspension of credit in the great financial markets. There followed the abandonment, by practically all banking institutions in the United States, of the requirements of cash in payment of debt balances between banks at the Clearing House…" (p. 188).

14. Deposit insurance is a worldwide phenomenon. See Demirgüc-Kunt, Karacaovali, and Laeven (2005).

15. Studies of the relation between stock and bond returns at the aggregate level include Keim and Stambaugh (1986) and Fama and French (1989, 1993), and at the firm level they include Blume, Keim, and Patel (1991) and Cornell and Green (1991); at the individual level, see, for example, Kwan (1996).

16. Securitization is a worldwide phenomenon. See, for example, Gyntelberg and Remolona (2006), Scatigna and Tovar (2007), and Wang (2004).

17. I do not mean to imply that buying on the rating is a bad thing. Rather, because debt is senior and relatively less sensitive to information, the level of due diligence is not as intense as with, say, equity.

18. Myron Scholes' and Robert Merton's Nobel Prize lectures discuss the history and growth of the derivatives market. See Scholes (1998) and Merton (1998).

19. Other credit enhancements include ratings triggers that terminate the transaction at market and third-party guarantees. See Litzenberger (1992). Also, see Bliss and Kaufman (2006).

20. A bank posts collateral by repoing eligible securities to the central bank.

21. There is a large academic literature on this topic, including Angelini (1998), Kahn and Roberds (2001), and Furfine and Stehm (1998).

22. See http://www.chips.org/home.php.

23. There were banking panics in the United States prior to the National Banking Era, but they are harder to study because banks were state-chartered then, and data is harder to collect. See, for example, Rezneck (1933), McGrane (1924), and Davis (2001).

24. Other citations to the empirical work on panics in the United States are given in Gorton (2008), but those are not exhaustive.

25. Fels (1951), speaking of the Panic of 1893, wrote: "there are many reasons for not accepting the Bureau's dates in blind faith. Not the least of which is the scarcity of monthly data for the 1870's" (p. 336). See Miron and Romer (1990), Romer (1994), and Davis (2006, 2004).

26. Miron and Romer (1990): "...there are some important differences between our index and various alternatives. These differences are especially noticeable around the dates of major financial panics. For example, following the banking panic of May 1884, our index shows a much more immediate fall in production than does the pig iron series that has been used in other analyses. This is also the case around the panic of October 1907. The new index, like the Babson and Persons indexes, turns down perceptibly before the panic, whereas the frequently used pig iron series does not turn down until November 1907. These differences in the timing of real output movements around financial panics could have large effects in studies that seek to identify the direction of causation between panics and recessions" (p. 332).

27. On the Panic of 1893 see, for example, Fels (1951), Noyes (1894), Rezneck (1953), and Stevens (1894); on the Panic of 1907 see, for example, Sprague (1908) and Moen and Tallman (1990). Also, see Calomiris and Gorton (1991).

28. Country banks also withdrew money on deposit with city banks, reminiscent of today's crisis.

29. Friedman and Schwartz (1971) discuss the currency premium during the Great Depression, p. 110.

30. The information about clearinghouses is drawn from Gorton (1985b) and Gorton and Mullineaux (1987). Also, see Cannon (1910) and Gorton and Huang (2006).

31. The Panic of 1914 involved the government issuing a kind of money that had been authorized under the Aldrich-Vreeland Act. See Sprague (1915) and Silber (2007a, b). When the Federal Reserve System came into existence, these features of the Aldrich-Vreeland Act were not incorporated. In this sense, the panics of the Great Depression were very special. See Gorton (1988).

32. New York Times, September 28, 1913, Society, Theaters, Schools, Real Estate, Financial, Business section, p. X15.

33. Ibid.

34. Ibid.

35. As discussed in Calomiris and Gorton (1991), banking panics only occurred in banking systems characterized by many smaller banks. Also see Gorton and Huang (2006). Banking systems with a few large banks, e.g., Canada, typically have no experience of panics.

36. The literature on financial innovation includes Miller (1986), Tufano (2004), Merton (1992), and Lerner (2006).

37. On money market mutual funds, see, for example, Gorton and Pennacchi (1993b). On junk bonds competing with bank loans, see Benveniste, Singh, and Wilhelm (1993) and Molyneux and Shamroukh (1996).

38. Strahan (2003) argues that deregulation was "followed by better performance of the real economy. State economies grew faster and had higher rates of new business formation after this deregulation. At the same time macroeconomic stability improved" (p. 111).

39. The assertion that there is a breakdown of incentives—the "originate-to-distribute" view—is discussed in chapter 4.

40. It may well be that "double-counting" is correct because of rehypothecation. With no data it is difficult to know the velocity of rehypothecation. For some evidence, see Singh and Aitken (2009).

41. Of course, the issue of whether the "bank" is solvent will arise. Repo is an exception to the U.S. Bankruptcy Code. If the lender fails, the nondefaulting party—the depositor in this case—has the option to unilaterally terminate the repo agreement and keep the bond (or go into chapter 11). The issue that arises in the next section concerns whether the bond is liquid.

42. Every six months, the indices are reconstituted based on a pre-identified set of rules, and a new vintage of the index and subindices are issued. Only four vintages were issued, two in 2006 and two in 2007. The index is overseen by Markit Partners. The dealers provide Markit Partners with daily and monthly marks. See http://www.markit.com/information/products/abx.html.

43. Keep in mind that house price indices, like the S&P Case-Shiller indices, are calculated with a two-month lag. Furthermore, house price indices are not directly relevant because of the complicated structure of subprime securitizations (see Gorton (2008)).

44. A collateralized debt obligation (CDO) is a special purpose vehicle (a separate legal entity), which buys a portfolio of fixed income assets, and finances the purchase of the portfolio by issuing bonds of different seniority (different tranches of risk) in the capital markets. These tranches are senior tranches, rated Aaa/AAA, mezzanine tranches, rated Aa/AA to Ba/BB, and equity tranches (unrated). Of particular interest are ABS CDOs, CDOs which have underlying portfolios consisting of asset-backed securities (ABS), including residential mortgage-backed securities (RMBS) and commercial mortgage-backed securities (CMBS).

45. The London Interbank Offered Rate (LIBOR) is a series of interest rates of different maturities and currencies at which banks offer to lend funds to each other. These rates are calculated by the British Bankers' Association as the averages of quotes contributed by a panel of banks. See Gyntelberg and Wooldridge (2008). An Overnight Indexed Swap (OIS) is a fixed/floating interest-rate swap where the floating leg of the

swap is tied to a published index of a daily overnight rate reference. The term ranges from one week to two years (sometimes more). At maturity, the two parties agree to exchange the difference between the interest accrued at the agreed fixed rate and interest accrued through geometric averaging of the floating index rate on the agreed notional amount. This means that the floating-rate calculation replicates the accrual on an amount (principal plus interest) rolled at the index rate every business day over the term of the swap. If cash can be borrowed by the swap receiver on the same maturity as the swap and at the same rate, and lent back every day in the market at the index rate, the cash payoff at maturity will exactly match the swap payout: the OIS acts as a perfect hedge for a cash instrument.

46. Hördahl and King (2008): "the (former) top US investment banks funded roughly half of their assets using repo markets, with additional exposure due to off-balance sheet financing of their customers" (p. 39).

47. Suspension of mark-to-market accounting might have been prudent to mitigate the effects of asset sales. See chapter 4.

48. The "lemons market" refers to a market in which one side of a transaction has information about the true value of something, but the other side does not. As a result, parties can try to sell overvalued cars or securities, or whatever. But then the parties with undervalued things to sell leave the market. See Akerlof (1970).

49. The Quiet Period also corresponds to a less skill-intensive, lower paid financial sector. See Philippon and Reshef (2008).

50. Insuring demand deposits, something we take for granted, was controversial at the time of adoption: "many bankers and economists protested" Taggart and Jennings (1934, p. 508).

51. For example, Pozdena (1986) discusses "the causes of rapid growth in securitization" almost 25 years ago. He writes: "Securitization is ... one manifestation of how financial innovation—driven by technological and other changes—is moving some parts of financing activity away from financial intermediaries."

52. *New York Times*, January 16, 1877, p. 4.

53. On the Aldrich-Vreeland Act, see Silber (2007a, b).

54. Demand deposits could reflect the risk of the bank failing if the face value was discounted when consumers wrote checks to buy things. This was, in fact, the case for the private bank money issued during the Free Banking Era in pre–Civil War America. This market was "efficient," but was being superseded by demand deposits. See Gorton (1996, 1999).

CHAPTER 3

1. My use of the phrase "no trade theorem" is an abuse of its original meaning. The "no trade theorem" is the theoretical result that in most circumstances it is not possible for an agent with superior information to profit from trading on that information. See Grossman and Stiglitz (1980) and Milgrom and Stokey (1982). Here, I mean to imply that counterparties assumed their trading partners were better informed and hence refused to trade. "Every banker knows that if he has to prove that he is worthy of

credit, however good may be his arguments, in fact his credit is gone." Walter Bagehot, *Lombard Street* (1873, chapter II, paragraph II): http://www.econlib.org/Library/Bagehot/bagLom.html.

2. See Gorton (1984, 1985, 1988) and Gorton and Mullineaux (1987) for discussions of the clearinghouses' issue of their own emergency currency. Gorton and Huang (2006) provide a theory.

3. I have described these changes in banking with various coauthors, including the rise of loan sales and securitization, the use of derivatives, and the regulatory implications of a declining bank charter values. See Gorton and Pennacchi (1989, 1995), Gorton and Souleles (2006), Gorton and Rosen (1995), Gorton (1994).

4. See Gorton (1988), Gorton and Mullineaux (1987), Calomiris and Gorton (1991), and Gorton and Huang (2006).

5. The details are also important in the study of historical panics generally. Little work has been done. Exceptions include, for example, Kelley and Ó Gráda (2000) and Ó Gráda and White (2003). Ó Gráda and White (2003) conclude: "The outcome is partly at variance with the stylized facts of the theoretical literature on banking panics. Banking panics were not characterized by an immediate mass panic of depositors..." (p. 238). Other examples of empirical work include Calomiris and Schweikart (1991), Moen and Tallman (1992), Calomiris and Mason (1997), Richardson (2005) and Richardson and Troost (2005).

6. I do not address the issue of bubbles in this paper. Although I have written about bubbles (see Allen and Gorton, 1993), I don't think we really understand how they start or are sustained or why they end. In any case, others are more capable than I have written on this topic. (See, e.g., Shiller, 2007, and Case and Shiller, 2003).

7. See *Inside Mortgage Finance, The 2007 Mortgage Market Statistical Annual,* Key Data (2006), Joint Economic Committee (October 2007).

8. Recall that a CDO is a special purpose vehicle, which buys a portfolio of fixed income assets and finances the purchase of the portfolio via issuing different tranches of risk in the capital markets. A residential mortgage-backed security is a bond backed by the cash flows from a pool of mortgages in a special purpose vehicle, rather than the general credit of a corporation.

9. See Gorton and Souleles (2006) for a discussion of off-balance-sheet vehicles and the implicit contracting between investors and vehicle sponsors.

10. Andrews (1908A), speaking of the Panic of 1907: "As there was no common market for money, there were no regular quotations..." (p. 292).

11. A survey of the panic is provided by the Bank of England (2008). Appendix A of this paper provides a chronology of events.

12. By "breakdown," I mean that the arbitrage relations between the ABX indices and the underlying cash bonds broke down, as described in Gorton (2008).

13. In fact, the first subprime crisis occurred in 1998, when a number of subprime originators failed. See Temkin et al. (2002) and Moody's (October 1998). This first crisis did not result in a systemic problem emanating from subprime mortgages, though it was part of the larger Asian and LTCM crises.

14. On automated credit evaluation and other technological change in mortgage underwriting, see LaCour-Little (2000), Straka (2000), and Gates, Perry, and Zorn (2002).

15. Smith (1998), a Bank of America national manager of community lending, was interviewed for the Listokin et al. study. The citations in the quotations are taken from that interview.

16. Raiter and Parisi (2004) find a significant nonlinear relationship between FICO scores and coupon differentials: "We find that risk-based pricing has become more rational since 1998. The data show a trend toward greater differentiation in mortgage coupons over time" (p. 1).

17. Some borrowers in the subprime market may have been "prime" borrowers, but some lacked documented income, for example.

18. FICO is a credit score developed by Fair Isaac & Co. (http://www.fairisaac .com/fic/en). FICO scores range from 300 to 850. The higher the score, the better the chances of repayment of a loan.

19. The difference between the original balance and the current balance is the amount that has defaulted or has prepaid. The factor is the percentage remaining (current balance divided by original balance). The factor varies from 65.8% to 90.5%, reflecting differing speeds of prepayment.

20. There are other types of subprime loans, such as hybrid, interest-only, 40-year hybrid ARMs, and piggyback second liens. These types are less important quantitatively.

21. There is also an option to delay payment, in which case the mortgage becomes delinquent.

22. The probability of default is also a function of other factors, but I do not include other variables, to ease notation.

23. To ease notation, I will omit the prepayment penalty.

24. There is no hard evidence on this that I know of, but casually, this seems to be the case. The initial bank may have an information advantage over competitors. Gross and Souleles (2002), for example, show the additional explanatory power of bank internal information over publicly available information like FICO scores in predicting consumer defaults in credit card accounts. Other evidence concerns the originating bank waiving prepayment fees. For example: "Some lenders may waive the prepayment penalty if you refinance your loan with them and you have held the mortgage for at least one year." Pena Lending Group, see http://www.penalending .com/cash-out_refinance.html. Or Mark Ross, president and CEO of Tucson lender Prime Capital Inc., who said, "Prepayment penalties are most often found on subprime loans made to buyers with less-than-perfect credit histories. However, some lenders may be willing to waive prepayment penalties to let borrowers refinance."

See http://www.azstarnet.com/business/226559. However, if a loan is securitized, then the prepayment fee cannot be waived because there is a claimant on that cash flow stream in the RMBS.

25. As far as I know, there is no data set which tracks this. Loan performance, the mortgage data set for securitized mortgages, is careful not to allow individual lenders to be identified.

26. Updated estimates provided by Jim Kennedy of the mortgage system presented in "Estimates of Home Mortgage Originations, Repayments, and Debt On One-to-Four-

Family Residences," Alan Greenspan and James Kennedy, Federal Reserve Board FEDS working paper no. 2005–41.

27. Their data set does not allow them to determine how much was extracted.

28. An interesting question is whether house price increases in some parts of the country were in part caused by the granting of mortgages. Mayer and Pence (2008) is relevant here.

29. Gorton and Souleles (2006) describe the mechanics of securitization.

30. A REMIC (real estate mortgage investment conduit), shown in the figures, is an investment vehicle, a legal structure that can hold commercial and residential mortgages in trust and issue securities representing undivided interests in these mortgages. A REMIC can be a corporation, trust, association, or partnership. REMICS were authorized under the Tax Reform Act of 1986.

31. This is true of securitization generally; see Gorton and Souleles (2007).

32. Two other features are: (1) the clean-up call and (2) compensating interest. (1) The clean-up call gives the owner of the call, generally the residual owner, the option to purchase the remaining bonds in a deal at a predetermined price when the collateral factor reaches a certain level, i.e., when the deal has amortized down to a sufficiently low level. Normally, the call is to purchase the bonds at par plus accrued interest, when the factor is at or below 10%. (2) The day that a borrower prepays his loan, interest payments on that loan stop. The mortgage servicer, in a nonagency deal, is normally required to compensate investors for this foregone interest, using funds paid to the servicer as fees.

33. Delinquency triggers are classified as either "soft" or "hard." The trigger is hit if serious delinquencies, defined as 60+ days, foreclosure, and REO, are at or exceed certain limits. With a soft trigger, the delinquency limit is defined relative to the current amount of senior credit enhancement: the balance of the mezz and subordinate classes, plus OC, expressed as a percentage of the balance of the collateral. For example, serious delinquencies exceed 50% of the senior credit enhancement. With a hard trigger, the delinquency limit is defined as a specific percentage of the current collateral balance, e.g., if serious delinquencies exceed 12% of the current balance.

34. See the prospectus: http://www.secinfo.com/d12atd.z3e6.htm#1stPage.

35. The weighted average weighting factor refers to a weighted average rating where ratings have been converted to numbers by a rating agency (in such a way that the ratings are not equidistant apart). Similarly, "correlation factors" refers to rating agency-stated correlation assumptions. The details do not concern us here.

36. During the panic, this will be problematic, as the senior investors may choose to liquidate, even though they know that the prices are fire-sale prices, and their sale will push prices down further, causing another round of marking down—as discussed later.

37. See Moody's, "Impact of Subprime Downgrades on OC-linked Events of Default in CDOs," *Special Report,* November 1, 2007.

38. As of January 10, 2008, about $58 billion worth of CDOs have hit "events of default" (EOD) (see *Financial Times,* January 10, 2008). Moody's reported on January 7,

2008 that "more than 50 structured CDOs ("ABS CDOs") have experienced an Event of Default ("EOD")…" (see Moody's, "Understanding the Consequences of ABS CDO Events of Default Triggered by Loss of Overcollateralization," *Special Report*, January 7, 2008).

39. When investors indicate an interest in investing in a CDO, and even when they invest, the CDO is not completely "ramped up"; that is, all the ABS bonds for the portfolio have not been purchased yet. Investment will be made based on the criteria restricting the portfolio's composition.

40. I recognize that this is a casual observation. Though I believe this view is widely held by traders, I know of no formal documentation of this.

41. Gorton (2008) discusses negative-basis trades in more detail.

42. We do know that these were a source of writedowns for banks. For example, UBS (2008): "Negative Basis Super Seniors: these were Super Senior positions where the risk of loss was hedged through so-called Negative Basis (or "NegBasis") trades where a counterparty, such as a monoline insurer provided 100% loss protection. The hedge resulted in a credit exposure towards the protection seller. As of the end of 2007, writedowns on these positions represented approximately 10% of the total Super Senior losses" (p. 14).

43. The difference between total issuance and structured finance issuance would be other categories, such as investment grade loans, high yield loans, investment grade bonds, high yield bonds, etc.

44. Synthetic CDOs are not inclued in the table.

45. The residual category, which has been excluded, consists of market value CDOs. Fully synthetic CDOs are not included.

46. See http://www.markit.com/information/products/abx.html.

47. The rule also restricts the credit quality of the securities that a money market fund may purchase.

48. There was a maximum of 30 SIVs that existed, of which 21 were run by 10 banks, including Citigroup, Dresdner, and Bank of Montreal. The approximate size of the SIV sector at its peak was $400 billion in November 2007, having grown from $200 billion three years earlier. See S&P, transcript of teleconference, "Update on U.S. Subprime and Related Matters, November 1, 2007, http://www2.standardandpoors .com/spf/pdf/media/teleconference_transcript_110107.pdf.

49. There were market value CDOs, but they died out.

50. The example is simplified with only one mortgage in the subprime RMBS, and only one RMBS tranche in the CDO. This ignores a number of important issues in practice, which need not concern us here.

51. The example does not display the "cliff" risk that can occur when the CDO contains many tranches of various ABS, RMBS, and CMBS bonds. "Cliff" risk refers to the phenomenon of a tranche being wiped out quickly once losses reach it.

52. Though note that the investor in a CDO tranche would know the underlying ABS, RMBS, and CMBS bonds, but would not know the underlying portfolios of those instruments.

53. When I say "value" I usually mean to compute an expected loss or expected payoff using historical information. "Marking-to-market" is another matter, briefly discussed later.

CHAPTER 4

1. The calculation is the percentage change in the seasonally adjusted OFHEO repeat-sales house price index for purchase transactions, only between the fourth quarters of 2000 and 2005. See www.ofheo.gov/HPLasp.

2. There are two indices that measure house price appreciation: S&P/Case-Shiller and the OFHEO House Price Index. Both of these indices are based on repeat sales. The two indices differ in important respects. Case-Shiller does not cover the entire United States, and the omitted areas seem to be doing better than the included areas. Case-Shiller omits 13 states altogether and has incomplete coverage of 29 other states (see Leventis (2007)). The OFHEO index is not value-weighted and only includes homes with conforming mortgages.

3. The United States has not experienced a large, nationwide decline in house prices since the Great Depression of the 1930s. In 1940, the median nonfarm housing value was 48.6% below the 1930 median value (based on the 1940 Housing Census). Over the same decade, the Consumer Price Index had fallen 17.4% and food prices had fallen 27%. In other words, even adjusting for the deflation during the period, housing prices had not recovered to the levels at the beginning of the Depression by 1940. See Fishback, Horrace, and Kantor (2001).

4. The trustees for transactions make monthly reports known as remittance reports. Remittance reports detail scheduled and unscheduled remittances of principal, servicer advances, loan repurchases, realized losses, delinquencies, and so on.

5. This is related to some ideas of Grossman (1988) about the 1987 stock market crash. Grossman argues that portfolio insurance, in synthetically creating a put option, does not reveal to market participants the amount of such puts outstanding, something that would be known if actual put options were traded.

6. The initial coupons for the BBB- and AAA tranches are shown below:

ABX-HE BBB-	Coupon (bps)
2006-1	267
2006-2	242
2007-1	389
2007-2	500
ABX-HE AAA	
2006-1	18
2006-2	11
2007-1	9
2007-2	76

Source: Markit.

7. "…as the ABX has widened and gone down in price, on some bad fundamental news, we've gotten quite a nice mark to market benefit on that move," Ralph Cioffi, manager of the Bear Stearns hedge funds that subsequently were liquidated; Bear Stearns investor conference call, April 25, 2007.

8. The "super SIV" was the Master-Liquidity Enhancement Conduit (M-LEC), which was an attempt to create the incentive-compatible structure of a 19th-century clearinghouse, but failed. See the *Economist,* October 18, 2007, "Curing SIV," http://www.economist.com/displaystory.cfm?story_id=9993423.

9. For background on repurchase agreements (repo), see Bank for International Settlements (1999).

10. See Mishkin (February 15, 2008) and Taylor and Williams (2008A, B). LIBOR stands for "London interbank offered rate." It is the most widely used benchmark for short-term interest rates in major currencies worldwide. LIBOR is compiled, for 10 currencies over a range of maturities from overnight to 12 months, by the British Bankers' Association (BBA) and is published daily between 11:00 a.m. and noon London time. LIBOR rates are averages of interbank rates submitted by a panel of banks. For each currency, panels comprise at least eight contributor banks. Sterling, dollar, euro, and yen panels contain 16 banks.

See http://www.bba.org.uk/bba/jsp/polopoly.jsp?d=141. An OIS is an interest rate swap in which the floating leg is linked to a published index of daily overnight rates. The two parties agree to exchange at maturity, on an agreed notional amount, the difference between interest accrued at the agreed fixed rate and interest accrued through the geometric average of the floating index rate.

11. The question of what the spread represents is addressed by Taylor and Williams (2008A, B), and Michaud and Upper (2008). I do not pursue this here.

12. In fact, there is a general question concerning double-entry bookkeeping as a paradigm in a world of derivatives.

13. I know of no direct evidence on either of these issues.

14. Many banks had implemented it earlier, in anticipation of the rule coming into effect.

15. Statement 157 defines "fair value" as: "The price that would be received to sell an asset or paid to transfer a liability in an orderly transaction between market participants at the measurement date." See Statement of Financial Standards No. 157 http://www.fasb.org/pdf/fas157.pdf.

16. See Gorton, He, and Huang (2008) and Plantin, Sapra, and Shin (2006) for discussions.

17. Haldeman (2007) provides background, dating back to Enron.

18. See Committee of European Banking Supervisors (2008) and Bond Market Association and the American Securitization Forum (2006) for descriptions of the marking process and the data inputs.

19. Obviously, this would not occur if there was another side to this market. But investors are the very agents facing asymmetric information.

20. On trends in the use of collateral, also see BIS (2001).

21. See http://www.sec.gov/Archives/edgar/data/1174735/000119312507138443/dsc14d9.htm#rom81455_10.

22. CSAs are used in documenting collateral arrangements between two parties that trade privately negotiated (over-the-counter) derivative securities. The trade is documented under a standard contract called a master agreement, developed by the

International Swaps and Derivatives Association (ISDA). The two parties must sign the ISDA master agreement and execute a credit support annex before they trade derivatives with each other. See also ISDA "2005 ISDA Collateral Guidelines," http://www.isda .org/publications/pdf/2005isdacollateralguidelines.pdf.

23. Keep in mind that long credit derivative positions cannot be delivered to the discount window.

24. In triparty repo, a custodian bank or clearing organization acts as an intermediary between the two repo parties. There is no data that I know of that quantifies the amount of bilateral repo.

25. Private communication from a repo trader.

26. See, for example, Bernanke (2008); Wellink (2007), president of the Netherlands Bank and chairman of the Basel Committee on Banking Supervision; Knight (2008), general manager of the BIS; Gieve (2008), deputy governor of the Bank of England.

27. See, for example, Gorton (1988), Berger, Kashyap, and Scalise (1995), and Boyd and Gertler (1994) for some discussion of these trends.

28. See Benveniste, Singh, and Wilhelm (1993) for a description of this competition.

29. For the sake of space, I do not review these developments.

30. Eighty subprime mortgage lenders have exited the business since the end of 2006—many going bankrupt (see Worth Civils and Mark Gongloff, "Subprime Shakeout," WSJ online, http://online.wsj.com/public/resources/documents/info-subprimeloans 0706-sort.html.

31. Mortgage servicing rights may also be securitized.

32. Note that losses can exceed exposures due to the timing of the numbers. Net losses are for the year ending December 28, while net exposure is for December 29.

33. In addition, the sponsors hold the residuals of the securitizations.

34. Frank Vanderlip was a member of the Jekyll Island group, which wrote the draft of the bill that would become the Federal Reserve Act.

CHAPTER 5

1. These trends do not mean the end of banking or even that banking is unimportant. They mean that firms other than "banks" can provide banking services. The problem, from the point of view of public policy, only arises if entry into banking by nonbanks makes banks riskier.

2. See Gorton and Rosen (1995) for an analysis of the risks posed by interest rate derivatives to the U.S. banking system.

3. I focus more on this issue than on the issue of regulating foreign banks. The former issue seems to me to be more difficult and to have received less attention.

4. See Calomiris and Gorton (1991) and Gorton (1988) for discussions of the historical experience of banking panics. Also, see Bordo (1985).

5. Bernanke (1983), studying the Great Depression in the United States, suggests that when there is no public or private deposit insurance, the costs of panic can be large.

6. Recently, a market for the sale of commercial and industrial loans has opened in the United States. This market is fairly sizeable. See Gorton and Pennacchi (1990b) for a discussion.

7. Of course, this raises the question of why demand deposits are created as claims on bank assets, since bank assets are particularly hard to value. I discuss this issue later.

8. Effective deposit insurance need not necessarily be provided by the government. Private insurance was effective in the United States during the 19th century. See Gorton and Mullineaux (1987).

9. As I discuss below, historically it has been necessary to finance nontraded bank loans by debt that is redeemable on demand. Redeemability creates an incentive for debt holders to monitor the otherwise unobservable actions of bankers.

10. Goodhart (1988) discusses this idea of "clubs" in banking.

11. The lack of good substitutes for bank loans basically says that bonds and bank loans are quite different securities. See Gorton and Kahn (2000).

12. Charter value is an asset and should be reflected in the value of the bank. But bank equity is usually assessed by regulators on a book-value basis, so charter value is not reflected.

13. Over 90% of all the loans are floating rate, so this is not much of a selection bias. The difficulty with fixed-rate loans is that the term structure of interest rate then matters, so that the date the loan is originated matters. But then it is difficult to find U.S. firms with which to match the entrants' loans.

14. The results of unsecured loans are not presented because it seems less persuasive that risk is being held constant in the comparison (though the results are no different from the other cases).

15. Gorton and Pennacchi (1993b) test for the presence of contagion effects in nonbanking and find no evidence for their presence.

16. It is worth stressing that in most cases of new activities, such as derivatives or foreign exchange trading, there is no reason for public policy concern per se. Risk is not the issue; information externalities are the issue, and these emanate from loans financed by deposits. See Gorton and Rosen (1995) for an analysis of these issues.

17. This section draws on results from Gorton and Winton (1994).

18. Another problem concerns the market for corporate control in banking. Bank equity holders face problems in disciplining bank managements in many banking systems because hostile takeovers are difficult in banking. As a result, even if equity holders want to unseat management and shrink the size of the bank, they may be unable to do so. These ideas are developed in more detail in Gorton and Rosen (1995b).

19. Alan Greenspan, the former chairman of the Federal Reserve, in a speech to members of the American Bankers Association, said: "Competition among banks and their non-bank counterparts has never been greater. We have been seeing for some months now the result of that competition in the form of easing of the price and non-price terms for credit for business loans." Eugene Ludwig, the U.S. comptroller of the currency, speaking to the same group, said: "We found signs that some banks have eased their underwriting standards over the last several quarters." See the *New York Times,* October 9, 1994.

20. In that case, the "narrow banking" proposal addresses the question of defining a bank very clearly. It focuses completely on the production of demand deposits, limiting entry into that industry and then requiring that deposits be claims on prespecified assets. Moreover, it might be argued that this would be the natural outcome in a less regulated world (see Gorton and Pennacchi, 1992). While a version of this view appears to have lost the debate (on political if not intellectual grounds), some attempt to delineate what is meant by banking is necessary if any regulatory outcome other than the present drift toward universal regulation is to occur.

21. There is also the issue of how to report the market value of positions.

CHAPTER 6

1. See Bernanke (2000), a collection of essays on the Great Depression.

2. See http://www.newyorkfed.org/markets/pridealers_current.html for the list of primary dealers. As of May 28, 2009, the primary dealers were BNP Paribas Securities Corp.; Banc of America Securities LLC; Barclays Capital Inc.; Cantor Fitzgerald & Co.; Citigroup Global Markets Inc.; Credit Suisse Securities (USA) LLC; Daiwa Securities America Inc.; Deutsche Bank Securities Inc.; Dresdner Kleinwort Securities LLC; Goldman Sachs & Co.; HSBC Securities (USA) Inc.; J.P. Morgan Securities Inc.; Mizuho Securities USA Inc.; Morgan Stanley & Co. Incorporated, RBS Securities Inc.; UBS Securities LLC.

3. See the St. Louis Federal Reserve Bank series MULT, M1 Money Multiplier. http://research.stlouisfed.org/fred2/series/MULT/.

4. Even at that low, there was more confidence in banks than in television news, newspapers, or the institution garnering the lowest level of confidence: Congress.

5. A Gallup poll found that confidence did increase slightly; see Jacobe (2009).

6. The full quotation is: "He who controls the present, controls the past. He who controls the past, controls the future." In the novel, the main character, Winston Smith, lives in a fictional totalitarian society where his job is to change history by changing old newspaper records to match whatever "truth" the Party has decided on.

7. Bray Hammond (1886–1968) was the assistant secretary of the Board of Governors of the Federal Reserve System from 1944–1950.

References

Adrian, Tobias, and Hyun Song Shin (2009a), "Liquidity and Leverage," *Journal of Financial Intermediation,* forthcoming (see Federal Reserve Bank of New York Staff Report, No. 328, May 2008).

Adrian, Tobias, and Hyun Song Shin (2009b), "Money, Liquidity and Monetary Policy," *American Economic Review Papers and Proceedings,* forthcoming (see Federal Reserve Bank of New York Staff Report, No. 360, January 2009).

Akerlof, George (1970), "The Market for 'Lemons': Quality Uncertainty and the Market Mechanism," *Quarterly Journal of Economics,* Vol. 84, No. 3, 488–500.

Allen, Franklin, and Gary Gorton (1993), "Churning Bubbles," *Review of Economic Studies,* Vol. 60, No. 4, 813–836.

Andrew, A. Piatt (1908a), "Hoarding in the Panic of 1907," *Quarterly Journal of Economics,* Vol. 22, No. 4, 497–516.

Andrew, A. Piatt (1908b), "Substitutes for Cash in the Panic of 1907," *Quarterly Journal of Economics,* Vol. 22, No. 2, 290–299.

Angelini, Paolo (1998), "An Analysis of Competitive Externalities in Gross Settlement Systems," *Journal of Banking and Finance,* Vol. 22, 1–18.

Baer, H., and McElravey J. (1992), "The Changing Impact of Capital Requirements on Bank Growth—1975 to 1991," Federal Reserve Bank of Chicago, working paper.

Bank of England (2008), *Financial Stability Report* (April), Issue No. 23.

Bank for International Settlements (1999), "Implications of Repo Markets for Central Banks," Report of a working group established by the Committee on the Global Financial System of the Central Banks of the Group of Ten Countries, March 9, 1999.

Bank for International Settlements (2001), "Collateral in Wholesale Financial Markets: Recent Trends, Risk Management and Market Dynamics," Report prepared by the Committee on the Global Financial System Working Group on Collateral (March 2001).

Bank for International Settlements, Committee on Payment and Settlement Systems (2005a), "New Developments in Large-Value Payment Systems."

Bank for International Settlements, Committee on Payment and Settlement Systems (2005b), "New Developments in Large-Value Payment Systems."

Bank for International Settlements (BIS) (2008a), "Semiannual OTC Derivatives Statistics at end-June 2008."

Bank for International Settlements (BIS) (2008b), "International Banking and Financial Market Developments," *BIS Quarterly Review* (December).

Basel Committee on Banking Supervision, Bank for International Settlements (2008c), The Joint Forum, "Credit Risk Transfer," Consultative Document (April).

Bank for International Settlements (BIS) (2009), Committee on Payment and Settlement Systems of the Group of Ten Countries, "Statistics on Payment and Settlement in Selected Countries" (March).

Bear Stearns (2006a), "Bear Stearns Quick Guide to Non-Agency Mortgage-Backed Securities" (September).

Bear Stearns (2006b), "RMBS Residuals: A Primer" (September).

Becketti, S., and Morris, C. (1992), "Are Bank Loans Still Special?" *Economic Review*, Vol. 77, No. 3, 71–84.

Benveniste, Lawrence, Manoj Singh, and William Wilhelm (1993), "The Failure of Drexel Burnham Lambert: Evidence on the Implications for Commercial Banks," *Journal of Financial Intermediation*, Vol. 3, 104–137.

Berger, Allen, Anil Kashyap, and Joseph Scalise (1995), "The Transformation of the U.S. Banking Industry: What a Long Strange Trip It's Been," *Brookings Papers on Economic Activity*, Vol. 2, 55–218.

Bernanke, Ben (2008), "Addressing Weaknesses in the Global Financial Markets: The Report of the President's Working Group on Financial Markets," speech at the World Affairs Council of Greater Richmond's Virginia Global Ambassador Award Luncheon, Richmond, Virginia, April 10, 2008.

Bernanke, Ben (2000), *Essays on the Great Depression* (Princeton, NJ: Princeton University Press).

Bernanke, Ben (1983), "Nonmonetary Effects of the Financial Crisis in Propagation of the Great Depression," *American Economic Review*, Vol. 73, No. 3, 257–276.

Bhardwaj, Geetesh, and Rajdeep Sengupta (2008a), "Prepaying Subprime Mortgages," Federal Reserve Bank of St. Louis, working paper.

Bhardwaj, Geetesh, and Rajdeep Sengupta (2008b), "Where's the Smoking Gun? A Study of Underwriting Standards for U.S. Subprime Mortgages," Federal Reserve Bank of St. Louis, working paper.

Black, H., Fields, M. A., and Schweitzer, R. (1990), "Changes in Interstate Banking Laws: The Impact on Shareholder Wealt," *Journal of Finance*, Vol. 45, No. 5, 1663–1671.

Bliss, Robert, and George Kaufman (2006), "Derivatives and Systemic Risk: Netting, Collateral and Closeout," *Journal of Financial Stability*, Vol. 2, No. 1, 55–70.

Blume, Marshall E., Donald B. Keim, and Sandeep A. Patel (1991), "Returns and Volatility of Low-grade Bonds: 1977–1989," *Journal of Finance* 46, 49–74.

Bond Market Association and the American Securitization Forum (2006), "An Analysis and Description of Pricing and Information Sources in the Securitized and Structured Finance Markets" (October).

Bond Market Association (2005), "Repo & Securities Lending Survey of U.S. Markets Volume and Loss Experience," *Research* (January).

Bordo, Michael (1986), "Financial Crises, Banking Crises, Stock Market Crashes and the Money Supply: Some International Evidence, 1870–1933," in *Financial Crises and the World Banking System* (London: MacMillan), eds. Forrest Capie and Geoffrey Wood, 190–248.

Bordo, Michael (1985), "The Impact and International Transmission of Financial Crises: Some Historical Evidence, 1870–1933," *Revista di Storia Economica* 2, 41–78.

Boyd, John, and Mark Gertler (1994), "Are Banks Dead? Or Are the Reports Greatly Exaggerated?" in *Proceedings of a Conference on Bank Structure and Competition,* Federal Reserve Bank of Chicago, 85–117.

Boyd, John, Sungkyu Kwak, and Bruce Smith (2005), "The Real Output Losses Associated with Modern Banking Crises," *Journal of Money, Credit, and Banking,* Vol. 37, No. 6, 977–999.

Burns, Arthur F., and Wesley C. Mitchell (1946), *Measuring Business Cycles* (New York: NBER).

Caballero, Ricardo (2006), "On the Macroeconomics of Asset Shortages," in *The Role of Money: Money and Monetary Policy in the Twenty-First Century,* The Fourth European Central Banking Conference 9–10, November 2006, eds. Andreas Beyer and Lucrezia Reichlin, 272–283.

Calomiris, Charles (1993), "Regulation, Industrial Structure, and Instability in U.S. Banking: An Historical Perspective," in *Structural Change in Banking* (Homewood, IL: Business One Irwin), eds. Michael Klausner and Lawrence White, 19–116.

Calomiris, Charles, and Gary Gorton (1991), "The Origins of Banking Panics: Models, Facts, and Bank Regulation," in *Financial Markets and Financial Crises* (University of Chicago Press), ed. Glenn Hubbard.

Calomiris, C., and Charles Kahn (1991), "The Role of Demandable Debt in Structuring Optimal Banking Arrangements," *American Economic Review,* Vol. 81, No. 3, 497–513.

Calomiris, Charles, and Joseph Mason (1997), "Contagion and Bank Failures during the Great Depression: The June 1932 Chicago Banking Panic," *American Economic Review,* Vol. 87, No. 5, 863–883.

Calomiris, Charles, and Joseph Mason (2004), "Credit Card Securitization and Regulatory Arbitrage," *Journal of Financial Services Research,* Vol. 26, No. 1, 5–27.

Calomiris, Charles, and Larry Schweikart (1991) "The Panic of 1857: Origins, Transmission, and Containment," *Journal of Economic History,* Vol. 51, No. 4, 807–834.

Canner, Glenn, and Wayne Passmore (1999), "The Role of Specialized Lenders in Extending Mortgages to Lower-Income and Minority Homebuyers," *Federal Reserve Bulletin* (November), 709–723.

Cannon, James G. (1910), *Clearing Houses* (Washington D.C.: Government Printing Office: U.S. National Monetary Commission).

Case, Karl, and Robert Shiller (2003), "Is There a Bubble in the Housing Market?" *Brookings papers on Economic Activity*, Vol. 2, 299–362.

Cerra, Valerie, and Sweta Chaman Saxena (2008), "Growth Dynamics: The Myth of Economic Recovery," *American Economic Review*, Vol. 98, No. 1, 439–457.

Chailloux, Alexandre, Simon Gray, and Rebecca McCaughrin (2008), "Central Bank Collateral Frameworks: Principles and Policies," International Monetary Fund, Working Paper # WP/08/222.

Chen, Weitzu, Chi-Chun Liu, and Stephen Ryan (2007), "Characteristics of Securitizations that Determine Issuers' Retention of Risks on the Securitized Assets" (http://papers.ssrn.com/s013/papers.cfm?abstract_id=1077798).

Chomsisengphet, Souphala, and Anthony Pennington-Cross (2007), "Subprime Refinancing: Equity Extraction and Mortgage Termination," *Real Estate Economics*, Vol. 35, No. 2, 233–263.

Chomsisengphet, Souphala, and Anthony Pennington-Cross (2006), "The Evolution of the Subprime Mortgage Market," Federal Reserve Bank of St. Louis *Review* (January/February).

Citibank (2007), "A Simple Guide to Subprime Mortgages, CDOs, and Securitization" (April 13).

Committee of European Banking Supervisors (2008), "Report on Issues Regarding the Valuation of Complex and Illiquid Financial Instruments" (June 18).

Cornell, Bradford, and Kevin Green (1991), "The Investment Performance of Low-grade Bond Funds," *Journal of Finance*, Vol. 46, 29–48.

Cowen, David, Richard Sylla, and Robert Wright (2006), "The U.S. Panic of 1792: Financial Crisis Management and the Lender of Last Resort," New York University, working paper.

Cuite, Cara, Sarah Condry, Mary Nucci, and William Hallman (2007), "Public Response to the Contaminated Spinach Recall of 2006," Food Policy Institute Report, Rutgers University.

Dang, Tri Vi, Gary Gorton and Bengt Holmström (2009), "Opacity and the Optimality of Debt for Liquidity."

Davis, Joseph (2006), "An Improved Annual Chronology of U.S. Business Cycles since the 1790s," *Journal of Economic History*, Vol. 66: 103–121.

Davis, Joseph (2004), "An Annual Index of U.S. Industrial Production, 1790–1915," *Quarterly Journal of Economics*, Vol. 119, No. 4, 1177–1215.

Demirgüc-Kunt, Asli, Baybars Karacaovali, and Luc Laeven (2005), "Deposit Insurance around the World: A Comprehensive Database," World Bank Policy Research Working Paper 3628.

Demyanyk, Yuliya, and Otto Van Hemert (2007), "Understanding the Subprime Mortgage Crisis" (December 10), Stern School of Business, New York University, working paper.

Deutsche Bundesbank (1987), "Longer-term Trends in the Banks' Investments in Securities," *Monthly Report* (May), 24–33.

Deutsche Bundesbank (1992), "Longer-term Trends in the Financing of West Germany Enterprises," *Monthly Report* (October), 25–39.

Domanski, Dietrich, and Uwe Neumann (2001), "Collateral in Wholesale Financial Markets," *BIS Quarterly Review* (September), 57–64.

Dunbar, Charles F. (1887), "Deposits as Currency," *Quarterly Journal of Economics*, Vol. 1, No. 4, 401–419.

Drucker, Steven, and Manju Puri (2007), "On Loan Sales, Loan Contracting, and Lending Relationships," Duke University, working paper.

Dwyer, Gerald, and R. Alton Gilbert (1989), "Bank Runs and Private Remedies," Federal Reserve Bank of St. Louis *Review* (May/June), 43–61.

Economist, The (2008), "Don't Mark to Markit" (May 6) (http://www.economist.co.uk/finance/displaystory.cfm?story_id=10809435).

Euromoney (2008), "Understanding the Mark-To-Market Meltdown" (March 3).

European Central Bank, (2007), *Financial Stability Review*.

Fama, E. (1985), "What's Different about Banks?" *Journal of Monetary Economics*, Vol. 15, 5–29.

Fama, Eugene F., and Kenneth R. French (1989), "Business Conditions and Expected Returns on Stocks and Bonds," *Journal of Financial Economics*, Vol. 25, 23–49.

Fama, Eugene F., and Kenneth R. French (1993), "Common Risk Factors in the Returns on Stock and Bonds," *Journal of Financial Economics*, Vol. 33, 3–56.

Farris, John, and Christopher Richardson (2004), "The Geography of Subprime Mortgage Prepayment Penalty Patterns," *Housing Policy Debate*, Vol. 15, No. 3, 687–714.

Federal Deposit Insurance Corporation (1998), *A Brief History of Deposit Insurance in the United States*, Prepared for the International Conference on Deposit Insurance, Washington D.C., September 1998.

Federal Reserve System (2006), "Consultation Paper on Intraday Liquidity Management and Payment System Risk Policy," *Federal Register*, Vol. 71, No. 119 (June 21), 35679–35687.

Fels, Rendigs (1951), "American Business Cycles, 1865–79," *The American Economic Review*, Vol. 41, No. 3, 325–349.

Fender, Ingo, and Peter Hördahl (2007), "Overview: Credit Retrenchment Triggers Liquidity Squeeze," *BIS Quarterly Review* (September), 1–16.

Fishback, Price, William Horrace, and Shawn Kantor (2001), "The Origins of Modern Housing Finance: The Impact of Federal Housing Programs during the Great Depression," University of Arizona, working paper.

Fitch Ratings (2008), "Fair Value Accounting: Is It Helpful in Illiquid Markets?" *Accounting Research Special Report* (April 28).

Fitch Ratings (2007), "The Impact of Poor Underwriting Practices and Fraud in Subprime RMBS Performance," *U.S. Residential Mortgage Special Report* (November 28).

Fleming, Michael, and Kenneth Garbade (2005), "Explaining Settlement Fails," *Current Issues in Economics and Finance* (September), Federal Reserve Bank of New York.

Flood, Mark D. (1992), "The Great Deposit Insurance Debate," Federal Reserve Bank of St. Louis *Review* (July/August), 51–77.

Frankel, Allen (2006), "Prime or Not so Prime? An Exploration of U.S. Housing Finance in the New Century," Bank for International Settlements, *Quarterly Review* (March).

Friedman, Milton, and Anna Schwartz (1971), *Monetary History of the United States, 1867–1960* (Princeton, NJ: Princeton University Press).

Frodin, J. (1980), "The Tax/Subsidy Relation between Member Banks and the Federal Reserve System," *Journal of Monetary Economics,* Vol. 6, 105–19.

Furfine, Craig, and Jeff Stehm (1998), "Analyzing Alternative Intraday Credit Policies in Real-Time Gross Settlement Systems," *Journal of Money Credit and Banking,* Vol. 30, No. 4, 832–48.

Gali, Jordi, and Luca Gambetti (2008), "On the Sources of the Great Moderation," National Bureau of Economic Research, Working Paper No. 14171.

Gates, Susan, Perry, Vanessa, and Zorn, Peter (2002), "Automated Underwriting in Mortgage Lending: Good News for the Underserved?" *Housing Policy Debate,* Vol. 13, No. 2, 369–391.

Geithner, Timothy (2008), Remarks at the Economic Club of New York, New York City, June 9, 2008.

Gieve, John (2008), "The Return of the Credit Cycle: Old Lessons in New Markets," speech at the Euromoney Bond Investors Congress, February 27, 2008 (http://www.bankofengland.co.uk/publications/speeches/2008/speech338.pdf).

Gilbert, A. (1977), "Utilization of Federal Reserve Bank Services by Member Banks: Implications for the Costs and Benefits of Membership," *Review,* Federal Reserve Bank of St Louis, 2–15.

Goodhart, C. (1988), *The Evolution of Central Banks* (Cambridge, MA: MIT Press).

Gordon, Brian (2008), "Hedges in the Warehouse: The Banks Get Trimmed," *Chicago Fed Letter,* Federal Reserve Bank of Chicago, April, Number 249.

Gorton, Gary, and Andrew Metrick (2009a), "Securitized Banking and the Run on Repo," Yale, working paper.

Gorton, Gary and Andrew Metrick (2009b), "Haircuts," Yale, working paper.

Gorton Gary (2008), "Information, Liquidity, and the (Ongoing) Panic of 2007," *American Economic Review, Papers and Proceedings,* Vol. 9, No. 2 (May), 567–572.

Gorton, Gary (1996), "Reputation Formation in Early Bank Note Markets," *Journal of Political Economy,* Vol. 104, No. 2, 346–397.

Gorton, Gary (1999), "Pricing Free Bank Notes," *Journal of Monetary Economics,* Vol. 44, 33–64.

Gorton, Gary (1994), "Bank Regulation When 'Banks' and 'Banking' Are Not the Same," *Oxford Review of Economic Policy,* Vol. 10, No. 4, 106–119.

Gorton, Gary (1988), "Banking Panics and Business Cycles," *Oxford Economic Papers,* Vol. 40, 751–781.

Gorton, Gary (1985), "Clearinghouses and the Origin of Central Banking in the U.S.," *Journal of Economic History,* Vol. 45, No. 2, 277–283.

Gorton, Gary (1984), "Private Bank Clearinghouses and the Origins of Central Banking," Federal Reserve Bank of Philadelphia *Business Review* (January–February), 3–12.

Gorton, Gary, Ping He, and Lixin Huang (2008), "Monitoring and Manipulation: Asset Prices When Agents are Marked-to-Market," working paper.

Gorton, Gary, and Lixin Huang (2006), "Banking Panics and Endogenous Coalition Formation," with Lixin Huang, *Journal of Monetary Economics,* Vol. 53, No. 7, 1613–1629.

Gorton, Gary, and James Kahn (2000), "The Design of Bank Loan Contracts," *Review of Financial Studies*, Vol. 13, 331–364.

Gorton, Gary, and Andrew Metrick (2009), "The Run on Repo and the Panic of 2007–2008," Yale, working paper.

Gorton, Gary, and Don Mullineaux (1987), "The Joint Production of Confidence: Endogenous Regulation and Nineteenth Century Commercial Bank Clearinghouses," *Journal of Money, Credit, and Banking*, Vol. 19, No. 4, 458–68.

Gorton, Gary, and George Pennacchi (1990a), "Financial Intermediaries and Liquidity Creation," *Journal of Finance*, Vol. 45, No. 1 (March), 49–72.

Gorton, Gary, and George Pennacchi (1990b), "Are Loan Sales Really Off-Balance Sheet?" *Journal of Accounting, Auditing and Finance*, Vol. 4, No. 2, 125–145.

Gorton, Gary, and George Pennacchi (1993a), "Security Baskets and Index-Linked Securities," *Journal of Business,* Vol. 66, No. 1, 1–29.

Gorton, Gary, and George Pennacchi (1993b), "Money Market Funds and Finance Companies: Are They the Banks of the Future?" in *Structural Change in Banking* (Homewood, IL: Irwin Publishing), Michael Klausner and Lawrence White, eds.

Gorton, Gary, and George Pennacchi (1993c), "Banks and Loan Sales: Marketing Non-Marketable Assets," *Journal of Monetary Economics*, Vol. 35, No. 3, 389–411.

Gorton, Gary, and George Pennacchi (1992), "Financial Innovation and the Provision of Liquidity Services." In *Reform of Federal Deposit Insurance* (HarperCollins), J. Barth, and D. Brumbaugh, eds.

Gorton, Gary, and George Pennacchi (1990a), "Financial Intermediaries and Liquidity Creation," *Journal of Finance*, Vol. 45, No. 1 (March), 49–72.

Gorton, Gary, and George Pennacchi (1989), "Are Loan Sales Really Off-Balance Sheet?" *Journal of Accounting, Auditing and Finance*, Vol. 4, No. 2 (Spring), 125–145.

Gorton, Gary, and Richard Rosen (1995a), "Banks and Derivatives," in National Bureau of Economic Research *Macroeconomics Annual 1995* (MIT Press).

Gorton, Gary, and Richard Rosen (1995b), "Corporate Control, Portfolio Choice, and the Decline of Banking," *Journal of Finance*, Vol. 50, No. 5, 1377–1420.

Gorton, Gary, and Nicholas S. Souleles (2006), "Special Purpose Vehicles and Securitization," in *The Risks of Financial Institutions,* (University of Chicago Press), Rene Stulz and Mark Carey, eds.

Gorton, Gary, and Andrew Winton (2000), "Liquidity Provision and the Social Cost of Bank Capital," working paper.

Gorton, Gary, and Andrew Winton (1994), "Bank Capital Regulation in General Equilibrium," Wharton School, University of Pennsylvania, working paper.

Greenspan, Alan, and James Kennedy (2007), "Sources and Uses of Equity Extracted from Homes," Board of Governors of the Federal Reserve System, Finance and Economics Discussion Series, Working Paper #2007–20.

Greenspan, Alan, and James Kennedy (2005), "Estimates of Home Mortgage Originations, Repayments, and Debt on One-to-Four Family Residences," Board of Governors of the Federal Reserve System, Finance and Economics Discussion Series, Working Paper #2005–41.

Gross, David, and Nicholas Souleles (2002), "An Empirical Analysis of Personal Bankruptcy and Delinquency," *Review of Financial Studies*, Vol. 15, 319–347.

Grossman Richard (1993), "The Macroeconomic Consequences of Bank Failures under the National Banking System," *Explorations in Economic History*, Vol. 30, No. 3, 294–320.

Grossman, Sanford (1988), "An Analysis of the Implications for Stock and Futures Price Volatility of Program Trading and Dynamic Trading Strategies," *Journal of Business*, Vol. 61, 275–298.

Grossman, Sanford, and Joseph Stiglitz (1980), "On the Impossibility of Informationally Efficient Markets," *American Economic Review*, Vol. 70, 393–408.

Guerrera, Francesco, and Deborah Brewster (April 30, 2008), "Pimco Scouts for Wall St Cast-offs," *Financial Times* (http://www.ft.com/cms/s/0/22861bb0–16f0–11dd-bbfc-0000779fd2ac.html).

Gyntelberg, Jacob, and Philip Wooldridge (2008), "Interbank Rate Fixings during the Recent Turmoil," Bank for International Settlements *Quarterly Review* (March), 59–72.

Haldeman, Robert (2007), "Fact, Fiction, and Fair Value Accounting at Enron," *The CPA Journal* (August 25).

Hammond, Bray (1957), *Banks and Politics in America from the Revolution to the Civil War* (Princeton, NJ: Princeton University Press; current edition 1991).

Hannan, Timothy, and Allen Berger (1991), "The Rigidity of Prices: Evidence from the Banking Industry," *American Economic Review*, Vol. 81, No. 4, 938–945.

Hester, Elisabeth, and Katherine Bureton (June 19, 2008), "Hedge Funds Hire from Wall Street as Jobs Disappear, Pay Falls," Bloomberg.com (http://www.bloomberg.com/apps/news?pid=20601087&sid=avItj3PPwSGk&refer=home).

Hollander, J.H. (1913), "Banking Reform—Discussion," *American Economic Review*, Vol. 3, No. 1, Supplement, Papers and Proceedings, 64–88.

Holmström, Bengt (2008), "Discussion of 'The Panic of 2007,' by Gary Gorton," in *Maintaining Stability in a Changing Financial System*, Proceedings of the 2008 Jackson Hole Conference, Federal Reserve Bank of Kansas City.

Hördahl, Peter, and Michael King (2008), "Developments in Repo Markets During the Financial Turmoil," Bank for International Settlements *Quarterly Review* (December), 37–53.

Hoshi, T., Kashyap, A., and Scharfstein, D. (1993), "The Choice Between Public and Private Debt: An Analysis of Post-Deregulation Corporate Financing in Japan," National Bureau of Economic Research, Working Paper 4421.

International Monetary Fund (April 2008), "Containing Systemic Risks and Restoring Financial Soundness," *Global Financial Stability Report*.

International Swaps and Derivatives Association (ISDA) (2009), "ISDA Margin Survey 2009."

International Swaps and Derivatives Association (ISDA) (2007), "ISDA Margin Survey 2007."

International Swaps and Derivatives Association (ISDA) (2005), "2005 ISDA Collateral Guidelines."

Jacobe, Dennis (2008), "Confidence in U.S. Banks Down Sharply" (June 23). See http://www.gallup.com/poll/108229/confidence-banks-down-sharply.aspx.

Jacobe, Dennis (2009), "Post-Stress Tests, Confidence in U.S. Banks Improves Slightly" (May 13). See http://www.gallup.com/poll/118384/Post-Stress-Tests-Confidence-Banks-Improves-Slightly.aspx.

James, Christopher (1987), "Some Evidence on the Uniqueness of Bank Loans," *Journal of Financial Economics*, Vol. 19, 217–235.

James, F. Cyril (1934), "The American Banking Problem," *Annals of the American Academy of Political and Social Science*, Vol. 171, 1–4.

Jiangli, Wenying, and Matt Pritsker (2008), "The Impacts of Securitization on U.S. Bank Holding Companies," Board of Governors of the Federal Reserve System, working paper.

Joint Economic Committee of the U.S. Congress (2007), "The Subprime Lending Crisis" (October).

Joint Forum, The (2008), "Credit Risk Transfer: Developments from 2005 to 2007" (April).

Johnson, Christian (1997), "Derivatives and Rehypothecation Failure: It's 3:00 P.M., Do You Know Where Your Collateral Is?" *Arizona Law Review*, Vol. 30, No. 949.

Kahn, Charles, and William Roberds (2001), "Real-Time Gross Settlement and the Costs of Immediacy," *Journal of Monetary Economics*, Vol. 47, 299–319.

Kau, J.B., and D.C. Keenan (1995), "An Overview of the Option-Theoretic Pricing in Mortgages," *Journal of Housing Research*, Vol. 6, No. 2, 217–244.

Keeley, Michael (1990), "Deposit Insurance, Risk, and Market Power in Banking," *American Economic Review*, Vol. 80, No. 5, 1183–1200.

Keim, Donald B., and Robert F. Stambaugh (1986), "Predicting Returns in the Stock and Bond Markets," *Journal of Financial Economics*, Vol. 17, 357–390.

Kelley, Morgan, and Cormac Ó Gráda (2000), "Market Contagion: Evidence from the Panics of 1854 and 1857," *American Economic Review*, Vol. 90, No. 5, 1110–1124.

Kemmerer, E.W. (1911), "American Banks in the Times of Crisis under the National Banking System," *Proceedings of the Academy of Political Science in the City of New York*, Vol. 1, No. 2, 233–253.

Kevin Kendra, Fitch (2007), "Tranche ABX and Basis Risk in Subprime RMBS Structured Portfolios" (February 20). See http://www.fitchratings.com/web_content/sectors/subprime/Basis_in_ABX_TABX_Bespoke_SF_CDOs.ppt.

Kiff, John, and Paul Mills (2007), "Lessons from Subprime Turbulence," *IMF Survey Magazine* (August 23).

Kiff, John, and Paul Mills (2007), "Money for Nothing and Checks for Free: Recent Developments in U.S. Subprime Mortgage Markets," July, IMP Working Paper #07–188.

Knigh, Malcom (2008), "Some Reflections on the Future of the Originate-to-Distribute Model in the Context of the Current Financial Turmoil," speech at the Euro 50 Group Roundtable, London, April 21, 2008 (http://www.bis.org/speeches/sp080423.htm).

Kohlbeck, Mark, and Terry Warfield (2002), "The Role of Unrecorded Intangible Assets in Residual Income Valuation: The Case of Banks." See http://papers.ssrn.com/s013/papers.cfm?abstract_id=296387&download=yes.

Krishnamurthy, Arvind, and Annette Vissing-Jorgensen (2008), "The Aggregate Demand for Treasury Debt," Kellogg School, Northwestern University, working paper.

Kwan, Simon H. (1996), "Firm-specific Information and the Correlation Between Individual Stocks and Bonds," *Journal of Financial Economics*, Vol. 40, 63–80.

LaCour-Little, Michael (2000), "The Evolving Role of Technology in Mortgage Finance," *Journal of Housing Research*, Vol. 11, No. 3, 173–205.

Laeven, Luc, and Stijn Claessens (2008), "The Use of Blanket Guarantees in Banking Crises," International Monetary Fund, Working Paper WP/08/250.

Lerner, Josh (2006), "The New New Financial Thing: The Origins of Financial innovations," *Journal of Financial Economics*, Vol. 79, 223–255.

Leventis, Andrew (2007), "A Note on the Differences Between the OFHEO and S&P/Case-Shiller House Prices Indexes," Office of Federal Housing Enterprise Oversight, working paper.

Levintal, Oren (2008), "The Real Effects of Banking Shocks: Evidence from OECD Countries," Hebrew University, working paper.

Listokin, David, Elvin Wyly, Larry Keating, Kristopher Rengert, and Barbara Listokin (2000), "Making New Mortgage Markets: Case Studies of Institutions, Home Buyers, and Communities," Fannie Mae Foundation Research Report.

Litzenberger, Robert (1992), "Swaps: Plain and Fanciful," *Journal of Finance*, Vol. 47, No. 3, 831–850.

Lonski, John (2008), "Market Breakdowns Prompt Fastest Bank C&I Growth Since 1973," Moody's *Credit Trends* (January 8).

Lorin, Janet Frankston (2007), "Consumers Still Worried about E. Coli," WashingtonPost .com (February 5).

Mansfield, Cathy Lesser (2000), "The Road to Subprime 'HEL' Was Paved with Good Congressional Intentions: Usury Deregulation and the Subprime Home Equity Market," *South Carolina Law Review*, Vol. 51 (Spring).

Marburg, Theodore (1908), "The Panic and the Present Depression," *Annals of the American Academy of Political Science*, Vol. 32, 55–62.

Marcus, Alan (1984), "Deregulation and Bank Financial Policy," *Journal of Banking and Finance*, Vol. 8, 557–565.

Mayer, Chris, and Karen Pence (2008), "Subprime Mortgages: What, Where, and to Whom?," Board of Governors, Federal Reserve System, Working Paper #2008–29.

McDermott, Gail, Leslie Albergo, and Natalie Abrams (2001), "NIMs Analysis: Valuing Prepayment Penalty Fee Income," Standard & Poor's, New York, January 3.

McGrane, Reginald (1924), *The Panic of 1837* (Chicago: University of Chicago Press).

Merton, Robert (1992), "Financial Innovation and Economic Performance," *Journal of Applied Corporate Finance*, Vol. 4, 12–22.

Merton, Robert (1998), "Option-Pricing Theory: Twenty-Five Years Later," *American Economic Review*, Vol. 88, No. 3, 323–349.

Michaud, François-Louis, and Upper, Christian (2008), "What Drives Interbank Rates? Evidence from the Libor Panel," BIS *Quarterly Review* (March), 47–58.

Milgrom, Paul, and Nancy Stokey (1982), "Information, Trade and Common Knowledge," *Journal of Economic Theory*, Vol. 26, 17–27.

Miller, Merton (1986), "Financial Innovation: The Last Twenty Years and the Next," *Journal of Financial and Quantitative Analysis*, Vol. 21, No. 4, 459–471.

Miron, Jeffrey, and Christina Romer (1990), "A New Index of Industrial Production, 1884–1940," *Journal of Economic History*, Vol. 50, No. 2, 321–337.

Mishkin, Frederic (2008), "On Leveraged Losses: Lessons From the Mortgage Meltdown," speech at the U.S. Policy Forum, New York, New York, February 29, 2008.

Mishkin, Frederic (2008), "The Federal Reserve's Tools for Responding to Financial Disruptions," speech at the Tuck Global Capital Markets Conference, Tuck School of Business, Dartmouth College, Hanover, New Hampshire, February 15, 2008.

Missal, Michael (2008), "Final Report of Michael Missal, Bankruptcy Court Examiner," United States Bankruptcy Court of the District of Delaware, In re: New Century Holdings, Inc. Chapter 11, Case No. 07–10416 (KJC), February 29, 2008.

Moen, Jon, and Ellis Tallman (1992), "The Bank Panic of 1907: The Role of Trust Companies," *Journal of Economic History*, Vol. 52, 611–30.

Molyneux, Phil, and Nidal Shamroukh (1996), "Diffusion of Financial Innovations: The Case of Junk Bonds and Note Issuance Facilities," *Journal of Money, Credit, and Banking*, Vol. 28, No. 3, 502–522.

Moody's Investors Service (2008), "Understanding the Consequences of ABS CDO Events of Default Triggered by Loss of Overcollateralization," *Structured Finance Special Report* (January 7).

Moody's Investors Service (2007), "Challenging Times for the U.S. Subprime Mortgage Market," *Structured Finance Special Report* (March 7).

Moody's Investors Service (2007), "Impact of Subprime Downgrades on OC-Linked Events of Default in CDOs," *Structured Finance Special Report* (November 1).

Moody's Investors Service (2006), "U.S. RMBS: Evaluating Alternative Performance Triggers," *Structured Finance Special Report* (September 26).

Moody's Investors Service (2006), "Moody's Cashflow Assumptions for RMBS Alt-A Transactions," *Structured Finance Special Report* (February 9).

Moody's Investors Service (2005), "Tranching Senior Classes in U.S. Overcollateralization Structures: A Distinct Loss Position May Warrant a Distinct Rating," *Structured Finance Special Report* (May 12).

Moody's Investors Service (2003), "Structural Nuances in RMBS," *Structured Finance Special Report* (May 30).

Moody's Investors Service (2003), "The Fundamentals of Asset-Backed Commercial Paper," *Structured Finance Special Report* (February 3).

Moody's Investors Service (2002), "Protected for Life? Weak Step-Down Triggers May Add Vulnerability in Some Home Equity Securitizations," *Structured Finance Special Report* (November 22).

Moody's Investors Service (2002), "An Introduction to Structured Investment Vehicles," *Structured Finance Special Report* (January 25).

Moody's Investors Service (1998), "Subprime Home Equity: The Party's Over," *Global Credit Research* (October).

Nash, William (1908), "Clearing-House Certificates and the Need for a Central Bank," *Annals of the American Academy of Political and Social Science*, Vol. 31, Lessons of the Financial Crisis (March), 61–66.

Neumark, David, and Steven Sharpe (1992), "Market Structure and the Nature of Price Rigidity: Evidence from the Market for Consumer Deposits," *Quarterly Journal of Economics,* Vol. 107, No. 2, 657–680.

Norris, Floyd (2007), "Reading the Tea Leaves of Financial Statements," *New York Times,* November 9.

Noyes, Alexander (1894), "The Banks and the Panic of 1893," *Political Science Quarterly,* Vol. 9, No. 1, 12–30.

Ó Gráda, Cormac, and Eugene White (2003), "The Panics of 1854 and 1857; A View from the Emigrant Industrial Savings Bank," *Journal of Economic History,* Vol. 63, No. 1, 213–240.

O'Hara, M., and Shaw, W. (1990), "Deposit Insurance and Wealth Effects: The Value of Being 'Too Big To Fail,'" *Journal of Finance,* 45, No. 5, 1587–600.

Pagano, Marco (1989), "Endogenous Market Thinness and Stock Price Volatility," *Review of Economic Studies,* Vol. 56, 269–288.

Peltzman, Sam (1965), "Entry into Commercial Banking," *Journal of Law and Economics,* Vol. 8, 11–50.

Philippon, Thomas, and Ariell Reshef (2008), "Wages and Human Capital in the U.S. Financial Industry," NYU, working paper, *Journal of Finance,* forthcoming.

Plantin, Guillaume, Haresh Sapra, and Hyun Song Shin, 2006, "Marking to Market: Panacea or Pandora's Box?" Princeton University, working paper.

Pollock, Alex (2008), "Conflicted Agents and Platonic Guardians: Interview with Alex Pollock," American Enterprise Institute Interview, posted May 15, 2008 (http://www.aei.org/publications/filter.all,pubID.28012/pub_detail.asp).

Pozdena, Randall (1986), "Securitization and Banking," *FRBSF Weekly Letter* (July 4).

President's Working Group on Financial Markets (March 2008), "Policy Statements on Financial Market Developments."

Raiter, Frank, and Francis Parisi (2004), "Mortgage Credit and the Evolution of Risk-Based Pricing," Joint Center for Housing Studies, Harvard University, BABC 04–23.

Redlich, Fritz (1947), *The Molding of American Banking: Men and Ideas* (New York and London: Johnson Reprint Corporation; 1968 reprint of 1947 original).

Rezneck, Samuel (1933), "The Depression of 1819–1822, A Social History," *American Historical Review,* Vol. 39, 28–47.

Rezneck, Samuel (1953), "Unemployment, Unrest, and Relief in the United States during the Depression of 1893–97," *Journal of Political Economy,* Vol. 61, No. 4, 324–345.

Richardson, Gary (2005), "Bank Distress during the Great Contraction, 1929 to 1933, New Evidence from the Archives of the Board of Governors," University of California-Irvine, Department of Economics, working paper.

Richardson, Gary, and William Troost (2005), "Monetary Intervention Mitigated Banking Panics During the Great Depression: Quasi-Experimental Evidence from the Federal Reserve District Border in Mississippi, 1929 to 1933," University of California-Irvine, Department of Economics, working paper.

Romer, Christina (1994), "Remeasuring Business Cycles," *Journal of Economic History,* Vol. 54, No. 3, 573–609.

Rose, P. (1991), *Japanese Banking and Investment in the United States* (New York, Quorum Books).

Rosengren, Eric (2007), "Subprime Mortgage Problems: Research, Opportunities, and Policy Considerations," speech by Eric Rosengren at The Massachusetts Institute for a New Commonwealth, December 3, 2007. See http://www.bos.frb.org/news/speeches/rosengren/2007/120307.htm.

Scatigna, Michela, and Camilo E. Tovar (2007), "Securitisation in Latin America," *BIS Quarterly Review* (September), 71–82.

Scholes, Myron (1998), "Derivatives in a Dynamic Environment," *American Economic Review*, Vol. 88, No. 3, 350–370.

Securities Industry and Financial Markets Association (2008), *Research Quarterly* (May).

Seward, Anne (1924), "Bank Runs Rare Now, Owing to Federal Reserve Law," *New York Times*, March 2, p. XXII.

Shell, Ellen Ruppel (1998), "Could Mad-Cow Disease Happen Here?" *Atlantic Monthly* (September), three parts.

Shiller, Robert (2007), "Understanding Recent Trends in House Prices and Homeownership," Kansas City Federal Reserve Bank, Jackson Hole Conference Proceedings.

Silber, William (2007a), "The Great Financial Crisis of 1914: What Can We Learn from Aldrich-Vreeland Emergency Currency?" *American Economic Review Papers and Proceedings*, Vol. 97, No. 2, 285–289.

Silber, William (2007b), *When Washington Shut Down Wall Street: The Great Financial Crisis of 1914 and the Origins of America's Monetary Supremacy* (Princeton, NJ: Princeton University Press).

Singh, Manmohan, and James Aitken (2009), "Deleveraging after Lehman—Evidence from Reduced Rehypothecation," International Monetary Fund, working paper, WP/09/42.

Slovin, M., Sushka, M., and Polonchek, J. (1993), "The Value of Bank Durability: Borrowers as Bank Stakeholders," *Journal of Finance*, Vol. 48, No. 1, 247–66.

Sprague, Isaac (1986), *Bailout: An Insider's Account of Bank Failures and Rescues* (New York: Basic Books).

Sprague, O.M.W. (1915), "The Crisis of 1914 in the United States," *American Economic Review*, Vol. 5, No. 3, 499–533.

Sprague, O.M.W. (1910), *History of Crises under the National Banking System*, National Monetary Commission, 61st Congress, 2nd Session, Senate document No. 538 (Washington, DC: Government Printing Office).

Sprague, O.M.W. (1908), "The American Crisis of 1907," *The Economic Journal*, Vol. 18, No. 71, 353–72.

Sprague, O.M.W. (1903), "The New York Money Market," *Economic Journal*, Vol. 13, No. 49, 30–57.

Standard and Poor's (2008), "Is It Time to Write Off Fair Value?" (May 27).

Standard and Poor's (2007), "Marking to Market When There Is No Market" (October 15).

Standard and Poor's (2007), "Structured Investment Vehicles: Under Stormy Skies, An Updated Look at the Weather," *Ratings Direct* (August 30).

Standard and Poor's (2003), "Structured Investment Vehicle Criteria: New Developments" (September 4).

Stenzel, Thomas (2008), Prepared statement, before the U.S. House of Representatives Committee on Agriculture, Subcommittee on Horticulture and Organic Agriculture, July 30, 2008.

Stock, James, and Mark Watson (2002), "Has the Business Cycle Changed and Why?" *NBER Macroeconomics Annual 2002* (MIT Press).

Strahan, Philip (2003), "The Real Effects of Bank Deregulation," Federal Reserve Bank of St. Louis *Economic Review*, Vol. 85, No. 4 (July/August), 111–128.

Straka, John (2000), "A Shift in the Mortgage Landscape: The 1990s Move to Automated Credit Evaluations," *Journal of Housing Research*, Vol. 11, No. 2, 207–232.

Summers, Peter (2005), "What Caused The Great Moderation? Some Cross-Country Evidence," *Economic Review*, Federal Reserve Bank of Kansas City (third quarter), 6–32.

Swanson, William Walker (1908a), "The Crisis of 1860 and the First Issue of Clearing-House Certificates: I," *Journal of Political Economy*, Vol. 16, No. 2, 65–75.

Swanson, William Walker (1908b), "The Crisis of 1860 and the First Issue of Clearing-House Certificates: II," *Journal of Political Economy*, Vol. 16, No. 4, 212–226.

Taggart, J.H., and L. D. Jennings (1934), "The Insurance of Bank Deposits," *Journal of Political Economy*, Vol. 42, No. 4, 508–516.

Taylor, John, and John Williams (2008A), "A Black Swan in the Money Market," Federal Reserve Bank of San Francisco, working paper.

Taylor, John, and John Williams (2008B), "Further Results on a Black Swan in the Money Market," Federal Reserve Bank of San Francisco, working paper.

Temkin, Kenneth, Jennifer Johnson, Diane Levy (2002), "Subprime Markets, the Role of GSEs, and Risk-Based Pricing," U.S. Department of Housing and Urban Development (March).

Thomas, R.G. (1935), "Bank Failures-Causes and Remedies," *The Journal of Business of the University of Chicago*, Vol. 8, No. 3, 297–318.

Tran, Kiet (no date), "The Sub-Prime Mortgage Market—A Rough Storm Ahead?" See http://www.markit.com/information/news/commentary/Structured-Finance/contentParagraphs/014/document/20071106%20ABX.pdf.

Tufano, Peter (2004), "Financial Innovation," in *The Handbook of the Economics of Finance* (North Holland), George Constantinides and Rene Stulz, eds.

UBS (2008), "Shareholder Report on UBS's Write-Downs" (April 18).

UBS (2007), "Mortgage Strategist," various issues: June 26, July 31, November 27, October 23, December 11.

UBS (2007), "Q-Series: Global Banking Crisis" (November 29).

U.S. Treasury (2008), "Blueprint for a Modernized Financial Regulatory Structure," The Department of Treasury, March.

Valencia, Fabian (2008), "Banks' Precautionary Capital and Persistent Credit Crunches," International Monetary Fund, Working Paper # WP/08/248.

Vanderlip, Frank (1908), "The Panic as a World Phenomenon," *Annals of the American Academy of Political and Social Science*, Vol. 31, Lessons of the Financial Crisis, (March), 2–7.

Wallis, John Joseph (2001), "What Caused the Crisis of 1839?" NBER Historical Paper No. 133.

Wang, Feng (2004), "Throwing Bricks, Attracting Jade—Securitization of Non-Performing Loans in China," working paper.

Wellink, Nout (2007), "Risk Management and Financial Stability-Basel II and Beyond," speech at the GARP 2007 8th Annual Risk Management Convention and Exhibition, February 27, 2007 (http://www.bis.org/review/r070228a.pdf?noframes=1).

Weston, N.A. (1922), "The Studies of the National Monetary Commission," *Annals of the American Academy of Political and Social Science*, Vol. 99, 17–26.

Yu, Fan (2005), "How Profitable is Capital Structure Arbitrage?" University of California, Irvine, working paper.

Zelmanovich, Mark, Quincy Tang, Sharon McGarvey, and Bernard Maas (2007), "RMBS NIMS: An Overview," *Journal of Structured Finance* (Spring), 65–68.

Zigas, Barry, Carol Parry, and Paul Weech (2002), "The Rise of Subprime Lending: Causes, Implications, and Proposals," Fannie Mae working paper.

Zingales, Luigi (2007), "Is the U.S. Capital Market Losing its Competitive Edge?" European Corporate Governance Institute, Finance Working Paper No. 192/2007.

Zhou, Ruilin (2000), "Understanding Intraday Credit in Large-Value Payment Systems," Federal Reserve Bank of Chicago, *Economic Perspectives*, Vol. 24, 29–44.

Index